# THE GERMAN SECRET
# SERVICE IN AMERICA

Count Johann von Bernstorff, the responsible director of Germany's secret policies in America

# THE GERMAN SECRET
# SERVICE IN AMERICA

BY

JOHN PRICE JONES
AUTHOR OF "AMERICA ENTANGLED"

AND

PAUL MERRICK HOLLISTER

**Fredonia Books**
**Amsterdam, The Netherlands**

The German Secret Service in America

by
John Price Jones
Paul Merrick Hollister

ISBN: 1-58963-720-8

Copyright © 2002 by Fredonia Books

Reprinted from the 1918 edition

Fredonia Books
Amsterdam, The Netherlands
http://www.fredoniabooks.com

"It is plain enough how we were forced into the war. The extraordinary insults and aggressions of the Imperial German Government left us no self-respecting choice but to take up arms in defense of our rights as a free people and of our honor as a sovereign government. The military masters of Germany denied us the right to be neutral. They filled our unsuspecting communities with vicious spies and conspirators and sought to corrupt the opinion of our people in their own behalf. When they found they could not do that, their agents diligently spread sedition amongst us and sought to draw our own citizens from their allegiance—and some of these agents were men connected with the official embassy of the German Government itself here in our own capital. They sought by violence to destroy our industries and arrest our commerce. They tried to incite Mexico to take up arms against us and to draw Japan into a hostile alliance with her—and that, not by indirection but by direct suggestion from the Foreign Office in Berlin. They impudently denied us the use of the high seas and repeatedly executed their threat that they would send to their death any of our people who ventured to approach the coasts of Europe. And many of our own people were corrupted. Men began to look upon their neighbors with suspicion and to wonder in their hot resentment and surprise whether there was any community in which hostile intrigue did not lurk. What great nation in such circumstances would not have taken up arms?  Much as we have desired peace, it was denied us, and not of our own choice.  This flag under which we serve would have been dishonored had we withheld our hand."

—WOODROW WILSON, Flag Day Address
June 14, 1917

# INTRODUCTION

A nation at war wants nothing less than complete information of her enemy. It is hard for the mind to conceive exactly what "complete information" means, for it includes every fact which may contain the lightest indication of the enemy strength, her use of that strength, and her intention. The nation which sets out to obtain complete information of her enemy must pry into every neglected corner, fish every innocent pool, and collect a mass of matter concerning the industrial, social and military organization of the enemy which when correlated, appraises her strength—and her weakness. Nothing less than full information will satisfy the mathematical maker of war.

Germany was always precociously fond of international statistics. She wanted—the present tense is equally applicable—full information of America and her allies so as to attack their vulnerable points. She got a ghastly amount of it, and she attacked. This book sets forth how secret agents of the Teutonic governments acting under orders have attacked our national life, both before and after our declaration of war; how men and women in Germany's employ on American

# INTRODUCTION

soil, planned and executed bribery, sedition, arson, the destruction of property and even murder, not to mention lesser violations of American law; how they sought to subvert to the advantage of the Central Powers the aims of the Government of the United States; how, in short, they made enemies of the United States immediately the European war had broken out.

The facts were obtained by the writer first as a reporter on the *New York Sun* who for more than a year busied himself with no other concern, and afterwards in an independent investigation. Some of them he has cited in a previous work. This book brings the story of Germany's secret agencies in America up to the early months of 1918. Because the writer during the past six months has devoted his entire time to the Liberty Loan, it became necessary for him to leave the rearrangement of the work entirely in the hands of the co-author, and he desires to acknowledge his complete indebtedness to the co-author for undertaking and carrying out an assignment for which the full measure of reward will be derived from a sharper American consciousness of the true nature of our enemy at home and abroad.

So we dedicate this chronicle to our country.

JOHN PRICE JONES.

New York, June 1, 1918.

# CONTENTS

CHAPTER                                                    PAGE

I   THE ORGANIZATION . . . . . . . . . . .   I

The economic, diplomatic and military aspects of secret warfare in America—Germany's peace-time organization—von Bernstorff, the diplomat—Albert, the economist—von Papen and Boy-Ed, the men of war.

II   THE CONSPIRATORS' TASK . . . . . . . 19

The terrain—Lower New York—The consulates—The economic problem of supplying Germany and checking supplies to the Allies—The diplomatic problem of keeping America's friendship—The military problem in Canada, Mexico, India, etc.—Germany's denial.

III   THE RAIDERS AT SEA . . . . . . . 28

The outbreak of war—Mobilization of reservists—The Hamburg-American contract—The *Berwind*—The *Marina Quezada*—The *Sacramento*—Naval battles.

IV   THE WIRELESS SYSTEM . . . . . . . 43

The German Embassy a clearing house—Sayville—German's knowledge of U. S. wireless—Subsidized electrical companies—Aid to the raiders—The *Emden*—The *Geier*—Charles E. Apgar—The German code.

V   MILITARY VIOLENCE . . . . . . . . 60

The plan to raid Canadian ports—The first Welland Canal plot—Von Papen, von der Goltz and Tauscher—The project abandoned—Goltz's arrest—The Tauscher trial—Hidden arms—Louden's plan of invasion.

# CONTENTS

**CHAPTER**  **PAGE**

VI  PAUL KOENIG . . . . . . . . . 73

Justice and Metzler—Koenig's personality—von Papen's checks—The "little black book"—Telephone codes —Shadowing—Koenig's agents—His betrayal.

VII  FALSE PASSPORTS . . . . . . . . . 82

Hans von Wedell's bureau—The traffic in false passports—Carl Ruroede—Methods of forgery— Adams' coup—von Wedell's letter to von Bernstorff— Stegler—Lody—Berlin counterfeits American passports —von Breechow.

VIII  INCENDIARISM . . . . . . . . . 100

Increased munitions production—The opening explosions—Orders from Berlin—Von Papen and Seattle—July, 1915—The Van Koolbergen affair—The Autumn of 1915—The Pinole explosion.

IX  MORE BOMB PLOTS . . . . . . . . 117

Kaltschmidt and the Windsor explosions—The Port Huron tunnel—Werner Horn—Explosions embarrass the Embassy—Black Tom—The second Welland affair —Harry Newton—The damage done in three years— Waiter spies.

X  FRANZ VON RINTELEN . . . . . . . 138

The leak in the National City Bank—The *Minnehaha* —Von Rintelen's training—His return to America— His aims—His funds—Smuggling oil—The Krag-Joergensen rifles—Von Rintelen's flight and capture.

XI  SHIP BOMBS . . . . . . . . . 154

Mobilizing destroying agents—The plotters in Hoboken—Von Kleist's arrest and confession—The *Kirk Oswald* trial—Further explosions—The *Arabic*—Robert Fay—His arrest—The ship plots decrease.

# CONTENTS

CHAPTER                                                          PAGE

XII  LAROR . . . . . . . . . . . . . . 171

    David Lamar—Labor's National Peace Council—The embargo conference—The attempted longshoremen's strike—Dr. Dumba's recall.

XIII  THE SINKING OF THE LUSITANIA . . . . 190

    The mistress of the seas—Plotting in New York—The *Lusitania's* escape in February, 1915—The advertised warning—The plot—May 7, 1915—Diplomatic correspondence—Gustave Stahl—The results.

XIV  COMMERCIAL VENTURES . . . . . . . 203

    German law in America—Waetzoldt's reports—The British blockade—A report from Washington—Stopping the chlorine supply—Speculation in wool—Dyestuffs and the *Deutschland*—Purchasing phenol—The Bridgeport Projectile Company—The lost portfolio—The recall of the attachés—A summary of Dr. Albert's efforts.

XV  THE PUBLIC MIND . . . . . . . . . 225

    Dr. Bertling—The *Staats-Zeitung*—George Sylvester Viereck and *The Fatherland*—Efforts to buy a press association—Bernhardi's articles—Marcus Braun and *Fair Play*—Plans for a German news syndicate—Sander, Wunnenberg, Bacon and motion pictures—The German-American Alliance—Its purposes—Political activities—Colquitt of Texas—The "Wisconsin Plan"—Lobbying—Misappropriation of German Red Cross funds—Friends of Peace—The American Truth Society.

XVI  HINDU-GERMAN CONSPIRACIES . . . . 252

    The Society for Advancement in India—"Gaekwar Scholarships"—Har Dyal and *Gadhr*—India in 1914—Papen's report—German and Hindu agents sent to the Orient—Gupta in Japan—The raid on von Igel's office—Chakravarty replaces Gupta—The *Annie Larsen* and *Maverick* filibuster—Von Igel's memoranda—Har Dyal in Berlin—A request for anarchist agents—Ram Chandra—Plots against the East and West Indies—Correspondence between Bernstorff and Berlin, 1916—Designs on China, Japan and Africa—Chakravarty arrested—The conspirators indicted.

# CONTENTS

CHAPTER                   PAGE

XVII Mexico, Ireland, and Bolo . . . . . . 228

Huerta arrives in New York—The restoration plot
—German intrigue in Central America—The Zimmer-
mann note—Sinn Fein—Sir Roger Casement and the
Easter Rebellion—Bolo Pacha in America and France
—A warning.

XVIII America Goes to War . . . . . . . 320

Bernstorff's request for bribe-money—The President on German spies—Interned ships seized—Enemy
aliens—Interning German agents—The water-front and
finger-print regulations—Pro-German acts since April,
1917—A warning and a prophecy.

Appendix . . . . . . . . . . . . . . 335

A German Propagandist.

# List of Illustrations

Count Johann von Bernstorff . . *Frontispiece*

PAGE

The German Embassy in Washington . . 2
Captain Franz von Papen . . . . . 12
Captain Karl Boy-Ed . . . . . 16
William J. Flynn . . . . . . 22
Thomas J. Tunney . . . . . . 26
Dr. Karl Buenz . . . . . . 32
Passport given to Horst von der Goltz . . 64
Paul Koenig . . . . . . . 74
Hans von Wedell and his wife . . . 84
Franz von Rintelen . . . . . . 138
Robert Fay . . . . . . . 166
Dr. Constantin Dumba . . . . . 184
The *Lusitania* . . . . . . . 190
Advertisement of the German Embassy . . 194
Checks signed by Adolf Pavenstedt . . 230
George Sylvester Viereck . . . . 234
Letter from Count von Bernstorff . . . 236
Check from Count von Bernstorff . . . 238
Letter-paper of "The Friends of Peace" . . 250
Dr. Chakravarty . . . . . . 284
Jeremiah A. O'Leary . . . . . 302
Paul Bolo Pacha . . . . . . 310

# THE GERMAN SECRET SERVICE IN AMERICA

## CHAPTER I

### THE ORGANIZATION

The economic, diplomatic and military aspects of secret warfare in America—Germany's peace-time organization—von Bernstorff, the diplomat—Albert, the economist—von Papen and Boy-Ed, the men of war.

When, in the summer of 1914, the loaded dice
fell for war, Germany began a campaign overseas as thoughtfully forecasted as that first head-
long flood which rolled to the Marne. World-
domination was the Prussian objective. It is
quite natural that the United States, whose influence affected a large part of the world, should
have received swift attention from Berlin.
America and Americans could serve Germany's
purpose in numerous ways, and the possible
assets of the United States had been searchingly
assayed in Berlin long before the arrival of "Der
Tag."

The day dawned—and Germany found herself

1

hemmed in by enemies.   Her navy did not control the oceans upon which she had depended for a large percentage of her required food and raw materials, and upon which she must continue to depend if her output were to keep pace with her war needs.   If surprise-attack should fail to bring the contest to a sudden and favorable conclusion, Germany was prepared to accept the more probable alternative of a contest of economic endurance.   Therefore, she reasoned, supplies must continue to come from America.

Of importance scarcely secondary to the economic phase of her warfare in the United States was the diplomatic problem.   Here was a nation of infinite resources, a people of infinite resource. This nation must be enlisted on the side of the Central Powers; failing that, must be kept friendly; under no circumstances was she to be allowed to enlist with the Allies.   One fundamental trait of Americans Germany held too lightly—their blood-kinship to Britons—and it is a grimly amusing commentary upon the confidence of the German in bonds Teutonic that he believed that the antidote to this racial "weakness" of ours lay in the large numbers of Germans who had settled here and become Americans of sorts.   But the German was alarmingly if not absolutely correct in his estimate, for upon the

The German Embassy in Washington, headquarters and clearing-house of German intrigue in the world outside Mittel-Europa, 1914-1917

conduct and zeal of Germans in America actually depended much of the success of Germany's diplomatic tactics in America.

The war, then, so far as the United States figured in Germany's plan, was economic and diplomatic. But it was also military. German representatives in the United States were bound by oath to coöperate to their utmost in all military enterprises within their reach. With a certain few notable exceptions, no such enterprises came within their reach, and if the reader anticipates from that fact a disappointing lack of violence in the narrative to follow, let him remember that "all's fair in war," and that every German activity in the United States, whether it was economic, diplomatic or military, was carried on with a certain Prussian thoroughness which was chiefly characterized by brutal violence.

We have come to believe that thoroughness is the first and last word in German organization. Any really thorough organization must be promptly convertible to new activities without loss of motion. If these new activities are unexpected, the change is more or less of an experiment, and its possibilities are not ominous. But truly dangerous is the organization which transfers suddenly to coping with the expected. Germany had expected war for forty years.

Her peace-time organization in America consisted of four executives: an ambassador, a fiscal agent, a military attaché, and a naval attaché. Its chief was the ambassador, comparable in his duties and privileges to the president of a corporation, the representative with full authority to negotiate with other organizations, and responsible to his board of directors—the foreign office in Berlin. Its treasurer was the fiscal agent. And its department heads were the military and naval attachés, each responsible in some degree to his superiors in matters of policy and finances, and answerable also to Berlin.

The functions of the chief were two-fold. Convincing evidence produced by the State Department has placed at his door the ultimate responsibility for executing Germany's commands not in the United States alone, but throughout all of the world excepting Middle Europe. Under his eyes passed Berlin's instructions to her envoys in both Americas, and through his hands passed their reports. He directed and delegated the administration of all German policy in the western world and the far east, and of course directed all strictly diplomatic enterprises afoot in the United States.

Germany could hardly have chosen an abler envoy than this latest of all the Bernstorffs, Jo-

hann, a statesman whose ancestors for genera-
tions had been Saxon diplomats. A glance at
the man's countenance convinced one of his powers of concentration: the many lines of his face
seemed to focus on a point between his eyebrows.
And yet his expression was hardly grim. The
modeling of his head was unusually strong, his
features sensitive, with no trace of weakness. If
there had been weakness about his mouth, it
was concealed by the conventional ferocity of a
Hohenzollern moustache, and yet those untruth-
ful lips could part in an ingratiating smile which
flashed ingenuous friendliness. His frame was
tall and slender, his mannerisms suggested carefully bridled nervous activity. The entire appearance of the man may best be described by a
much-abused term—he was "distinguished."

Count von Bernstorff, once his nation had declared war upon France and England, went to
war with the United States. As ambassador,
diplomatic courtesy gave him a scope of observation limited only by the dignity of his position.
A seat in a special gallery in the Senate and
House of Representatives was always ready for
his occupancy; he could virtually command the
attention of the White House; and senators, congressmen and office-holders from German-American districts respected him. Messengers kept

him in constant touch with the line-up of Congress on important issues, and two hours later that line-up was known in the Foreign Office in Berlin. As head and front of the German spy system in America, he held cautiously aloof from all but the most instrumental acquaintances: men and women of prominent political and social influence who he knew were inclined, for good and sufficient reasons, to help him. One woman, whose bills he paid at a Fifth Avenue gown house, was the wife of a prominent broker and another woman of confessedly German affiliations who served him lived within a stone's throw of the Metropolitan Museum and its nearby phalanx of gilded dwellings (her husband's office was in a building at 11 Broadway, of which more anon); a third woman intimate lived in a comfortable apartment near Fifth Avenue—an apartment selected for her, though she was unaware of it, by secret agents of the United States. During the early days of the war the promise of social sponsorship which any embassy in Washington could extend proved bait for a number of ingénues of various ages, with ambition and mischief in their minds, and the gracious Ambassador played them smoothly and dexterously. Mostly they were not German women, for the German women of America were not so likely to be useful socially, nor as a type so astute as to qualify them for von Bernstorff's delicate work. To those whom he chose to see he was courteous, and superficially frank almost to the point of naïveté. The pressure of negotiation between Washington and Berlin became more and more exacting as the war progressed, yet he found time to command a campaign whose success would have resulted in disaster to the United States. That he was not blamed for the failure of that campaign when he returned to Germany in April, 1917, is evidenced by his prompt appointment to the court of Turkey, a difficult and important post, and in the case of Michaelis, a stepping-stone to the highest post in the Foreign Office.

Upon the shoulders of Dr. Heinrich Albert, privy counsellor and fiscal agent of the German Empire, fell the practical execution of German propaganda throughout America. He was the American agent of a government which has done more than any other to coöperate with business towards the extension of influence abroad, on the principle that "the flag follows the constitution." As such he had had his finger on the pulse of American trade, had catalogued exhaustively the economic resources of the country, and held in his debt, as his nation's treasurer in America, scores of bankers, manufacturers and traders to whom Germany had extended subsidy. As such also he was the paymaster of the Imperial secret diplomatic and consular agents.

You could find him almost any day until the break with Germany in a small office in the Hamburg-American Building (a beehive of secret agents) at No. 45 Broadway, New York. He was tall and slender, and wore the sombre frock coat of the European business man with real grace. His eyes were blue and clear, his face clean-shaven and faintly sabre-scarred, and his hair blond. He impressed one as an unusual young man in a highly responsible position. His greeting to visitors, of whom he had few, was punctilious, his bow low, and his manner altogether polite. He encouraged conversation rather than offered it. He had none of the "hard snap" of the energetic, outspoken, brusque American man of business. Dr. Albert was a smooth-running, well-turned cog in the great machine of Prussian militarism.

Upon him rested the task of spending between $2,000,000 and $3,000,000 a week for German propaganda. He spent thirty millions at least—and only Germany knows how much more—in secret agency work, also known by the uglier names of bribery, sedition and conspiracy. He admitted that he wasted a half million or more. He had a joint account with Bernstorff in the Chase National Bank, New York, which amounted at times to several millions. His resources gave weight to his utterances in the quiet office overlooking Broadway, or in the German Club in Central Park South, or in the consulates or hotels of Chicago and New Orleans and San Francisco, to which he made occasional trips to confer with German business men.

His colleagues held him in high esteem. His methods were quiet and successful, and his participation in the offences against America's peace might have passed unproven had he not been engaged in a too-absorbing conversation one day in August, 1915, upon a Sixth Avenue elevated train. He started up to leave the train at Fiftieth Street, and carelessly left his portfolio behind him—to the tender care of a United States Secret Service man. It contained documents revealing his complicity in enterprises the magnitude of which beggars the imagination. The publication of certain of those documents awoke the slumbering populace to a feeling of chagrin and anger almost equal to his own at the loss of his dossier. And yet he stayed on in America, and returned with the ambassadorial party to Germany only after the severance of diplomatic relations in 1917, credited with expert generalship on the economic sector of the American front.

Germany's military attaché to the United States was Captain Franz von Papen. His mission was the study of the United States army. In August, 1914, it may be assumed that he had absorbed most of the useful information of the United States army, which at that moment was no superhuman problem. In July of that year he was in Mexico, observing, among other matters, the effect of dynamite explosions on railways. He was quite familiar with Mexico. According to Admiral von Hintze he had organized a military unit in the lukewarm German colony in Mexico City, and he used one or more of the warring factions in the southern republic to test the efficacy of various means of warfare.

The rumble of a European war sent him scurrying northward. From Mexico on July 29 he wired Captain Boy-Ed—of whom more presently —in New York to

". . . arrange business for me too with Pavenstedt,"

which referred to the fact that Boy-Ed had just engaged office space in the offices of G. Amsinck & Company, New York, which was at that time a German house of which Adolph Pavenstedt was the president, but which has since been taken over by American interests. And he added:

"Then inform Lersner. The Russian attaché ordered back to Washington by telegraph. On outbreak of war have intermediaries locate by detective where Russian and French intelligence office."

The latter part of the message is open to two interpretations: that Boy-Ed was to have detectives locate the Russian and French secret service officers; or that Boy-Ed was to place German spies in those offices.

Captain von Papen reported to his ministry of war anent the railway explosions:

"I consider it out of the question that explosives prepared in this way would have to be reckoned with in a European war . . ."

a significant opinion, which he changed later.

What of the man himself? He was all that "German officer" suggested at that time to any one who had traveled in Germany. His military training had been exhaustive. Though he had not seen "active service," his life, from the early youth when he had been selected from his gymnasium fellows for secret service in Abteilung III of the great bureau, had been unusually active. He had traveled as a civilian over various countries, drawing maps, harking to the sentiment of the people, and checking from time to time the operations of resident German agents abroad. His disguises were thorough, as this incident will illustrate: In Hamburg, at the army riding school where von Papen was trained, young officers are taught the French style. Yet one fine morning in Central Park he stopped to chat with an acquaintance who had bought a mare. Von Papen admired the mount, promptly named its breed, and told in what counties in Ireland the best specimens of that breed could be found—information called up from a riding tour he had made over the length and breadth of Ireland. It is commonly said that horsemen trained in the French style cling to its mannerisms, but a cavalier revealing those mannerisms in Ireland, where the style is exclusively English, would have attracted undue attention. So he had disguised even his horsemanship!

A man who moves constantly about among more or less unsuspecting peoples seeking their military weakness becomes intolerant. Tolerance is scarcely a German military trait, and in that respect Captain von Papen was consistently loyal to his own superior organization. "I always say to those idiotic Yankees they had better hold their tongues," he wrote to his wife in a letter which fell later into the hands of those same

Captain Franz von Papen

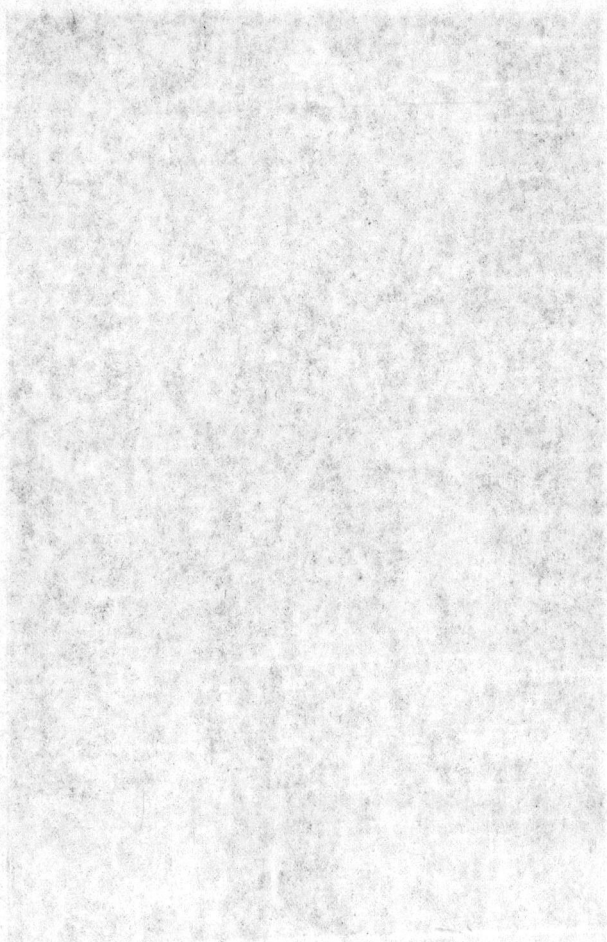

"bloedsinnige" Yankees. He was inordinately proud of his facility in operating unobserved, arrogant of his ability, and blunt in his criticism of his associates. He telegraphed Boy-Ed on one occasion to be more cautious. The gracious colleague replied, in a letter:

"Dear Papen: A secret agent who returned from Washington this evening made the following statement: 'The Washington people are very much excited about von Papen and are having a constant watch kept on him. They are in possession of a whole heap of incriminating evidence against him. They have no evidence against Count B. and Captain B-E ( !).' "

And Boy-Ed, a trifle optimistically, perhaps, added:

"In this connection I would suggest with due diffidence that perhaps the first part of your telegram is worded rather too emphatically."

Von Papen was a man of war, a Prussian, the Feldmarschal of the Kaiser in America. In appearance he bespoke his vigor: he was well set up, rawboned, with a long nose, prominent ears, keen eyes and a strong lower jaw. He was energetic in speech and swift in formulating daring plans. In those first frantic weeks after the declaration of war he reached out in all directions to snap taut the strings that held his organization together—German reservists who had been peaceful farmers, shopkeepers or waiters, all over the United States, were mobilized for service, and paraded through Battery Park in New York shouting "Deutschland, Deutschland ueber alles!" to the strains of the Austrian hymn, while they waited for Papen's orders from a building near by, and picked quarrels with a counter procession of Frenchmen screaming the immortal "Marseillaise." Up in his office sat the attaché, summoning, assigning, despatching his men on missions that were designed to terrorize America as the spiked helmets were terrorizing Belgium at that moment.

And he, too, failed. Although von Papen marshaled his consuls, his reservists, his thugs, his women, and his skilled agents, for a programme of violence the like of which America had never experienced, the military phase of the war was not destined for decision here, and there is again something ironical in the fact that the arrogance of Captain von Papen's outrages hastened the coming of war to America and the decline of Captain von Papen's style of warfare in America.

The Kaiser's naval attaché at Washington was Karl Boy-Ed, the child of a German mother and a Turkish father, who had elected a naval career and shown a degree of aptitude for his work which qualified him presently for the post of chief lieutenant to von Tirpitz. He was one of the six young officers who were admitted to the chief councils of the German navy, as training for high executive posts. In the capacity of news chief of the Imperial navy, Boy-Ed carried on two highly successful press campaigns to influence the public on the eve of requests for heavy naval appropriations, the second, in 1910, calling for 400,000,000 marks. He spread broadcast through cleverly contrived pamphlets and through articles placed in the subsidized press, a national resentment against British naval dominion. His duties took him all over the world as naval observer, and he may be credited more than casually with weaving the plan-fabric of marine supremacy with which Germany proposed in due time to envelop the world.

So he impressed diplomatic Washington in 1911 as a polished cosmopolite. Polished he was, measured by the standards of diplomatic Washington, for rare was the young American of Boy-Ed's age who had his cultivation, his wide experience, and his brilliant charm. He was sought after by admiring mothers long before he was sought after by the Secret Service; he moved among the clubs of Washington and New York making intimates of men whose friendship and confidence would serve the Fatherland, cloaking his real designs by frivolity and frequent attendances at social functions. His peace-time duties had been to study the American navy; to familiarize himself with its ship power and personnel, with its plans for expansion, its theories of strategy, its means of supply, and finally, with the coast defenses of the country. He had learned his lesson, and furnished Berlin with clear reports. On those reports, together with those of his colleagues in other countries, hinged Germany's readiness to enter war, for it would have been folly to attempt a war of domination with America an unknown, uncatalogued naval power. (It will be well to recall that the submarine is an American invention, and that Germany's greatest submarine development took place in the years 1911–1914.)

And then, suddenly, he dropped the cloak. The Turk in him stood at attention while the German in him gave him sharp orders—commands to be carried out with Oriental adroitness and Prussian finish. Then those who had said lightly that "Boy-Ed knows more about our navy than Annapolis itself" began to realize that they had spoken an alarming truth. His war duties were manifold. Like von Papen, he had his corps of reservists, his secret agents, his silent

Captain Karl Boy-Ed (on the right)

forces everywhere ready for active coöperation in carrying out the naval enterprises Germany should see fit to undertake in Western waters.

America learned gradually of the machinations of the four executives, Bernstorff, Albert, Papen and Boy-Ed. America had not long to wait for evidences of their activity, but it was a long time before the processes of investigation revealed their source. It was inevitable that they could not work undiscovered for long, and they seem to have realized that they must do the utmost damage at top speed. Their own trails were covered for a time by the obscure identities of their subordinates. The law jumps to no conclusions. Their own persons were protected by diplomatic courtesy. It required more than two years of tedious search for orthodox legal evidence to arraign these men publicly in their guilt, and when that evidence had finally been obtained, and Germany's protest of innocence had been deflated, it was not these men who suffered, but their country, and the price she paid was war with America.

A hundred or more of their subordinates have been convicted of various criminal offenses and sent to prison. Still more were promptly interned in prison camps at the outbreak of war in 1917. The secret army included all types, from bankers to longshoremen. Many of them were conspicuous figures in American public life, and of these no small part were allowed to remain at large under certain restrictions—and under surveillance. Germany's army in the United States was powerful in numbers; the fact that so many agents were working destruction probably hastened their discovery; the loyalty of many so-called German-Americans was always questionable. The public mind, confused as it had never been before by the news of war, was groping about for sound fundamentals, and was being tantalized with false principles by the politicians. Meanwhile Count von Bernstorff was watching Congress and the President, Dr. Albert was busy in great schemes, Captain von Papen was commanding an active army of spies, and Captain Boy-Ed was engaged in a bitter fight with the British navy.

# CHAPTER II

## THE CONSPIRATORS' TASK

The terrain—Lower New York—The consulates—The economic problem of supplying Germany and checking supplies to the Allies—The diplomatic problem of keeping America's friendship—The military problem in Canada, Mexico, India, etc.—Germany's denial.

The playwright selects from the affairs of a group of people a few characters and incidents, and works them together into a three-hour plot. He may include no matter which is not relevant to the development of his story, and although in the hands of the artist the play seems to pierce clearly into the characters of the persons involved, in reality he is constructing a framework, whose angles are only the more prominent salients of character and episode. The stage limits him, whether his story takes place in the kitchen or on the battlefield.

The drama of German spy operations in America is of baffling proportions. Its curtain rose long before the war; its early episodes were grave enough to have caused, any one of them, a nine-days' wonder in the press, its climax was rather a huge accumulation of intolerable disasters than a single outstanding incident, and its dénouement continued long after America's declaration of war.   In the previous chapter we have accepted our limitations and introduced only the four chief characters of the play.   It is necessary, in describing the motives for their enterprises, to appreciate the problems which their scene of operations presented.

The world was their workshop.   Plots hatched in Berlin and developed in Washington and New York bore fruit from Sweden to India, from Canada to Chili.   The economic importance of the United States in the war needs no further proof than its vast area, its miles of seacoast, its volume of export and import, and its producing power.   As a diplomatic problem it offered, among other things, a public opinion of a hundred million people of parti-colored temperament, played upon by a force of some 40,000 publications.   As a military factor, the United States possessed a strong fleet, owned the only Atlantic-Pacific waterway, was bounded on the south by Mexico and the coveted Gulf, and on the north by one of Germany's enemies.   There was hardly a developed section of the nation which did not require prompt and radical German attention, or one which did not receive it in proportion to its industrial development. Washington, as the governmental capital, and New York as the real capital became at once the headquarters of German operations in the western world.

Count von Bernstorff directed all enterprises from the Imperial Embassy in Washington, and from the Ritz-Carlton in New York. An ambassador was once asked by an ingenuous woman at a New York dinner whether he often ran counter of European spies. "Oh, yes," he replied. "I used to stop at the ——, but my baggage was searched by German agents so often that I moved to the ——. But there it was just as bad." "Didn't you complain to the management?"—the lady wanted particulars. "No," the diplomat answered naturally, "for you see every time Bernstorff stops at the —— I have his baggage searched, too!"

The strands of intrigue focussed from every corner of America upon the lower tip of Manhattan. In a tall building at 11 Broadway, which towers over Bowling Green and confronts the New York Custom House, Captain Boy-Ed had his office. A long stone's throw to the northward stood the Hamburg-American building; there Dr. Albert carried on much of his business. Captain von Papen had offices on the twenty-fifth floor of No. 60 Wall Street. If we regard 11 Broadway as the tip of a triangle, with Wall Street and Broadway forming its right angle and 60 Wall Street as its other extremity, we find that its imaginary hypotenuse travels through the building of J. P. Morgan & Company, chief bankers for the Allies; through the New York Stock Exchange, where the so-called "Christmas leak" turned a pretty penny for certain German sympathizers in 1916; through the home of the Standard Oil Companies, as well as through several great structures of less strategic importance. There is more than mere coincidence in this geometrical freak—Germany held her stethoscope as close as possible to the heart of American business. Fortunately, however, the offices of Chief William J. Flynn—until January, 1918, head of the United States Secret Service—were in the Custom House near by.

After business hours these men met their subordinates at various rendezvous in the city; the hotels were convenient, the Manhattan was frequently appointed, and the Deutscher Verein at 112 Central Park South was the liveliest ganglion of all the nerve centers of a system of communication which tapped every section of the great community.

In the lesser cities the German consulate served

William J. Flynn, chief of the United States Secret Service
until 1918, who led the hunt of the German spy

as the nucleus for the organization. That in San Francisco is conspicuous for its activity, for it prosecuted its own warfare on the entire Pacific coast. Wherever it was necessary German sympathizers furnished accommodations for offices and storage room. Headquarters of every character dotted the country from salons to saloons, from skyscrapers to cellars, each an active control in the manipulation of Germany's almost innumerable enterprises.

Those enterprises may be best outlined perhaps, by recalling the three phases of warfare which Germany had to pursue. America had shipped foodstuffs and raw materials in enormous quantities for many years to Germany. Dr. Albert must see to it that she continue to do so. The Imperial funds were at his disposal. He had already the requisite contact with American business. But let him also exert his utmost influence upon America to stop supplying the Allies. If he could do it alone, so much the better; if not, he was at liberty to call upon the military and naval attachés. But in any case "food and arms for Germany and none for the Allies" was the economic war-cry.

American supplies must be purchased for Germany and shipped through the European neutral nations, running the blockade. If capital proved obstinate and the Allies covered the market, it would be well to remember that labor produced supplies; labor must therefore be prevented from producing or shipping to the Allies. If labor refused to be interfered with, the cargoes should be destroyed.

His enormous task would depend, of course, very much upon the turn of affairs diplomatic. The State Department must be kept amicable. The Glad Hand was to be extended to official America, while the Mailed Fist thrashed about in official America's constituencies. Thus also with Congress, through influential lobbying or the pressure of constituents. Count von Bernstorff knew that the shout raised in a far-off state by a few well-rehearsed pacifists, reinforced by a few newspaper comments, would carry loud and clear to Washington. Upon his shoulders rested the entire existence of the German plan, and he spent a highly active and trying thirty months in Washington in an attempt to avoid the inevitable diplomatic rupture.

The military problem quickly resolved itself into two enterprises: carrying war to the enemy, and giving aid and comfort to its own forces— in this case the German navy. As the war progressed, and the opportunity for strictly military operations became less likely, the two Captains occupied their time in injecting a quite military flavor into the enterprises Bernstorff and Albert had on foot. As a strategic measure Mexico must divert America's attention from Europe and remove to the border her available forces. Meanwhile, German reservists must be supplied to their home regiments. Failing that they must be mobilized for service against Germany's nearest enemy here—Canada. German raiders at sea must be supplied. German communication with her military forces abroad must be maintained uninterrupted.

Long after the departure of the principals for their native land the enterprises persisted. It may be well here to extend to the secret agents of the United States the tribute which is their due. To Chief Flynn, of the United States Secret Service of the Treasury Department, to A. Bruce Bielaski, head of the special agents of the Department of Justice, to W. M. Offley, former Superintendent of the New York Bureau of Special Agents, to Roger B. Wood, Assistant United States District Attorney, to his successor, John C. Knox, (now a Federal judge), to Raymond B. Sarfaty, Mr. Wood's assistant who developed the Rintelen case, to former Police Commissioner Arthur Woods of New York, his deputy, Guy Scull, his police captain, Thomas J. Tunney, and to the men who worked obscurely and tirelessly with them to avert disasters whose fiendish intention shook the faith if not the courage of a nation. Those men found Germany out in time.

Germany was fluent in her denials. When the President in his message to Congress in December, 1915, bitterly attacked Germans and German-Americans for their activities in America, accusing the latter of treason, the German government authorized a statement to the Berlin correspondent of the New York *Sun* on December 19, 1915, to the effect that it

"naturally has never knowingly accepted the support of any person, group of persons, society or organization seeking to promote the cause of Germany in the United States by illegal acts, by counsels of violence, by contravention of law, or by any means whatever that could offend the American people in the pride of their own authority. If it should be alleged that improper acts have been committed by representatives of the German Government they could be easily dealt with. To any complaints upon proof as may be submitted by the American Government suitable response will be duly made. . . . Apparently the enemies of Germany have succeeded in creating the impression that the German Government is in some way, morally or otherwise, responsible for what Mr. Wilson has characterized as anti-American activities, comprehending attacks upon property in violation of the rules which the American Government has seen fit to impose upon the course of neutral trade. This

Inspector Thomas J. Tunney of the New York Police Department, head of the "Bomb Squad" and foremost in apprehending many important German agents

the German Government absolutely denies. It cannot specifically repudiate acts committed by individuals over whom it has no control, and of whose movements it is neither officially nor unofficially informed."

To this statement there is one outstanding answer. It is an excerpt from the German book of instructions for officers:

"Bribery of the enemy's subjects with the object of obtaining military advantages, acceptances of offers of treachery, reception of deserters, utilization of the discontented elements in the population, support of the pretenders and the like are permissible; indeed international law is in no way opposed to the exploitation of the crimes of third parties (assassination, incendiarism, robbery and the like) to the prejudice of the enemy. Considerations of chivalry, generosity and honor may denounce in such cases a hasty and unsparing exploitation of such advantages as indecent and dishonorable, but law, which is less touchy, allows it. The ugly and inherently immoral aspect of such methods cannot affect the recognition of their lawfulness. The necessary aim of war gives the belligerent the right and imposes upon him, according to circumstances, the duty not to let slip the important, it may be decisive, advantages to be gained by such means."

("The War Book of the German General Staff," translated by J. H. Morgan, M.A., pp. 113–114.)

# CHAPTER III

The outbreak of war—Mobilization of reservists—The Hamburg-American contract—The *Berwind*—The *Marina Quezada*—The *Sacramento*—Naval battles.

A fanatic student in the streets of Sarajevo, Bosnia, threw a bomb at a visiting dignitary, and the world went to war. That occurred on the sunny forenoon of June 28, 1914. The assassin was chased by the police, the newspaper men, and the photographers, who reached him almost simultaneously, and presently the world knew that the Archduke Francis Ferdinand, of Austria, was the victim, and that a plain frightened fellow, struggling in the shadow of a doorway, was his assailant.

Austria's resentment of the crime mounted during July and boiled over in the ultimatum of July 23. Five days later, with Germany's permission, Austria declared war on Servia. By this time continental tempers had been aroused, and the Central Empires knew that "Der Tag"

had come.  Austria, Russia, Germany, England,
France and Belgium entered the lists within a
fortnight.

By mid-July Germany had warned her agents
in other lands of the imminence of war and a
quiet mobilization had begun of the more important reservists in America.  Captain von Papen,
after dispatching his telegram from Mexico via
El Paso to Captain Boy-Ed, hurried to Washington, arriving there on August 3.  He began to
weld together into a vast band the scientists, experts, secret agents and German army-reservists,
who were under German military oaths, and were
prepared to gather information or to execute a
military enterprise "zu Befehl!"  How rapidly
he assembled his staff is shown in testimony given
on the witness stand by "Horst von der Goltz,"
alias Bridgeman Taylor, alias Major Wachen-
dorf, a German spy who had been a major in a
Mexican army until July.

A German consul in El Paso had sounded out
Goltz's willingness to return to German service.
"A few days later, the 3rd of August, 1914,
license was given by my commanding officer to
separate myself from the service of my brigade
for the term of six months.  I left directly for
El Paso, Texas, where I was told by Mr. Kueck,
German  Consul  at  Chihuahua,  Mexico,  who

stayed there, to put myself at the disposition of Captain von Papen." This was two days before the final declaration of war.

All German and Austro-Hungarian consulates received orders to coördinate their own staffs for war service. Germany herself supplied the American front with men by wireless commands to all parts of the world. Captain Hans Tauscher, who enjoyed the double distinction of being agent in America for the Krupps and husband of a noted operatic singer, Mme. Johanna Gadski, chanced to be in Berlin when war broke out, reported for duty and was at once detailed to return to the United States and report to von Papen, as Wilhelmstrasse saw the usefulness of an ordnance expert in intimate touch with our Ordnance Department and our explosives plants. Two German officers detailed to topographical duty, who had spent years mapping Japan, and were engaged in the same work in British Columbia, jumped the border to the United States, taking with them their families, their information and their fine surveying and photographic instruments, and in the blocking out of the country which the wise men in the East were performing, were assigned to the White Mountains. Railroads and ships to the Atlantic seaboard bore every day new groups of reserve officers from the

Orient and South America to New York for sailing orders.

They found von Papen already there. He established a consultation headquarters at once with Boy-Ed in a room which they rented in the offices of G. Amsinck & Co., at 6 Hanover Street. From that time forward, New York was to be his base of operations, and it was at that moment especially convenient to von Bernstorff's summer establishment at Newport.

The naval situation at once became active. In the western and southern Atlantic a scattered fleet of German cruisers was still at large. The British set out eagerly to the chase. Security lay in southern waters, and the German craft dodged back and forth through the Straits of Magellan. From time to time the quarry was forced by the remoteness of supply to show himself, and a battle followed; in the intervals, the Germans lay *perdu*, dashing into port for supplies and out again to concealment, or wandering over seldom traveled ocean tracks to meet coal and provision ships sent out from America.

Captain Boy-Ed received from Berlin constant advices of the movements of his vessels. On July 31, Dr. Karl Buenz, the American head of the Hamburg-American Line, had a cable from Berlin which he read and then forwarded to the

Embassy in Washington for safekeeping. Until 1912 Buenz had had no steamship experience, having been successively a judge in Germany, a consul in Chicago and New York, and minister to Mexico. When at the age of 70 he was appointed Hamburg-American agent, one of the first matters which came to his attention was the consummation of a contract between the Admiralty Division of the German government and the steamship line, which provided for the provisioning, during war, of German ships at sea, using America as a base. This contract was jealously guarded by the Embassy.

The cablegram of July 31 called on Dr. Buenz to carry out this contract. There was consultation at once with Boy-Ed for the location of the vessels to be supplied, merchant ships were chartered or purchased, then loaded, and despatched. The first to leave New York harbor was the *Berwind*. There was hesitancy among the conspirators as to who should apply for her clearance papers—documents of which Dr. Buenz protested he knew nothing. They finally told G. B. Kulenkampff, a banker and exporter, that the *Berwind* was loaded with coal, and directed him to get the clearance papers. He swore to a false manifest of her cargo and got them. The *Berwind* carried coal to be sure—but she also carried

Dr. Karl Buenz, managing director of the
Hamburg-American Line

food for German warships, and she was not
bound for Buenos Aires, as her clearance papers
stated. Thus the United States, by innocently
issuing false papers, made herself, on the third
day of the war, a party to German naval operations.

The steamship *Lorenzo* dropped down the harbor, ostensibly for Buenos Aires, on the following day, August 6, cleared by a false manifest,
and bearing coal and food for German sailors.
On these ships, and on the *Thor* (from Newport
News for Fray Bentos, Uruguay), on the *Heine*
(from Philadelphia on August 6 for La Guayra),
on the *J. S. Mowinckel* and the *Nepos* (out of
Philadelphia for Monrovia) and others Boy-Ed
and Buenz had placed supercargoes bearing secret
instructions. These men had authority to give
navigating orders to the captains once they were
outside the three-mile limit—orders to keep a rendezvous with German battleships by wireless
somewhere in the Atlantic wastes.

The *Berwind* approached the island of Trinidad and Herr Poeppinghaus, who was her supercargo, directed the captain to lie to. Five German ships, the *Kap Trafalgar, Pontus, Elinor
Woerman, Santa Lucia* and *Eber,* approached
and the transfer of supplies started. It was interrupted by the British converted cruiser *Car-*

*mania.* She engaged in a brisk two-hour duel with the *Kap Trafalgar* which ended only when the latter sank into the tropical ocean. The *Berwind* meanwhile put the horizon between herself and the *Carmania.*

Few of the chartered ships carried out their intentions, although their adventures were various. Hear the story of the *Unita:* Her skipper was Eno Olsen, a Canadian citizen born in Norway. Urhitzler, the German spy placed aboard, made the mistake of assuming that Olsen was friendly to Germany. He gave him his "orders," and the skipper balked. " 'Nothing doing,' I told the supercargo," Captain Olsen testified later, with a Norwegian twist to his pronunciation. "She's booked to Cadiz, and to Cadiz she goes! So the supercargo offered me $500 to change my course. 'Nothing doing—nothing doing for a million dollars,' I told him. The third day out he offered me $10,000. Nothing doing. So," announced Captain Olsen with finality, "I sailed the *Unita* to Cadiz and after we got there I sold the cargo and looked up the British consul."

One picturesque incident of the provisioning enterprise was the piratical cruise of the good ship *Gladstone,* rechristened, with a German benediction, *Marina Quezada.* Under the name of *Gladstone,* the ship had flown the Norwegian flag on a route between Canada and Australia, but shortly after the outbreak of war she put into Newport News. Simultaneously a sea captain, Hans Suhren, a sturdy German formerly of the Pacific coast, appeared in New York, called upon Captain Boy-Ed, who took kindly interest in him, and then departed for Newport News. Here he assumed charge of the *Marina Quezada*.

"I paid $280,000 in cash for her," he told First Officer Bentzen. After hiring a crew, he hurried back to New York, where he received messages in care of "Nordmann, Room 801, 11 Broadway, N. Y. C."—Captain Boy-Ed's office. Captain Boy-Ed had already told him to erect a wireless plant on his ship—the equipment having been shipped to the *Marina Quezada*—and to hire a wireless operator. He then handed Suhren a German naval code book, a chart with routes drawn, and sailing instructions for the South Seas, there to await German cruisers. Food supplies, ordered for the steamer *Unita* (which at that time had been unable to sail) were wasting on the piers at Newport News and Captain Boy-Ed ordered them put in the *Marina Quezada*. Two cases of revolvers also were sent to the boat.

Again Suhren went back to the ship and kept his wireless operators busy and speeded up the

loading of the cargo, which was under the supervision of an employee of the North German Lloyd.
Needing more money before sailing in December,
1914, he drew a draft for $1,000 on the Hamburg-
American Line, wiring Adolf Hachmeister, the
purchasing agent, to communicate with "Room
801, 11 Broadway."

Then trouble arose over the ship's registry.
Though Suhren insisted that he owned her, a
corporation in New York whose stockholders
were Costa Ricans were laying claim to owner-
ship, for they had christened her and had secured provisional registration from the Costa Rican minister in Washington. Permanent registry, however, required application at Port Limon,
Costa Rica. So hauling down the Norwegian
ensign that had fluttered over the ship as the
*Gladstone,* Captain Suhren ran up the Costa
Rican emblem. He had obtained false clearance
papers stating his destination as Valparaiso.
They were based upon a false manifest, and he
sailed for Port Limon. The Costa Rican authorities declined to give Suhren permanent
papers, and he found himself master of a ship
without a flag, and in such status not permitted
under international law to leave port. He waited
for a heavy storm and darkness, then quietly
slipping his anchor, he sped out into the high seas,

a pirate. Off Pernambuco he ran up the Norwegian flag, put into port and got into such difficulties with the authorities that his ship and he were interned. His supplies never reached the raiders and Boy-Ed learned of another fiasco.

The *Lorenzo, Thor* and *Heine* were seized at sea. The *Bangor* was captured in the Straits of Magellan. Out of twelve shiploads of supplies, only some $20,000 worth were ever transshipped to German war vessels. This involved a considerable loss, as the following statement of expenditures for those vessels made by the Hamburg-American Line will show:

| Steamer | Total payment |
| --- | --- |
| *Thor* ................... | $113,879.72 |
| *Berwind* ............... | 73,221.85 |
| *Lorenzo* ................ | 430,182.59 |
| *Heine* .................. | 288,142.06 |
| *Nepos* .................. | 119,037.60 |
| *Mowinckel* ............. | 113,367.18 |
| *Unita* ................... | 67,766.44 |
| *Somerstad* ............. | 45,826.75 |
| *Fram* ................... | 55,053.23 |
| *Craecia* ................ | 29,143.59 |
| *Macedonia* ............. | 39,139.98 |
| *Navarra* ................ | 44,133.50 |
| Total .............. | $1,419,394.49 |

Where did the money come from? The Hamburg-American Line, under the ante-bellum contract, placed at Captain Boy-Ed's disposal three payments of $500,000 each from the Deutsches Bank, Berlin; the Deutsches Bank forwarded through Wessells, Kulenkampff & Co., credit for $750,000 more. "I followed the instructions of Captain Boy-Ed," Kulenkampff testified. "He instructed me at different times to pay over certain amounts either to banks or firms. I transferred $350,000 to the Wells-Fargo Nevada National Bank in San Francisco, $150,000 to the North German Lloyd, then $63,000 to the North German Lloyd. The balance of $160,000 I placed to the credit of the Deutsches Bank with Gontard & Co., successors to my former firm. That was reduced to about $57,000 by payments drawn at Captain Boy-Ed's request to the order of the Hamburg-American Line."

The North German Lloyd was serving as the Captain's Pacific operative, which accounts for the transfer of the funds to the West. (The same line, through its Baltimore agent, Paul Hilken, was also coöperating at this time, but not to an extent which brought the busy Hilken into prominence as did his later connection with the merchant submarine, *Deutschland*.) Following the course of the funds, federal agents eventually uncovered the operations of Germans on the Pacific coast, and secured the arrest and convictions of no less personages than the consular staff in San Francisco.

The steamship *Sacramento* left San Francisco with a water-line cargo of supplies. A firm of customs brokers in San Francisco was given a fund of $46,000 by the German consulate to purchase supplies for her; a fictitious steamship company was organized to satisfy the customs officials; on September 23 an additional $100,000 was paid by the Germans for her cargo; a false valuation was placed on her cargo, and she was cleared on October 3. Two days later Benno Klocke and Gustav Traub, members of the crew, broke the wireless seals and got into communication with the *Dresden*. Klocke usurped the position of master of the vessel, and steered her to a rendezvous on November 8 with the *Scharnhorst*, off Masafueros Island, in the South Pacific; six days later she provisioned and coaled the German steamship *Baden*. She reached Valparaiso empty. Captain Anderson said he could not help the fact that her supplies were swung outboard and into the *Scharnhorst* and *Dresden*.

Captain Fred Jebsen, who was a lieutenant in the German Naval Reserve, took out a cargo of coal, properly bonded in his ship, the *Mazatlan*, for Guaymas, Sonora, Mexico. Off the mouth of Magdalena Bay the *Mazatlan* met the *Leipzig,* a German cruiser, and the cargo of coal was transferred to the battleship. One of Jebsen's men, who had signed on as a cook, was an expert wireless operator, and he went to the *Leipzig* with three cases of "preserved fruits"—wireless apparatus forwarded by German agents in California. Jebsen, after an attempt to smuggle arms into India, which will be discussed later, made his way to Germany in disguise, and was reported to have been drowned in a submarine. The *Nurnberg* and *Leipzig* lay off San Francisco for days in August, the former finally entering the Golden Gate for the amount of coal allowed her under international law. The *Olson* and *Mahoney,* a steam schooner, was laden with supplies for the German vessels and prepared to sail, but after a considerable controversy with the customs officials, was unloaded.

Perhaps the most bizarre attempt to spirit supplies to the Imperial navy was that in which the little barkentine *Retriever* figured as heroine. Wide publicity was given the announcement that she was to be sailed out to sea and used as the locale of a motion picture drama. The Government found out, however, that her hull was well down with coal, which did not seem vital to the scenario, and she was not permitted to leave port.

The major portion of Germany's naval strength lay corked in the Kiel Canal, where, except for a few indecisive sorties, Germany's visible fleet was destined to remain for more than three years. At the outbreak of war, the *Emden, Dresden, Scharnhorst, Gneisenau* and *Nurnberg* were at large in the southern oceans. On November 1 the German cruisers met the British *Monmouth, Good Hope, Glasgow* and *Otranto* off Coronel, the Chilean coast. The *Monmouth* and *Good Hope* were struck a mortal blow and sunk. The *Glasgow* and *Otranto* barely escaped. In a battle off the Falkland Islands on December 7, as the German army was being thrown back from Ypres, the *Scharnhorst, Leipzig, Gneisenau* and *Nurnberg* were sunk by a reinforced British fleet. (Walter Peters, one of the crew of the *Leipzig,* floated about for six hours after the engagement, was picked up, made his way to Mexico, and for more than three years was employed by a German vice-consul in Mexico in espionage in the United States. Peters was arrested as a dangerous enemy alien in Crockett, California, in April, 1918.) The *Dresden* and *Karlsruhe* escaped, and the former hid for two months in the fjords of the Straits of Magellan. On February 26, 1915, an American tourist vessel, the *Kroonland,* passed east through the Straits and into Punta Arenas harbor, while out of the harbor sneaked the little *Glasgow,* westward bound. The *Dresden,* after the American had passed, had run for the open Pacific; the *Glasgow,* hot on her trail, engaged her off the Chilean coast five days later and sank her, leaving only the *Emden* and *Karlsruhe* at large. The *Karlsruhe* disappeared.

The last lone member of the pack was hunted over the seas for months, and finally was beached, but long before her activities became public the necessity for supplying the German ships expired, from the simple elimination of German ships to supply. Captain Boy-Ed's first enterprise had been frustrated by the British navy and he turned to other and more sinister occupations. Buenz, Koetter and Hachmeister were sentenced to eighteen months in Atlanta, and Poeppinghaus to a year and a day—terms which they did not begin to serve until 1918.[1]

---

[1] Dr Buenz' case is an enlightening example of the use made by German agents in America of the law's delays. He was sentenced in December, 1915, for an offence committed in September, 1914. He at once appealed his case to the higher courts, going freely about meanwhile on bail furnished by the Hamburg American Line. In March, 1918, the Supreme Court of the United States, to which his case had finally been pressed, denied his appeal. His attorneys at once placed before President Wilson, through Attorney-General Gregory, a request for a respite, or commutation of his sentence, which the President, on April 23, 1918, denied. Buenz pleaded the frailty of his 79 years—which had not prevented him from keeping his social engagements while his appeal was pending.

# CHAPTER IV

## THE WIRELESS SYSTEM

The German Embassy a clearing house—Sayville—
Germany's knowledge of U. S. wireless—Subsidized elec-
trical companies—Aid to the raiders—The *Emden*—The
*Geier*—Charles E. Apgar—The German code.

The coördination of a nation's fighting forces
depends upon that nation's system of communication. In no previous war in the world's history
has a general staff known more of the enemy's
plans. We look back almost patronizingly across
a century to the semaphore which transmitted
Napoleon's orders from Paris to the Rhine in
three hours; we can scarcely realize that if the
report of a scout had ever got through to General Hooker, warning him that a suspicious
wagon train had been actually sighted a few miles
away, Stonewall Jackson's flanking march at
Chancellorsville would have been checked in its
first stages. In this greatest of all wars a British battery silences a German gun within two
minutes after the allied airman has "spotted" the
Boche. The air is "Any Man's Land." What

lies beyond the hill is no longer the great hazard, for the wireless is flashing.

If the Allied general staffs had been provided with X-ray field-glasses, and had trained those glasses on a certain brownstone house in Massachusetts Avenue, between Fourteenth and Fifteenth Streets, in Washington, they would have been interested in the perfection of the German system of communication. They would have observed the secretarial force of the Imperial Embassy opening and sorting letters from confederates throughout the country, many so phrased as to be quite harmless, others apparently meaningless. The Embassy served as a clearing-house for all German and Allied air messages.

Long before the war broke out the German government had seen the military necessity for a complete wireless system. Subsidies were secretly granted to the largest of the German electrical manufacturers to establish stations all over the globe. Companies were formed in America, ostensibly financed with American funds, but on plans submitted to German capitalists and through them to the German Foreign Office for approval. Thus was the Sayville station erected. As early as 1909 a German captain, Otto von Fossberg, had been sent to America to select a site on Long Island for the station. "The German government is backing the scheme," he told a friend, although the venture was publicly supposed to be under the auspices of the "Atlantic Communication Company," in which certain prominent German-Americans held stock and office. In 1911 an expert, Fritz von der Woude, paid Sayville a visit long enough to install the apparatus; he came under strict injunctions not to let his mission become generally known.

Boy-Ed watched the progress of the Sayville station with close interest and considerable authority, and his familiarity with wireless threw him into frequent and cordial relationship with the United States naval wireless men and the Department of Commerce. On one occasion the Department requested a confidential report from a radio inspector of the progress made by foreign interests in wireless; the report prepared went to Germany before it came to the hands of the United States government. Again: the German government was informed in 1914 by Boy-Ed in Washington that the United States intended to erect a wireless station at a certain point in the Philippines; full details, as the Navy Department had developed them, were forwarded, and the German government immediately directed a large electrical manufacturer in Berlin to bid for the work. The site the United States had selected was not altogether satisfactory to Germany, for some reason, so the German government added this delicious touch: a confidential map of the Philippines was turned over to the electrical house, with orders to submit a plan for the construction of the American station on a site which had been chosen by the German General War Staff!

The *Providence Journal* claims to have discovered an interesting German document—probably genuine—which reveals the scope of the Teutonic wireless project. It was a chart, bearing a rectangle labeled in German with the title of the German Foreign Office. From this "trunk" radiated three "branches," each bearing a name, and each terminating in the words "Telefunken Co." The first branch was labeled "Gesellschaft für Drahtlose Telegraphie, Berlin"; the second, "Siemens & Halske, Siemens-Schuckert-Werke, Berlin"; the third, "Allgemeine Elektrizitäts-Gesellschaft, Berlin."

From each branch grew still further subdivisions, labeled with the names of electrical firms or agents all over the world, and all subject to the direction of the German government. These names follow:

From No. 1: Atlantic Communication Co. (Sayville), New York; Australasian Wireless

Co., Ltd., Sydney (Australia); Telefunken East Asiatic Wireless Telegraph Co., Ltd., Shanghai; Maintz & Co. (of Amsterdam, Holland), Batavia (Java); Germann & Co. (of Hamburg), Manila; B. Grimm & Co., Bangkok; Paetzold & Eppinger, Havana; Spiegelthal, La Guayra; Kruger & Co., Guayaquil; Brahm & Co., Lima; E. Quicke, Montevideo; R. Schulbach, Thiemer & Co. (of Hamburg), Central America; Sesto Sesti, Rome; A. D. Zacharion & Cie., Athens; J. K. Dimitrijievic, Belgrade.

From No. 2: Siemens Bros. & Co., Ltd., London; Siemens & Halske, Vienna; Siemens & Halske, Petrograd; Siemens & Halske (K. G. Frank), New York; Siemens-Schuckert-Werke, Sofia; Siemens-Schuckert-Werke, Constantinople; Siemens-Schuckert-Werke (Dansk Aktsielskab), Copenhagen; Siemens-Schuckert-Werke (Denki Kabushiki Kaishe), Tokio; Siemens-Schuckert-Werke (Companhia Brazileira de Electricidade), Rio de Janeiro; Siemens-Schuckert, Ltd., Buenos Ayres; Siemens-Schuckert, Ltd., Valparaiso.

From No. 3: A. E. G. Union Electrique, Brussels; Allgemeine Elektrizitäts-Gesellschaft, Basel; A. E. G. Elecktriska Aktiebolaget, Stockholm; A. E. G. Electricitats Aktieselskabet, Christiania; A. E. G. Thomson-Houston Iberica, Madrid; A. E. G. Compania Mexicana, Mexico; A. E. G. Electrical Company of South Africa, Johannesburg.

The German manufacturers evinced a keen interest in the project of a wireless plant in Nicaragua, laying special stress on the point that "permanent stations in this neighborhood" would be valuable "if the Panama Canal is fortified." From Sayville station the German plan projected powerful wireless plants in Mexico, at Para, Brazil; at Paramaribo, Dutch Guiana; at Cartagena, Colombia, and at Lima, Peru. A point in which Captain H. Retzmann, the German naval attaché in 1911, was at one time interested was whether signals could be sent to the German fleet in the English Channel from America without England's interference. German naval wireless experts supervised the construction, and although the stations were nominally civilian-manned, and purely commercial, in reality the operators were often men of unusual scientific intellect, whose talents were sadly underpaid if they received no more than operators' salaries.

Gradually and quietly, Germany year by year spread her system of wireless communication over Central and South America, preparing her machinery for war. Over her staff of operators and mechanics she appointed an expert in the full confidence of the Embassy at Washington, and in close contact with Captain Boy-Ed. To the system of German-owned commercial plants in the United States he added amateur stations of more or less restricted radius, as auxiliary apparatus.

When the war broke out, and scores of German merchantmen were confined to American ports by the omnipresence of the British fleet at sea, the wireless of the interned ships was added to the system. Thus in every port lay a source of information for the Embassy. The United States presently ordered the closing of all private wireless stations, and those amateurs who had been listening out of sheer curiosity to the air conversation cheerfully took down their antennae. Not so, however, a prominent woman in whose residence on Fifth Avenue lay concealed a powerful receiving apparatus. Nor did the interned ships obey the order: apparatus apparently removed was often rigged in the shelter of a funnel, and operated by current supplied from an apparently innocent source. And the secret service discovered stations also in the residences of wealthy Hoboken Germans, and in a German-American "mansion" in Hartford, Connecticut.

The operators of these stations made their reports regularly through various channels to the

Embassy. There the messages were sorted, and it is safe to say that Count von Bernstorff was cognizant of the position of every ship on the oceans. He was in possession of both the French and British secret admiralty codes. In the light of that fact, the manœuvres of the British and German fleets in the South Atlantic and Pacific became simply a game of chess, Germany following every move of the British fleet under Admiral Cradock, knowing the identity of his ships, their gun-power, and their speed. When she located the *Good Hope, Monmouth, Glasgow* and *Otranto* off Coronel, Berlin, through von Bernstorff, gave Admiral von Spee the word to strike, with the results which we have observed: the sinking of the *Monmouth* and *Good Hope,* and the crippling of the *Glasgow* and *Otranto.*

Throughout August, September and October, 1914, the system operated perfectly. Bernstorff and Boy-Ed were confronted with the problem of keeping the German fleet alive as long as possible, and inflicting as much damage as possible on enemy shipping. Allied merchantmen left port almost with impunity, and were gathered in by German raiders who had been informed from Washington of the location of their prey. But the defeat off Chile apparently was conclusive proof to England that Germany knew her naval code, and the events of November and December indicate that England changed her code.

It was while engaged in escort duty to the first transport fleet of the Australian Expeditionary Force that the Australian crusier *Sydney* received wireless signals from Cocos Island shrieking that the *Emden* was near by. The *Emden,* having been deprived for some time of news of enemy ships, had gone there to destroy the wireless station, having in the past three months sunk some $12,500,000 of British shipping. Even while the island's distress signals were crashing out, the *Emden* had her own wireless busy in an effort to drown the call for help, or "jam" the air. On the following morning, November 9, the *Sydney* came up with the enemy. A sharp action followed. The *Sydney's* gunfire was accurate enough to cause the death of 7 officers and 108 men; her own losses were 4 killed and 12 wounded; the *Emden* fled, ran aground on North Keeling Island, one of the Cocos group, and ultimately became a total wreck.

In the same month the cruiser *Geier* fled the approach of the British and found refuge in Honolulu harbor. Her commander, Captain Karl Grasshof, made the mistake of keeping a diary. That document, which later fell into the hands of the Navy Intelligence Service, revealed a complete disrespect for the hospitality which the American government afforded the refugees. The *Geier's* band used to strike up for an afternoon concert, and under cover of the music, the wireless apparatus sent out messages to raiders at sea or messages in English so phrased as to start rumors of trouble between Japan and the United States. The *Geier* was the source of a rumor to the effect that Japanese troops had landed in Mexico; the *Geier* gave what circulation she could to a report that Germans in the United States were planning an invasion of Canada and was ably assisted in this effort by George Rodiek, German consul at Honolulu; the *Geier* caught all trans-Pacific wireless messages, and intercepted numerous United States government despatches. Captain Grasshof also spread a report quoting an American submarine commander as saying he would "like to do something to those Japs outside" (referring to the Japanese Pacific patrol) provided he (the American commander) and the German could reach an agreement. This report Grasshof attributed to von Papen, and later retracted, admitting that it was a lie. Grasshof's courier to the consulate in San Francisco was A. V. Kircheisen, a quartermaster on the liner *China,* a German secret service agent bearing the number K-17. Kircheisen frequently used the *China's* wireless to send German messages.

On December 8 occurred the engagement off the Falklands, which resulted in the defeat of the German fleet. The *Karlsruhe* within a short time gave up her aimless wanderings and disappeared. In February the *Glasgow* avenged herself on the *Dresden,* and the *Prinz Eitel Friedrich* and the *Kronprinz Wilhelm* fled into the security of Hampton Roads for the duration of war.

The United States' suspicions had been aroused by the activity of the German wireless plants, but the arm of the law did not remove at once the German operators at certain commercial stations. They were the men who despatched communications to Berlin and to the raiders. Interspersed in commercial messages they sprinkled code phrases, words, numbers, a meaningless and innocent jargon. The daily press bulletin issued to all ships at sea was an especially adaptable vehicle for this practice, as any traveler who has been forced to glean his news from one of these bulletins will readily appreciate. There were Americans shrewd enough, however, to become exceedingly suspicious of this superficially careless sending, and their suspicions were confirmed through the invention of another shrewd American,

Charles E. Apgar. He combined the principles of the phonograph and the wireless in such a way as to record on a wax disc the dots and dashes of the message, precisely as it came through the receiver. The records could be studied and analyzed at leisure. And the United States government has studied them.

At three o'clock every morning, the great wireless station at Nauen, near Berlin, uttered a hash of language into the ether. It was apparently not directed to any one in particular, nor did it contain any known coherence. Unless the operator in America wore a DeForest audian detector, which picks up waves from a great distance, he could not have heard it, and certainly during the early part of the war he paid no attention to it. The United States decided, however, that it might be well to eavesdrop, and so for over two years every utterance from Nauen was transcribed and filed away, or run off on the phonograph, in the hope that repetition might reveal the code. Until the code was discovered elsewhere, the phonographic records told no tales, but then the State Department found that it had a priceless library of Prussian impudence.

The diplomatic code was a dictionary, its pages designated by serial letters, its words by serial numbers. Thus the message

## "12-B-15-C-7"

signified the twelfth and fifteenth words on the second page, and the seventh word on the third page. This particular dictionary was one of a rare edition.

To complement the diplomatic code the Deutches Bank, the German Foreign Office, and their commercial representatives, Hugo Schmidt and Dr. Albert, had agreed upon an arbitrary code which proved one of the most difficult which the American authorities have ever had to decipher. Solution would have been impossible without some of the straight English or German confirmations which followed by mail, but as most of these documents were lost or destroyed, the deciphering had to be done by astute construction of testimony taken from Schmidt as late as the fall of 1917. He had made the work doubly difficult by burning the cipher key and most of his important papers in the furnace of the German Club.

Simple phrases, such as might readily pass any censor without arousing suspicion, passed frequently through Sayville station. The message "Expect father to-morrow" meant "The political situation between America and Germany grows worse. It is imperative that you take care of your New York affairs." "Depot" meant "Securities"; "Depot Pritchard" meant "Securities to be held in Germany"; "Depot Cooper" meant "Securities to be forwarded to some neutral country in Europe." Schmidt himself had the following aliases: "John Maley," "Roy Woolen," "Sidney Pickford," "George Brewster," "175 Congress Street, Brooklyn," "James Frasier," or "Andrew Brodie." Dr. Albert was mentioned as "John Herbinsen," "Howard Ackley," "Leonard Hadden," or "Donald Yerkes." James W. Gerard, the American ambassador at Berlin, was "Wilbur McDonald"; America was "Fremessi" or "Alfred Lipton." To throw any suspicion off the scent, the phrase "Hughes recovered" was translatable simply as "agreed," whereas "Percy died" meant "disagreed." Amounts of money were to be multiplied by one thousand.

This cipher code, so far as it had any system at all, showed a skilful choice of arbitrary proper names, than which there is nothing less suggestive or significant when the name is backed up by no known or discoverable personality. These names met two requirements: they carefully avoided any names of personages, and they sounded English or American. Following is a table of the commoner symbols used:

| CODE | TRANSLATION |
|---|---|
| Alcott | Hugo Reisinger |
| Andeo | Payments are |
| John Hazel: Chapman; | |
| Thos. Hadley | G. Amsinck & Co. |
| Pythagoras Errflint | Argentine Finance Minister |
| Lawrence McKay | Austrian Ambassador at Washington. |
| John Hastings; Fred Holden; Wm. Lounsbury | |
| Flagside; Chas. Hall | Bankers Trust Co. |
| Henry Galloway | Belgium |
| Frenchlike; Blake | Berlin |
| Flammigere | Bethlehem Steel Co. |
| Percy Bloomfield | Reichsbank |
| Gobber Milbank or John Childs | Capt. Boy-Ed |
| George Mallery | British Ambassador at Washington |
| Charles Thurston: | |
| Caffney Richard | British Government |
| Ernest Whiskard | Central Bank of Norway |
| Frederick Chappell, | The Submarine *Deutschland* |
| Walter Harris; Edmund Hutton | Chase National Bank |
| Mills Edgar | Dr. Dernberg |
| Albert Hardwood | Empire Trust Co. |
| Herbert Hastings, Langman Howard, Luckett Ernest | Equitable Trust Co. |
| Eversleigh | New York |
| Sidney Farmer and others | Speyer & Co. |
| Francis Hawkins | Farmers Loan & Trust Co. |
| Francis Manuel; | |
| Edward Gary | German Government |
| Fleshquake | Kuhn, Loeb & Co. |
| Clarence Hadden | First National Bank |
| Floezanbel | George J. Gould |
| Floezuise | J. P. Morgan |
| Wm. Gerome | J. P. Morgan & Co. |
| Fluitkoker | Wm. Barclay Parsons |

| CODE | TRANSLATION |
|---|---|
| Fleuxerimus | High Official of Bethlehem Steel Co. |
| Fogarizers | Chas. M. Schwab |
| John Hayward | Norwegian Government |
| Franklin Giltrap | Hamburg-American Line |
| Theodore Hooper | Capt. von Papen |
| 15 Code names represented the | Guaranty Trust Co. |
| Paul Overton; Robt. Hopkins | Hanover Nat. Bank |
| George Hedding | Standard Mercantile Agency |
| Hugh Sturges | Paul Hilken (*Deutschland*) |
| Clarence Marsh | Japanese Ambassador at Washington |
| Howard Howe | Irving Nat. Bank |
| Herbert Miller | President of U. S. |
| Andrew Mills | Secretary of Commerce and Labor |
| Theodore Mitchell | Secretary of Agriculture |
| Robert Moffatt | Secretary of State |
| Frank Monroe | Secretary of Treasury |
| Walter Montgomery | Secretary of Navy |
| Dolling | London |
| Robert London | North German Lloyd |
| Steven Morgan | United States Congress |
| Frank Mountcastle | The name of the Deutsches Bank is not to be mentioned |
| Steven Lawson | Royal Bank of Canada |
| Gafento | Toluol (High explosive) |

The chief significance of the discovery of the two codes is their conclusive proof that while von Bernstorff was protesting to the American government that he could not get messages through to Berlin, nor replies from the foreign office, he was actually in daily, if not hourly, communica-

tion with his superiors. Messages were sent out
by his confidential operators under the very eyes
of the American naval censors. After the break
of diplomatic relations with Berlin, in February,
1917, the authorities set to work decoding the
messages, and the State Department from time to
time issued for publication certain of the more
brutal proofs of Germany's violation of American neutrality. The ambassador and his Washington establishment had served for two years
and a half as the "central exchange" of German
affairs in the western world. After his departure communication from German spies here was
handicapped only by the time required to forward
information to Mexico; from that point to Berlin
air conversation continued uninterrupted.

# CHAPTER V

## MILITARY VIOLENCE

The plan to raid Canadian ports—The first Welland
Canal plot—Von Papen, von der Goltz and Tauscher—
The project abandoned—Goltz's arrest—The Tauscher
trial—Hidden arms—Louden's plan of invasion.

Underneath the even surface of American life
seethed a German volcano, eating at the upper
crust, occasionally cracking it, and not infrequently bursting a great gap.  When an eruption
occurred, America stopped work for a moment,
stared in surprise, sometimes in horror, at the
external phenomena, discussed them for a few
days, then hurried back to work.  More often
than not it saw nothing sinister even in the phenomena.

Less than ten hours from German headquarters in New York lay Canada, one of the richest
possessions of Germany's bitter enemy England.
Captain von Papen had not only full details of all
points of military importance in the United
States, but had made practical efforts to utilize

them. He knew where his reservists could be found in America. When the Government, shortly after the outbreak of war, forbade the recruiting of belligerents within its boundaries, and then refused to issue American passports for the protection of soldiers on the way to their commands, Captain von Papen planned to mobilize and employ a German army on American soil in no less pretentious an enterprise than a military invasion of the Dominion.

The first plan was attributed to a loyal German named Schumacher, whose ambiguous address was "Eden Bower Farm, Oregon." He outlined in detail to von Papen the feasibility of obtaining a number of powerful motor-boats, to be manned by German-American crews, and loaded with German-American rifles and machine guns. From the ports on the shores of the Great Lakes he considered it practicable to journey under cover of darkness to positions which would command the waterfronts of Toronto, Sarnia, Windsor and Kingston, Ontario, find the cities defenseless, and precipitate upon them a fair storm of bullets. A few Canadian lives might be lost, which did not matter; an enormous hue and cry would be raised to keep the Canadian troops at home to guard the back door.

Von Papen entertained the plan seriously, and

submitted it to Count von Bernstorff, who for obvious diplomatic reasons did not care to sponsor open violence when its proponent's references were unreliable, its actual reward was at best doubtful, and when subtle violence was equally practicable. Von Papen then produced an alternative project.

Cutting through the promontory which separates Lake Erie from the western end of Lake Ontario runs the Welland Canal, through which all shipping must pass to avoid Niagara Falls. This waterway is one of Canada's dearest properties, and is no mean artery of supply from the great grain country of the Northwest.

Its economic importance, however, was secondary in the German mind to the psychological effect upon Canada which a dynamite calamity to the Canal would certainly cause. The first expeditionary force of Canadian troops was training frantically at Valcartier, Quebec. They must be kept at home. Whether or not the idea originated with Captain von Papen is of little consequence (it may be safely assumed that Berlin had long had plans for such an enterprise); the fact is that it devolved upon him as military commander to crystallize thought in action. The plot is ascribed to "two Irishmen, prominent members of Irish associations, who had both fought during the Irish rebellion," and was to include destruction of the main railway junctions and the grain elevators in the vicinity of Toronto.

The picturesque renegade German spy commonly known as Horst von der Goltz is responsible for the generally accepted version of incidents which followed his first interview with von Papen on August 22 at the German Consulate in New York. He was sent to Baltimore under the assumed name of Bridgeman H. Taylor, with a letter to the German Consul there, Karl Luederitz, calling for whatever coöperation Goltz might need. He was to recruit accomplices from the crew of a German ship then lying at the North German Lloyd docks in the Patapsco River. With a man whom he had hired in New York, Charles Tucker, alias "Tuchhaendler," he visited the ship and selected his men. He then returned to New York, where Papen placed three more men at his disposal, one of them being A. A. Fritzen, of Brooklyn, a discharged purser on a Russian liner; another Frederick Busse, an "importer," with offices in the World Building, New York; and the third man Constantine Covani, a private detective, of New York. After a few days the sailors from Baltimore reported for duty, but were sent back, as Goltz noticed that his movements were being watched.

Papen sent Goltz to Captain Tauscher's office at 320 Broadway for explosives. On September 5, Captain Tauscher ordered 300 pounds of 60 per cent. dynamite to be delivered by the E. I. du Pont de Nemours Company to Mr. Bridgeman Taylor. In a motor-boat Goltz applied at a du Pont barge near Black Tom Island and the Statue of Liberty and took away his three hundred pounds of dynamite in suitcases. The little craft made its way up the river to 146th Street. The conspirators then carried their burden to the German Club in Central Park South and later in a taxicab to Goltz's home, where it was stored with a supply of revolvers and electrical apparatus for exploding the charges.

A passport for facile entrance into Canada had been applied for by one of Luederitz's henchmen in Baltimore in the name of "Bridgeman Taylor," and had been forwarded in care of Karl W. Buck, who lived at 843 West End Avenue, New York. With this guerdon of American protection Goltz set out for Buffalo about September 10—the last day of the Battle of the Marne—Busse and Fritzen carrying the dynamite and apparatus, and Covani, as Goltz naïvely related, "attending to me." He found rooms at 198 Delaware Avenue, in the heart of Buffalo. He learned of the terrain for the enterprise from a German of myste-

Passport given to Horst von der Goltz under the
*alias* of Bridgeman H. Taylor

rious occupation, who had lived in Buffalo for several years. Within a few days Goltz and his companions moved on to Niagara Falls—a move made easier by an exchange of telegraphic communications between Papen and himself. It is only necessary to quote, from the British Secret Service report to Parliament, those messages which Goltz received from the attaché, or "Steffens," as Papen chose to sign himself:

New York, N. Y. Sept. 15, 14

Mr. Taylor, 198 Delaware Ave. Buffalo

Sent money today. Consult lawyer John Ryan six hundred thirteen Mutual Life Building Buffalo not later than seventeenth.

STEFFENS, 112 Central Park South

12.45 p.

New York, N. Y. Sept. 16–14

Mr. Taylor, 198 Delaware Avenue, Bflo.

Ryan got money and instructions.

STEFFENS,

1.14 p.

Goltz and Covani "consulted" Mr. Ryan, who had received $200 on September 16 from Papen through Knauth, Nachod & Kuhne.

Then Goltz claimed that he made two aeroplane flights over Niagara Falls, and "reconnoitered the ground." Something went wrong, for after a week arrived the following telegrams:

New York, N. Y. Sept. 24–14.
John T. Ryan, 613 Mutual Life Bldg. Buffalo.

Please instruct Taylor cannot do anything more for him.

STEFFENS.

12:51 p.

New York, N. Y. Sept. 26–14.
Mr. Taylor, care Western Union, Niagara Falls, N. Y.

Do what you think best.  Did you receive dollars two hundred

RYAN

9.45 A.

These messages are open to several constructions.  They do not contradict Goltz's claim that he "learned that the first contingent of Canadian troops had left the camp."  They could indicate that his chief was not fully satisfied with his technique.  Perhaps the most intriguing feature of the telegrams is their presence in a safe-deposit vault in Holland when Goltz was captured months later.  It may be assumed that if (as he maintained) he was being watched constantly in Buffalo by the United States Secret Service, one of the first things he would have done is to destroy any messages received.  We leave the reader to decide—after he has traced Goltz's history a step or two further.

Whatever the occasion, the Welland enterprise

was dismissed; the dynamite was left with an aviator in Niagara Falls; Fritzen and Busse were discharged from service, and Covani and Goltz left for New York. In a letter dated December 7, from Buffalo, poor Busse wrote to Edmund Pavenstedt, at 45 William Street, New York, pleading that he had been left without any money in Niagara Falls; that he had written to von Papen and had been compelled to wait two weeks before he got $20. His expenses had accumulated during the fortnight, he could not find work, he even had sold his overcoat, and he begged Pavenstedt to send him money to come back to New York. "My friend Fritzen," he added, "was sent back some weeks ago by a gentleman in the German-American Alliance. . . . I would appreciate anything you can do for me, especially since I enlisted in such a task . . . Von Papen signs himself Stevens."

The military attaché was frankly disgusted at the failure of the undertaking. Goltz claims to have explained everything satisfactorily, and to have been given presently a new commission—that of returning to Germany for further instructions from Abteilung III of the General Staff, the intelligence department of the Empire.

On October 8 Goltz sailed for Europe, armed with his false passport, and a letter of introduction to the German Consul-General in Genoa. He reached Berlin safely, received his orders, returned to England, and was arrested on November 13. The public was not informed of his arrest, yet in Busse's letter from Buffalo of December 7, he mentioned Goltz's capture in London. News traveled fast in German channels.

Examination of his papers resulted in a protracted imprisonment, which daily grew more painful, and finally Goltz agreed to turn state's evidence against his former confrères. It was not until March 31, 1916, that Captain Tauscher was interrupted at his office by the arrival of agents of the Department of Justice, who placed him under arrest. He was held in $25,000 bail on a charge of having furthered a plot to blow up the Welland Canal.

Meanwhile Goltz's confession had implicated him in something more than a casual acquaintance with the plot; stubs in the check-book of Captain von Papen established payment made by the latter to Tauscher of $31.13, which happened to be the exact total of two bills from the du Pont Company to Captain Tauscher for dynamite and hemp fuses delivered on September 5 and 13 to "Bridgeman Taylor." Prior to the trial in June and July, 1916, Tauscher offered to plead guilty for a promise of the maximum fine without imprisonment, but his offer was rejected by the United States attorneys. A letter was introduced as testimony to his good character from General Crozier, the then head of the Ordnance Department at Washington. Goltz made an unimpressive witness, and Captain Tauscher, protesting his innocence as a mere intermediary in the affair, was acquitted of the charge.

Of the smaller fry Fritzen was arrested in Los Angeles in March, 1917. He stated then to officers that he had made trips to Cuba after the outbreak of war in 1914, had traveled over southern United States in two attempts to reach Mexico City, and had finally found employment on a ranch. He was sentenced to 18 months in prison. Tucker and Busse were witnesses at the Tauscher trial and were treated leniently. Covani turned from his previous occupation as hunter to that of quarry, and was not apprehended.

Information gathered by the Federal authorities and produced in court proved that Captain von Papen and reservist German army officers in the country planned a second mobilization of German reservists to attack Canadian points. That the project was seriously considered for a time is evidenced by a note in the diary found on the commander of the *Geier*, in Honolulu, in which he said that the German consul in Honolulu, George Rodiek, had had orders from the San Francisco consulate to circulate a report to that effect. Hundreds of thousands of rifles and hundreds of rounds of ammunition that were to be available for German reservists were stored in New York, Chicago and other cities on the border. Many a German-American brewery concealed in the shadows of its storehouses crates of arms and ammunition. Tauscher stored in 200 West Houston Street, New York, on June 21, 1915, 2,000 45-calibre Colt revolvers, 10 Colt automatic guns, 7,000 Springfield rifles, 3,000,000 revolver cartridges and 2,500,000 rifle cartridges. When the New York police questioned him about this arsenal, he said he had purchased them in job lots, for speculation. As a matter of fact they had been intended for use in India, but had been diverted on the Pacific coast and returned to New York.

A bolder version of the plot of invasion came from Max Lynar Louden, known to the Federal authorities as "Count Louden." He was a man of nondescript reputation, who had secret communications with the Germans in the early part of the war. He confessed that he was party to a scheme for the quick mobilization and equipment of a full army of German reservists. Louden was consistently annoying to the Secret Service in that he refused openly to violate the neutrality laws, but the moment the authorities learned of the fact that he was supposed to have two or three wives they made an investigation which resulted in his imprisonment. His story, if not altogether reliable, is interesting.

Through German-American interests, the plans were made in 1914, he said, and a fund of $16,000,000 was subscribed to carry out the details. Secret meetings were held in New York, Buffalo, Philadelphia, Detroit, Milwaukee, and other large cities, and at these meetings it was agreed that a force of 150,000 reservists was available to seize and hold the Welland Canal, strategic points and munitions centers.

"We had it arranged," said Louden, "to send our men from large cities following announcements of feasts and conventions, and I think we could have obtained enough to carry out our plans had it not been for my arrest on the charge of bigamy. The troops were to have been divided into four divisions, with six sections. The first two divisions were to have assembled at Silvercreek, Mich. The first was to have seized the Welland Canal. The second was to have taken Wind Mill Point, Ontario. The third was to go from Wilson, N. Y., to Port Hope. The fourth was to proceed from Watertown, N. Y., to Kingston, Ontario. The fifth was to assemble near Detroit and land near Windsor. The sixth section was to leave Cornwall and take possession of Ottawa.

"It had been planned to buy or charter eighty-four excursion and small boats to use in getting into Canada. All of the equipment was to have been put aboard the boats, and when quarters for 120,000 men had been found it would have been easy to continue the expedition. The German government was cognizant of the plan and maps, etc., were to have been furnished by the German government. A representative of the British Ambassador offered $20,000 for our plans."

But none of the first German-American expeditionary forces left for their destinations. Their project was innocently foiled by Amelia Wendt, Rose O'Brien and Nella Florence Allendorf. These ladies were Louden's wives.

# CHAPTER VI

## PAUL KOENIG

Justice and Metzler—Koenig's personality—von Papen's checks—The "little black book"—Telephone codes —Shadowing—Koenig's agents—His betrayal.

In a narrative which attempts so far as possible to proceed chronologically, it becomes necessary at this point to introduce Paul Koenig. For, on September 15, 1914, he sent an Irishman, named Edmund Justice, who had been a dock watchman, and one Frederick Metzler to Quebec for information of the number of Canadian troops in training. On September 18 Koenig left New York and met Metzler in Portland, Maine. He received his report, and on September 25 was in Burlington, Vt., where he conferred with Justice, and learned that the two spies had inspected the fortifications in Quebec, and had visited the training camps long enough to estimate the number and condition of the men. (Their information Koenig reported at once to von Papen, and it is possible that it dictated Papen's recall of Goltz from Buffalo the next day.)

Who was Paul Koenig? His underlings knew him as "P. K.," and called him the "bull-headed Westphalian" behind his back. He had a dozen aliases, among them Wegenkamp, Wagener, Kelly, Winter, Perkins, Stemler, Rectorberg, Boehm, Kennedy, James, Smith, Murphy, and W. T. Munday.

He was a product of the "Kaiser's Own"—the Hamburg-American Line. He had been a detective in the service of the Atlas Line, a subsidiary of the Hamburg-American, and for some years before the war was superintendent of the latter company's police. In that capacity he bossed a dozen men, watching the company's laborers and investigating any complaints made to the line. His work threw him into constant contact with sailors, tug-skippers, wharf-rats, longshoremen, and dive-keepers of the lowest type, and there was little of the criminal life of the waterfront that he had not seen.

He had arms like an ape, and the bodily strength of one. His expression suggested craft, ferocity, and brutality. Altogether his powerful frame and lurid vocabulary made him a figure to avoid or respect. Waterfront society did both —and hated him as well.

Von Papen saw in Koenig's little police force the nucleus of just such an organization as he

Paul Koenig, the Hamburg-American emlpoye, who supplied
and directed agents of German violence in America

needed. The Line put Koenig at the attaché's disposal in August, 1914, and straightway von Papen connected certain channels of information with Koenig's own system. He supplied reservists for special investigations and crimes, and presently Koenig became in effect the foreman of a large part of Germany's secret service in the East. As his activities broadened, he was called upon to execute commissions for Bernstorff, Albert, Dr. Dumba, the Austro-Hungarian ambassador, and Dr. Alexander von Nuber, the Austrian consul in New York, as well as for the attachés themselves. He acted as their guard on occasion, served as their confidential messenger, and made himself generally useful in investigation work.

The guilt-stained check-book of the military attaché contained these entries:

March 29, 1915. Paul Koenig (Secret Service Bill) $509.11

April 18, Paul Koenig (Secret Service Bill) $90.94

May 11, Paul Koenig (Secret Service) $66.71

July 16, Paul Koenig (Compensation for F. J. Busse) $150 00

August 4, Paul Koenig (5 bills secret service) $118.92

Those entries represent only the payments made Koenig by check for special work done for von Papen. Koenig received his wages from the

Line. When he performed work for any one else he rendered a special bill. This necessitated his itemizing his expenditures, and this Germanly thorough and thoroughly German system of petty accounting enabled our secret service later to trace his activities with considerable success. Koenig and von Papen used to haggle over his bills—on one occasion the attaché felt he was being overcharged, and accordingly deducted a half-dollar from the total.

"P. K." also had an incriminating book—a carefully prepared notebook of his spies and of persons in New York, Boston and other cities who were useful in furnishing him information. In another book he kept a complete record of the purpose and cost of assignments on which he sent his men. He listed in its pages the names of several hundred persons—army reservists, German-Americans and Americans, clerks, scientists and city and Federal employees—showing that his district was large and that his range for getting information and for supervising other pro-German propaganda was broad. For his own direct staff he worked out a system of numbers and initials to be used in communication. The numbers he changed at regular intervals and a system of progression was devised by which each agent would know when his number changed.

He provided them with suitable aliases. These men had alternative codes for writing letters and for telephone communication to be changed automatically by certain fixed dates.

Always alert for spies upon himself, Koenig suspected that his telephone wire was tapped and that his orders were being overheard. So he instructed his men in various code words. If he told an agent to meet him "at 5 o'clock at South Ferry" he meant: "Meet me at 7 o'clock at Forty-second Street and Broadway." His suspicions were well-grounded, for his wire was tapped, and Koenig led the men who were spying on him an unhappy dance.

For example: he would receive a call on the telephone and would direct his agent, at the other end of the wire, to meet him in fifteen minutes at Pabst's, Harlem. It is practically impossible to make the journey from Koenig's office in the Hamburg-American Building to 125th Street in a quarter of an hour. After a time his watchers learned that "Pabst's, Harlem" meant Borough Hall, Brooklyn.

He never went out in the daytime without one or two of his agents trailing him to see whether he was being shadowed. He used to turn a corner suddenly and stand still so that an American detective following came unexpectedly face to face with him and betrayed his identity. Koenig would laugh heartily and pass on. Thus he came to know many agents of the Department of Justice and many New York detectives. When he started out at night he usually had three of his own men follow him and by a pre-arranged system of signals inform him if any strangers were following him.

The task of keeping watch of Koenig's movements required astute guessing and tireless work on the part of the New York police. So elusive did he become that it was necessary for Captain Tunney to evolve a new system of shadowing him in order to keep him in sight without betraying that he was under surveillance. One detective, accordingly, would be stationed several blocks away and would start out ahead of Koenig. The "front shadow" was signaled by his confederates in the rear whenever Koenig turned a corner, so that the man in front might dart down a cross-street and manœuvre to keep ahead of him. If Koenig boarded a street car the man ahead would hail the car several blocks beyond, thus avoiding suspicion. In more than one instance detectives in the rear, guessing that he was about to take a car, would board it several blocks before it got abreast of Koenig. His alertness kept Detectives Barnitz, Coy, Terra, and Corell on edge for months.

It was impossible to overhear direct conversation between Koenig and any man to whom he was giving instructions. Some of his workers he never permitted to meet him at all, but when he kept a rendezvous it was in the open, in the parks in broad daylight, or in a moving-picture theatre, or in the Pennsylvania Station, or the Grand Central Terminal. There he could make sure that nobody was eavesdropping. If he met an agent in the open for the first time he gave him some such command at this:

"Be at Third Avenue and Fifty-ninth Street at 2:30 to-morrow afternoon beside a public telephone booth there. When the telephone rings answer it."

The man would obey. On the minute the telephone would ring and the man would lift the receiver. A strange voice told him to do certain things—either a definite assignment, or instructions to be at a similar place on the following day to receive a message. Or he might be told to meet another man, who would give him money and further orders. The voice at the other end of the wire spoke from a public telephone booth and was thus reasonably sure that the wire was not tapped.

And Koenig trusted no man. He never sent an agent out on a job without detailing another man to shadow that man and report back to him in full the operations of the agent and of any persons whom he might deal with. He was brutally severe in his insistence that his men do exactly what he told them without using their own initiative.

Koenig had spies on every big steamship pier. He had eavesdroppers in hotels, and on busy telephone switchboards. He employed porters, window-cleaners, bank clerks, corporation employees and even a member of the Police Department.

This last, listed in his book as "Special Agent A. S.," was Otto F. Mottola, a detective in the warrant squad. The notebook revealed Mottola as "Antonio Marino," an alias later changed to Antonio Salvatore. Evidence was produced at Mottola's trial at Police Headquarters that Koenig paid him for investigating a passenger who sailed on the *Bergensfjord;* that he often called up Mottola, asked questions, and received answers which Koenig's stenographer took down in shorthand. Through him Koenig sought to keep closely informed of developments at Police Headquarters in the inquiry being made by the police into the activities of the Germans. Mottola was dismissed from the force because of false statements made to his superiors when they questioned him about Koenig.

Koenig's very caution was the cause of his undoing. The detectives who shadowed him learned that he "never employed the same man more than once," which meant simply that he was careful to place no subordinate in a position where blackmail and exposure might be too easy. To this fact they added another trifling observation; they noticed that as time went on he was seen less in the company of one George Fuchs, a relative with whom he had been intimate early in the war. They cultivated the young man's acquaintance to the extent that he finally burst out with a recitation of his grievances against Koenig, and betrayed him to the authorities.

"P. K." was defiant always. "They did get Dr. Albert's portfolio," he said one day, "but they won't get mine. I won't carry one."

# CHAPTER VII

## FALSE PASSPORTS

Hans von Wedell's bureau—The traffic in false passports—Carl Ruroede—Methods of forgery—Adams' coup—von Wedell's letter to von Bernstorff—Stegler—Lody—Berlin counterfeits American passports—Von Breechow.

Throughout August, 1914, it was comparatively easy for Germans in America who wished to respond to the call of the Fatherland to leave American shores. A number of circumstances tended swiftly to make it more hazardous. The British were in no mind to permit an influx of reservists to Germany while they could blockade Germany. The cordon tightened, and soon every merchant ship was stopped at sea by a British patrol and searched for German suspects. German spies here took refuge in the protection afforded by an American passport. False passports were issued by the State Department in considerable quantities during the early weeks of war—issued unwittingly, of course, for the applicant in most cases underwent no more than the customary peace-time examination.

We have already seen that von der Goltz easily secured a passport. The details of his application were these: Karl A. Luederitz, the German consul at Baltimore, detailed one of his men to supply Goltz with a lawyer and an application blank (then known as Form 375). The lawyer was Frederick F. Schneider, of 2 East German Street, Baltimore. On that application Goltz swore that his name was Bridgeman H. Taylor, his birthplace San Francisco, his citizenship American, his residence New York City, and his occupation that of export broker. Charles Tucker served as witness to these fantastic sentiments. Two days later (August 31) the State Department issued passport number 40308 in the name of Taylor, and William Jennings Bryan signed the precious document.

It was not necessary at that time to state the countries which the applicant intended to visit. Within a few weeks, however, that information was required on the passport.

Each additional precaution taken by the Government placed a new obstacle in the way of unlimited supply of passports. The Goltz method was easy enough, but it soon became impossible to employ it. The necessity for sending news through to Berlin by courier was increasingly urgent and it devolved upon Captain von Papen to systematize the supply of passports. The military attaché in November selected Lieutenant Hans von Wedell, who had already made a trip as courier to Berlin for his friend, Count von Bernstorff. Von Wedell was married to a German baroness. He had been a newspaper reporter in New York, and later a lawyer. He opened an office in Bridge Street, New York, and began to send out emissaries to sailors on interned German liners, and to their friends in Hoboken, directing them to apply for passports. He sent others to the haunts of tramps on the lower East Side, to the Mills Hotel, and other gathering places of the down-and-outs, offering ten, fifteen or twenty dollars to men who would apply for and deliver passports. And he bought them! He spent much time at the Deutscher Verein, and at the Elks' Club in 43rd Street where he often met his agents to give instructions and receive passports. His bills were paid by Captain von Papen, as revealed by the attaché's checks and check stubs; on November 24, 1914, a payment in his favor of $500; on December 5, $500 more and then $300, the latter being for "journey money." Von Wedell's bills at the Deutscher Verein in November, 1914, came to $38.05, according to

Hans von Wedell and his wife. He was an important member
of the false-passport bureau and she a messenger
from von Papen to Germany

another counterfoil. The Captain in the meantime employed Frau von Wedell as courier, sending her with messages to Germany. On December 22, 1914, he paid the baroness, according to his check-book, $800.

The passports secured by von Wedell, and by his successor, Carl Ruroede, Sr., a clerk in Oelrichs & Co., whom he engaged, were supplied by the dozens to officers whom the General Staff had ordered back to Berlin. Not only American passports, but Mexican, Swiss, Swedish, Norwegian and all South American varieties were seized eagerly by reservists bound for the front. Germans and Austrians, who had been captured in Russia, sent to Siberia as prisoners of war, escaped and making their way by caravan through China, had embarked on vessels bound for America. Arriving in New York they shipped for neutral European countries. Among them was an Austrian officer, an expert aeroplane observer whose feet were frozen and amputated in Siberia, but who escaped to this country. He was ordered home because of his extreme value in observation, and after his flight three-fourths of the way round the world, the British took him off a ship at Falmouth to spend the remainder of the war in a prison camp.

Captain von Papen used the bureau frequently

for passports for spies whom he wished to send to England, France, Italy or Russia. Anton Kuepferle and von Breechow were two such agents. Both were captured in England with false passports in their possession. Both confessed, and the former killed himself in Brixton Jail.

Von Wedell and Ruroede grew reckless and boastful. Two hangers-on at the Mills Hotel called upon one of the writers of this volume one day and told him of von Wedell's practices, related how they had blackmailed him out of $50, gave his private telephone numbers and set forth his haunts. When this and other information reached the Department of Justice, Albert G. Adams, a clever agent, insinuated himself into Ruroede's confidence, and offered to secure passports for him for $50 each. Posing as a pro-German, he pried into the inner ring of the passport-buyers, and was informed by Ruroede just how the stock of passports needed replenishing.

Though in the early days of the war it had not been necessary for the applicant to give more than a general description of himself, the cry of "German spies!" in the Allied countries became so insistent that the Government added the requirement of a photograph of the bearer. The Germans, however, found it a simple matter to

give a general description of a man's eyes, color
of hair, and age to fit the person who was actually
to use the document; then forwarded the picture of the applicant to be affixed. The applicant receiving the passport, would sell it at once.
Even though the official seal was stamped on the
photograph the Germans were not dismayed.

Adams rushed into Ruroede's office one day
waving a sheaf of five passports issued to him by
the Government. Adams was ostensibly proud
of his work, Ruroede openly delighted.

"I knew I could get these passports easily," he
boasted to Adams. "Why, if Lieutenant von
Wedell had kept on here he never could have done
this. He always was getting into a muddle."

"But how can you use these passports with
these pictures on them?" asked the agent.

"Oh, that's easy," answered Ruroede. "Come
in the back room. I'll show you." And Ruroede, before the observant eyes of the Department of Justice, patted one of the passports with
a damp cloth, then with adhesive paste fastened
a photograph of another man over the original
bearing the imprint of the United States seal.

"We wet the photograph," said Ruroede, "and
then we affix the picture of the man who is to
use it. The new photograph also is dampened,
but when it is fastened to the passport there still

remains a sort of vacuum in spots between the new picture and the old because of ridges made by the seal. So we turn the passport upside down, place it on a soft ground—say a silk handkerchief—and then we take a paper-cutter with a dull point, and just trace the letters on the seal. The result is that the new photograph dries exactly as if it had been stamped by Uncle Sam. You can't tell the difference."

Adams never knew until long afterward that when he met Ruroede by appointment in Bowling Green, another German atop 11 Broadway was scrutinizing him through field-glasses, and examining every one who paused nearby, who might arouse suspicion of Adams' ingenuous part in the transaction.

Through Adams' efforts Ruroede and four Germans, one of them an officer in the German reserves, were arrested on January 2, on the Scandinavian-American liner *Bergensfjord* outward bound to Bergen, Norway. They had passports issued through Adams at Ruroede's request under the American names of Howard Paul Wright, Herbert S. Wilson, Peter Hanson and Stanley F. Martin. Their real names were Arthur Sachse, who worked in Pelham Heights, N. Y., and who was returning to become a lieutenant in the German Army; Walter Miller, August R.

Meyer and Herman Wegener, who had come to New York from Chile, on their way to the Fatherland.

On the day when Ruroede, his assistant, and the four men for whom he obtained passports were arrested, Joseph A. Baker, assistant superintendent of the Federal agents in New York, took possession of the office at 11 Bridge Street. As he was sorting papers and making a general investigation, a German walked in bearing a card of introduction from von Papen, introducing himself as Wolfram von Knorr, a German officer who up to the outbreak of the war had been naval attaché in Tokio. The officer desired a passport. Baker, after a conversation in which von Knorr revealed von Papen's connection with the passport bureau, told him to return the next day. When the German read the next morning's newspapers he changed his lodging-place and his name.

Von Wedell himself was a passenger on the *Bergensfjord,* but when he was lined up with the other passengers, the Federal agents, who did not have a description of him, missed him and left the vessel. He was later (January 11) taken off the ship by the British, however, and transferred to another vessel for removal to a prison camp. She struck a German mine and sank, and von Wedell is supposed to have drowned.

A few days before he sailed, he wrote a letter to von Bernstorff which fixes beyond question the responsibility for his false passport activities. The letter, dated from Nyack, where he was hiding, on December 26, 1914, follows:

"His Excellency The Imperial German Ambassador. Count von Bernstorff, Washington, D. C. Your Excellency: Allow me most obediently to put before you the following facts: It seems that an attempt has been made to produce the impression upon you that I prematurely abandoned my post, in New York. That is not true.

"I—My work was done. At my departure I left the service, well organized and worked out to its minutest details, in the hands of my successor, Mr. Carl Ruroede, picked out by myself, and, despite many warnings, still tarried for several days in New York in order to give him the necessary final directions and in order to hold in check the blackmailers thrown on my hands by the German officers until after the passage of my travelers through Gibraltar; in which I succeeded. Mr. Ruroede will testify to you that without my suitable preliminary labors, in which I left no conceivable means untried and in which I took not the slightest consideration of my personal weal or woe, it would be impossible for him, as well as for Mr. von Papen, to forward officers and 'aspirants' in any number whatever, to Europe. This merit I lay claim to and the occurrences of the last days have unfortunately compelled me, out of sheer self-respect, to emphasize this to your Excellency.

"II—The motives which induced me to leave New

York and which, to my astonishment, were not communicated to you, are the following:

"1. I knew that the State Department had, for three weeks, withheld a passport application forged by me. Why?

"2. Ten days before my departure I learnt from a telegram sent me by Mr. von Papen, which stirred me up very much, and further through the omission of a cable, that Dr. Stark had fallen into the hands of the English. That gentleman's forged papers were liable to come back any day and could, owing chiefly to his lack of caution, easily be traced back to me.

"3. Officers and aspirants of the class which I had to forward over, namely the people, saddled me with a lot of criminals and blackmailers, whose eventual revelations were liable to bring about any day the explosion of the bomb.

"4. Mr. von Papen had repeatedly urgently ordered me to hide myself.

" 5. Mr. Igel had told me I was taking the matter altogether too lightly and ought to—for God's sake—disappear.

"6. My counsel . . . had advised me to hastily quit New York, inasmuch as a local detective agency was ordered to go after the passport forgeries.

"7. It had become clear to me that eventual arrest might yet injure the worthy undertaking and that my disappearance would probably put a stop to all investigation in this direction.

"How urgent it was for me to go away is shown by the fact that, two days after my departure, detectives, who had followed up my telephone calls, hunted up my wife's harmless and unsuspecting cousin in Brooklyn, and subjected her to an interrogatory.

"Mr. von Papen and Mr. Albert have told my wife that I forced myself forward to do this work. That is not true. When I, in Berlin, for the first time heard of this commission, I objected to going and represented to the gentleman that my entire livelihood which I had created for myself in America by six years of labor was at stake therein. I have no other means, and although Mr. Albert told my wife my practice was not worth talking about, it sufficed, nevertheless, to decently support myself and wife and to build my future on. I have finally, at the suasion of Count Wedell, undertaken it, ready to sacrifice my future and that of my wife. I have, in order to reach my goal, despite infinite difficulties, destroyed everything that I built up here for myself and my wife. I have perhaps sometimes been awkward, but always full of good will, and I now travel back to Germany with the consciousness of having done my duty as well as I understood it, and of having accomplished my task.

"With expressions of the most exquisite consideration, I am, your Excellency,

"Very respectfully,
"(Signed) HANS ADAM VON WEDELL."

Ruroede was sentenced to three years in Atlanta prison. The four reservists, pleading guilty, protested they had taken the passports out of patriotism and were fined $200 each.

The arrest of Ruroede exposed the New York bureau, and made it necessary for the Germans to shift their base of operations, but it did not put an end to the fraudulent passport conspiracies. Captain Boy-Ed assumed the burden, and hired men to secure passports for him. One of these men was Richard Peter Stegler, a Prussian, 33 years old, who had served in the German Navy and afterward came to this country to start on his life work. Before the war he had applied for his first citizenship papers but his name had not been removed from the German naval reserve list.

"After the war started," Stegler said, "I received orders to return home. I was told that everything was in readiness for me. I was assigned to the naval station at Cuxhaven. My uniform, my cap, my boots and my locker would be all set aside for me, and I was told just where to go and what to do. But I could not get back at that time and I kept on with my work."

He became instead a member of the German secret service in New York. "There is not a ship that leaves the harbor, not a cargo that is loaded or unloaded, but that some member of this secret organization watches and reports every detail," he said. "All this information is transmitted in code to the German Government." In January, 1915, if not earlier, Stegler was sent by the German Consulate to Boy-Ed's office, where he received instructions to get a passport and make arrangements to go to England as a spy. Boy-Ed paid him $178, which the attaché admitted. Stegler immediately got in touch with Gustave Cook and Richard Madden, of Hoboken, and made use of Madden's birth certificate and citizenship in obtaining a passport from the American Government. Stegler paid $100 for the document. Stegler pleaded guilty to the charge and served 60 days in jail; Madden and Cook were convicted of conspiracy in connection with the project, and were sentenced to 10 months' imprisonment.

"I was told to make the voyage to England on the *Lusitania*," continued Stegler. "My instructions were as follows: 'Stop at Liverpool, examine the Mersey River, obtain the names, exact locations and all possible information concerning warships around Liverpool, ascertain the amount of munitions of war being unloaded on the Liverpool docks from the United States, ascertain their ultimate destination, and obtain a detailed list of all the ships in the harbor.'

"I was to make constant, though guarded inquiries, of the location of the dreadnought squadron which the Germans in New York understand was anchored somewhere near St. George's Channel. I was to appear as an American citizen soliciting trade. Captain Boy-Ed advised me to get letters of introduction to business firms. He made arrangements so that I received such letters and in one letter were enclosed some rare stamps which were to be a proof to certain persons in England that I was working for the Germans.

"After having studied at Liverpool I was to go to London and make an investigation of the Thames and its shipping. From there I was to proceed to Holland and work my way to the German border. While my passport did not include Germany, I was to give the captain of the nearest regiment a secret number which would indicate to him that I was a reservist on spy duty. By that means I was to hurry to Eisendal, head of the secret service in Berlin."

Stegler did not make the trip because his wife learned of the enterprise and begged him not to go. He too had run afoul of the vigilant Adams, and was placed under arrest in February, 1915, shortly after he decided to stay at home. In his possession were all the letters and telegrams exchanged between him and Boy-Ed, and one telegram from "Winkler," Captain Boy-Ed's servant.

Stegler also said that he had been told by Dr. Karl A. Fuehr. one of Dr. Albert's assistants, that Boy-Ed previously had sent to England Karl Hans Lody, the German who in November, 1915, was put to death as a spy in the Tower of London. Lody had been in the navy, had served on the Kaiser's yacht and then had come to this country and worked as an agent for the Hamburg-American Line, going from one city to another. Shortly after the war started Lody had gone on the mission of espionage which cost him his life.

Captain Boy-Ed authorized the commander of the German cruiser *Geier,* interned in Honolulu, to get his men back to Germany as best he could, by providing them with false passports. Still another of Boy-Ed's protégés was a naval reservist, August Meier, who shipped as a hand on the freighter *Evelyn* with a cargo of horses for Bermuda. On the voyage practically all of the horses were poisoned. Meier, however, was arrested by the Federal authorities on the charge of using the name of a dead man in order to get an American passport. In supplying passports and in handling spies, Captain Boy-Ed was more subtle than his colleague, von Papen. Nevertheless the Government officials succeeded in getting a clear outline of his activities. The exposure of Boy-Ed's connection with Stegler made it necessary for the German Government to change its system once more.

The Wilhelmstrasse had a bureau of its own. Reservists from America reported in Berlin for duty in Belgium and France, and their passports ceased to be useful, to them. The intelligence department commandeered the documents for agents whom they wished to send back to America. Tiny flakes of paper were torn from the body of the passport and from the seal, in order that counterfeiters might match them up. On January 14, 1915, an American named Reginald Rowland obtained a passport from the State Department for safe-conduct on a business trip to Germany. While it was being examined at the frontier every detail of the document was closely noted by the Germans. Some months later Captain Schnitzer, chief of the German secret service in Antwerp, had occasion to send a spy to England. He chose von Breechow, a German whom von Papen had forwarded from New York, and who had his first naturalization papers from the United States. To Breechow he gave a facsimile of Rowland's passport identical with the original in every superficial respect except that the spy's photograph had been substituted for the original, and the age of the bearer set down as 31—ten years older than Rowland.

Von Breechow passed the English officials at Rotterdam and at Tilbury. He soon fell under suspicion, however, and his passport was taken away. When the British learned that the real Rowland was at home in New Jersey, and in possession of his own passport, they sent for it, and compared the two. Breechow's revealed a false watermark, stamped on in clear grease, which made the paper translucent, but which was soluble in benzine. The stamp, ordinarily used to countersign both the photograph and the paper in a certain way, had been applied in a different position. With those exceptions, and the suspicious Teutonic twist to a "d" in the word "dark," the counterfeit was regular.

The Rosenthal case was the first to bring to light the false passport activities in Berlin. Rosenthal, posing as an agent for gas mantles, traveled in England successfully as a spy under an emergency passport issued by the American Embassy in Berlin. Captain Prieger, the chief of a section in the intelligence department of the General Staff, asked Rosenthal to make a second trip. The spy demurred, doubting whether his passport might be accepted a second time. The Captain turned to a safe, extracted a handful of false American passports, and said: "I can fit you out with a passport in any name you wish." Rosenthal decided to employ his own. He was arrested and imprisoned in England.

As the State Department increased its vigilance the evil began to expire. It was further stifled by concerted multiplication by the Allies of the examinations which the stranger had to undergo. But during its course it made personal communication between Berlin and lower Broadway almost casual.

# CHAPTER VIII

## INCENDIARISM

Increased munitions production—The opening explosions—Orders from Berlin—Von Papen and Seattle—July, 1915—The Van Koolbergen affair—The autumn of 1915—The Pinole explosion.

A bomb is an easy object to manufacture. Take a section of lead pipe from six to ten inches long, and solder into it a partition of thin metal, which divides the tube into two compartments. Place a high explosive in one compartment and seal it carefully (the entire operation requires a gentle touch) and in the other end pour a strong acid; cap it, and seal it. If you have chosen the proper metal for the partition, and acid of a strength to eat slowly through it to the explosive, you have produced a bomb of a type which German destroying agents were fond of using in America from the earliest days of their operation.

When the first panic of war had passed, the Allied nations took account of stock and sent their purchasing agents to America for war materials. Manufacturers of explosives set to work at once to fill contracts of unheard-of size. They built new factories almost overnight, hired men broadcast, and sacrificed every other consideration to that of swift and voluminous output. Accidents were inevitable. Probably we shall never know what catastrophes were actually wrought by German sympathizers, for the very nature of the processes and the complete ruin which followed an explosion guarded the secret of guilt. No doubt carelessness was largely to blame for the earlier explosions, but instead of diminishing as the new hands became more skillful, and as greater vigilance was employed everywhere, the number of disasters increased. The word "disaster" is used advisedly. Powder, gun-cotton, trinitrotoluol (or TNT, as it is better known), benzol (one of the chief substances used in the manufacture of TNT) and dynamite were being produced in great volume for the Allies in American plants within a comparatively short time—all powerful explosives even in minute quantity.

At sea the German navy was losing control daily. It therefore behooved the German forces in America to stop the production of munitions at its source. It may be well, for the force which such presentation carries, to recount very briefly the major accidents which occurred in America in the first few months after August, 1914.

On August 30 one powder mill of the du Pont Powder company (strictly speaking the E. I. du Pont de Nemours Company) at Pompton Lakes, New Jersey, blew up. In September a guncotton explosion in the Wright Chemical Works caused the death of three people, and a large property damage. In October the factory of the Pain Fireworks Display Company was destroyed, and several people were killed. In the same month the fireworks factory of Detwiller and Street in Jersey City suffered an explosion and the loss of four lives. These explosions were the opening guns.

Throughout August and September most of these accidents may be attributed to the inexperience and confusion which followed greatly increased production in the powder mills. But a circular dated November 18, issued by German Naval Headquarters to all naval agents throughout the world, ordered mobilized all "agents who are overseas and all destroying agents in ports where vessels carrying war material are loaded in England, France, Canada, the United States and Russia."

Followed these orders:

"It is indispensable by the intermediary of the

third person having no relation with the official representatives of Germany to recruit progressively agents to organize explosions on ships sailing to enemy countries in order to cause delays and confusion in the loading, the departure and the unloading of these ships. With this end in view we particularly recommend to your attention the deckhands, among whom are to be found a great many anarchists and escaped criminals. The necessary sums for buying and hiring persons charged with executing the projects will be put at your disposal on your demand."

Equally incriminating proof that the "destroying agents" were active in and about the factories lies in a circular intercepted by the French secret service in Stockholm, in a letter addressed by one Dr. Klasse in Germany to the Pan-German League in Sweden, in which he said:

"Inclosed is the circular of November 22, 1914, for information and execution upon United States territory. We draw your attention to the possibility of recruiting destroying agents among the anarchist labor organization." This circular was signed by Dr. Fischer, Councillor General of the German Army.

In the first six months of 1915 the du Pont factories at Haskell, N. J., Carney's Point, N. J., Wayne, Pa., and Wilmington, Del., experienced explosions and fires; a chemical explosion occurred in a factorý in East 19th Street, New York; the Anderson Chemical Company, at Wallington, N. J., was rocked on May 3 by an explosion of guncotton which cost three lives; five more lives were flashed out in a similar accident in the Equitable powder plant at Alton, Ill. On New Year's Day, the Buckthorne plant of the John A. Roebling Company, manufacturers of shell materials, at Trenton, was completely destroyed by fire, the property loss estimated at $1,500,000. And on June 26, the Ætna Powder plant at Pittsburgh suffered a chemical explosion which killed one man and injured ten others.

Most of these "accidents" had taken place near the Atlantic seaboard. Yet Germany was active in the far West. On May 30 a barge laden with a large cargo of dynamite lay in the harbor of Seattle, Washington. The dynamite was consigned to Russia and was about to be transferred to a steamer, when it exploded with a shock of earthquake violence felt many miles inland, and comparable to the explosion in the harbor of Halifax in December, 1917. Two counterfoils in von Papen's check-book cast some light on the activities of the consulate in Seattle, the first dated February 11, 1915, the amount $1,300, the payee "German Consulate, Seattle," the penned notation "Angelegenheit" (affair) preceded by a mysterious "C"; the second dated May 11, 1915, for $500, payable to one "Schulenberg" [1] through the same consulate.

The month of July was a holocaust. A tank of phenol exploded in New York, the benzol plant of the Semet Solvay Company was destroyed at Solvay, N. Y.; on the 7th serious explosions occurred at the du Pont plant at Pompton Lakes and at the Philadelphia benzol plant of Harrison Brothers (the latter causing $500,000 damage); on the 16th five employees were killed in an explosion and fire at the Ætna plant at Sinnemahoning, Pa., three days later there was another at the du Pont plant in Wilmington; on the 25th a munitions train on the Pennsylvania line was wrecked at Metuchen, N. J.; on the 28th the du Pont works at Wilmington suffered again; and

[1] Franz Schulenberg was a deserter from the German army who advertised in the Spokane newspapers in February, 1915, for land on which to colonize a number of Spanish families. These families turned out to be Hindus, whom he proposed to employ in obtaining information of Canadian shipping, to be relayed by secret wireless to German raiders in the Pacific. Schulenberg was captured on December 5, 1917, in an automobile on the road from Santa Cruz to San Francisco, two days after he had left a woman spy who was associated with von Papen's office, and who directed Schulenberg's movements in the United States. He admitted having bought, in 1915, a ton of dynamite, fifty Maxim silencers, fifty rifles, and a quantity of fuse for shipment to Hindus near the Canadian border, between Victoria and Vancouver.

the month came to a fitting close with the destruction of a glaze mill in the American Powder Company at Acton, Mass., on the 29th. (The British army in Mesopotamia had just entered Kut-el-Amara at this time, and far to the northward Germany was prosecuting a successful campaign to force a Russian retirement from Poland.)

Each incident raised havoc in its immediate vicinity. Each represents a carefully worked-out plan involving a group of destroying agents. There is not space here to describe the plots in detail, nor to picture the horror of their results. But the affidavit of Johannes Hendrikus Van Koolbergen, dated San Francisco, August 27, 1915, may serve to show typical methods of operation, as well as to provide a story more than usually melodramatic.

Van Koolbergen was a Hollander by birth, and a British subject by naturalization. In April, 1915, he met in the Heidelberg Café, in San Francisco, a man named Wilhelm von Brincken, who lived at 303 Piccadilly Apartments, and who asked Van Koolbergen to call on him there. The latter, however, was leaving for Canada, and it was not until some five weeks later that he returned and found that in his absence von Brincken had twice telephoned him to pursue the acquaintance.

Van Koolbergen called. Von Brincken explained that he was a German army officer, on secret service, and employed directly by Franz Bopp, the German consul in San Francisco. His visitor's identity and personality was apparently well known to him, for he offered Van Koolbergen $1,000 for the use of his passport into Canada, "to visit a friend, to assist him in some business matters." Van Koolbergen refused to rent his passport, but volunteered to go himself on any mission. This offer was discussed at a later meeting at the consulate with Herr Bopp, and accepted, after, as Koolbergen said, "I became suspicious, and upon different questions being asked me . . . I became very pro-German in the expression of my sentiments."

He was shown into an adjoining office, and von Brincken popped in, and "asked me if I would do something for him in Canada . . . and I answered: 'Sure, I will do something, even blow up bridges, if there is any money in it.' (This struck my mind because of what I had read of what had been done in Canada of late—something about a bridge being blown up—) And he said: 'If that is so, you can make good money.'"

Von Brincken made an appointment with his newly engaged destroying agent for the following day. On the window-sill of 303 Piccadilly Apartments sat a flower pot with a tri-colored band around its rim. If the red was turned outward towards Van Koolbergen as he came along the street, he was to come right upstairs. If he saw the blue, he was to loiter discreetly about until the red was turned; if the white area showed, he was to return another day.

The red invitation signaled him to come up, and the two bargained for some time over Van Koolbergen's Canadian mission, without coming to an understanding. Once safely out of von Brincken's sight, the "destroying agent" pattered to the British Consulate and betrayed to Carnegie Ross, the consul, what was afoot. Ross urged him to advise Canada at once, so Van Koolbergen retold his story in a letter to Wallace Orchard, in the freight department of the Canadian Pacific Railway at Vancouver, B. C.

Orchard telegraphed back demanding Van Koolbergen's presence at once, and furnished money and transportation. Meanwhile the latter had pretended to accept von Bricken's commission to go to Canada and blow up a military train, bridge, or tunnel on the Canadian Pacific line between Revelstoke and Vancouver, for which he was to receive a fee of $3,000. The German exhibited complete maps of the railroad, told when a dynamite train might be expected to pass over that section of the road, and outlined to Van Koolbergen just where and when he could procure dynamite for the job. So on a Sunday morning in early May Van Koolbergen arrived in Vancouver, and lost no time in getting in touch with Orchard and the British Secret Service, with whom he framed the following plan:

Van Koolbergen was to send a letter to von Brincken warning him that something would happen in a day or two. The Vancouver newspapers would then carry a prepared story to the effect that a tunnel had caved in in the Selkirk mountains, whereupon Van Koolbergen was to collect for his services, and to secure incriminating evidence in writing from von Brincken if possible.

The plot worked well. The news story appeared, and cast a mysterious air over the accident. Van Koolbergen at once wrote a postcard to von Brincken:

"On the front page of Vancouver papers of (date) news appears of a flood in Japan. Our system may be in trouble, so wire here at the Elysium Hotel."

A few days later Van Koolbergen returned to San Francisco and met von Brincken. who told

him that he had replied to the postcard by telegram:

"Would like to send some flowers to your wife but do
not know her address,"

which meant simply that he had wished to communicate with Van Koolbergen through the latter's wife. (These messages, by the way, were
despatched from Oakland by Charles C. Crowley, who will appear again.) And von Brincken
paid Van Koolbergen $200 in bills, and asked him
to come to the consulate for the balance of his
fee.

Franz Bopp was skeptical. For some reason
he mistrusted Van Koolbergen. He produced a
map of British Columbia and asked him to describe what he had accomplished. Van Koolbergen, confused for a moment, suggested that
he would be unwise to go into detail before three
witnesses (Bopp, von Brincken, and von Schack,
the vice-consul). Bopp rose indignantly and
said that his secret was safe with three who had
been sworn to serve the Vaterland. So Van
Koolbergen invented and related the story of The
Dynamiting That Never Was, supporting it with
copies of the Vancouver newspapers. Bopp
wanted more proof; at Van Koolbergen's suggestion, he wrote one Van Roggenen, the Dutch

vice-consul at Vancouver, asking him to "inquire of the General Superintendent of the Canadian Pacific Railway Company why a car of freight which I expected from the East had not arrived yet, and to kindly wire me at my expense." Van Roggenen happened to be a friend of Van Koolbergen's, and of course any inquiry made of the railroad for Van Koolbergen's car of freight would have been tactfully construed and properly answered. But to make assurance doubly sure, Van Koolbergen wired Orchard in Vancouver to send him the following telegram:

"Superintendent refuses information. Found out however that freight has been delayed eleven days on account of accident. Signed V. R."

Armed with this fictitious reply, which Orchard soon sent him, Van Koolbergen called at the consulate, and was paid $300 more in cash. In order to get as much money as possible as soon as possible, the "destroying agent" agreed to cut his price from $3,000 to $1,750, and was promised the money the next day. The next day came, but no money. Van Koolbergen sent a sharp note to the Consul, suggesting blackmail, and the German Empire in San Francisco capitulated; von Brincken met Van Koolbergen at the Palace Hotel and paid him $1,750, (of which he extracted $250 as commission!). He made Koolbergen sign a receipt for $700, as he said a payment of $1,750 would look bad on the books, was much too high —even seven hundred was high, but could be justified if any one higher up complained. "And," concluded the thrifty Van Koolbergen in his affidavit written August 27, "I have some of the greenbacks given me by von Brincken now in my possession."

The San Franciscan participants in the episode were finally brought to justice. Bopp, Baron Eckhardt, von Schack, Lieutenant von Brincken, Crowley, and Mrs. Margaret Cornell, Crowley's secretary, were indicted, tried, and convicted. The men received sentences of two years and fines of $10,000 each; Mrs. Cornell was sentenced to a year and a day. The three members of the consulate, thanks to their other activities, involved themselves in a series of charges for which the maximum punishment was something more than the average man's lifetime in prison. Certain of their adventures will appear in other phases of German activity to be discussed. They may be dismissed here, however, with the statement that the California consulate also planned the destruction of munitions plants at Ætna, Indiana, and at Ishpeming, Michigan.

The State Department released on October 10,

1917, a telegram from the Foreign Office in Berlin, addressed to Count von Bernstorff, which established beyond question the chief's familiarity with these operations, and more especially the continued desire of the Foreign Office to interrupt transcontinental shipping in Canada. It is dated January 2, 1916. Its text follows:

"Secret. General staff desires energetic action in regard to proposed destruction of the Canadian Pacific Railroad at several points, with a view to complete and protracted interruption of traffic. Captain Boehm, who is known on your side, and is shortly returning, has been given instructions. Inform the military attaché and provide the necessary funds.

"Zimmermann."

The factory explosions continued. The Midvale Steel Company suffered incendiary fires; a Providence warehouse containing a consignment of cotton for Russia was burned; there were fires in the shell plant of the Brill Car Company, in the Southwark Machinery Company, and in the shell department of the Diamond Forge and Steel Company. For August the ghastly recitation proceeds somewhat as follows: Bethlehem Steel Company, powder flash, ten killed; League Island Navy Yard, Philadelphia, fire on battleship *Alabama;* Newport News Navy Yard, three fires in three weeks. In September an explosion in the aeroplane factory of the Curtiss plant at Depew, New York, a German suspected; explosions in the shell factory of the National Cable and Conduit Company at Hastings, New York; an explosion of benzol and wax in the plant of Smith and Lenhart, New York, in which two people were seriously injured; an explosion in a fireworks factory at North Bergen, N. J., in which two people were killed; an explosion which cost two lives in the shell factory of the Westinghouse Electric Company at Pittsburgh. Scarcely a week went by during the autumn without an explosion and fire which wiped out from one to a dozen lives, and from one hundred thousand to a million dollars. Munitions plants were blown to atoms in a moment, and hardly before the charred ground had cooled, were being rebuilt, for the guns in France were hungry.

Out of the mass of munitions accidents in the year 1915 stands sharp and clear the Bethlehem Steel fire of November 10—of which all Germany had had warning, and on which the German press was forbidden to comment—when 800 big guns were destroyed. The du Pont and Ætna organizations suffered again and again; a chemical plant had two fires which cost three-quarters of a million dollars; two explosions in the Tennessee Coal and Iron Works at Birmingham, Alabama, did considerable property damage, and assisted Germany further by frightening labor away from work. Suspects were arrested here and there, and always their trails led back to German or Austrian nationality or sympathy.

Their chiefs were elusive. Captain von Papen sauntered out of the Ritz-Carlton into Madison Avenue, New York, one afternoon. He idled down to Forty-second Street, and paused, as if undecided where to promenade. He turned east, walked a block, and turned again down the ramp into the Grand Central Station. Quickening his pace—he had only a minute more—he crossed the great waiting-room, presented a ticket at the train gate, and a moment later was in the Twentieth Century Limited, the last passenger aboard. He was seen next day in Chicago. And for a month thereafter he was completely lost to the authorities, while, as they found out later, he made a grand tour of the country, going first to Yellowstone Park, then down the Pacific Coast to Mexico, where he joined Boy-Ed, and finally returning to New York through San Francisco. He had ample opportunity to confer with his consular deputies, and his destroying agents. In August a train loaded with 7,000 pounds of dynamite from the du Pont works at Pinole, California, was destroyed; in the evidence against von Papen is this letter concerning the price to be paid for the Pinole job:

"Dear S.:  Your last letter with clipping today, and note what you have to say.  I have taken it up with them and 'B'" (who was Franz Bopp) "is awaiting decision of 'P'" (who was von Papen) "in New York, so cannot advise you yet, and will do so as soon as I get word from you.  You might size up the situation in the meantime."

Glancing back over the record of 1915—which was hardly mitigated in the succeeding years of war—one is inclined to marvel at the hardy perennial pose of the deported attaché, who said as he left the United States:

"I leave my post without any feeling of bitterness, because I know that when history is once written, it will establish our clean record despite all the misrepresentations and calumnies spread broadcast at present."

# CHAPTER IX

## MORE BOMB PLOTS

Kaltschmidt and the Windsor explosions—The Port Huron tunnel—Werner Horn—Explosions embarrass the Embassy—Black Tom—The second Welland affair—Harry Newton—The damage done in three years—Waiter spies.

In the check-book of the military attaché was a counterfoil betraying a payment of $1,000 made on March 27, 1915, to "W. von Igel (for A. Kaltschmidt, Detroit)." That stub was part of a bomb plot.

A young German named Charles Francis Respa was employed in 1908 by Albert Carl Kaltschmidt in a Detroit machine shop. Seven years later Kaltschmidt had occasion to hire Respa again. To a group which included Respa, his brother-in-law Carl Schmidt, Gus Stevens and Kaltschmidt's own brother-in-law, Fritz Neef, he outlined a plan for destroying factories in Canada. Neef was the Detroit agent for the Eisemann magneto, and had a machine shop of his own.

"We are not citizens of this country," Kaltschmidt reiterated to his accomplices. "It is our duty to stand by the Fatherland. The Americans would throw us out of work after war started." (The Americans, on the contrary, gave the ringleaders of the conspiracy plenty of hard labor after the war started.) To seal the bargain Kaltschmidt paid the men a retainer, and sent Stevens and Respa to Winnipeg to see whether it might not be feasible to blow up the railroad bridge there.

Respa reported back. His next assignment was to go to Port Huron and determine whether enough dynamite might be attached to the rear of a passenger train bound through the international tunnel under the St. Clair River to destroy the tube. Respa came to the conclusion that it was not practicable, for the authorities were taking precautions against just such an operation. Respa and Stevens were then despatched to Duluth, where they met Schmidt and a fourth member of the group, each carrying a suitcase containing numerous sticks of dynamite, and the quartette returned with its explosives to Detroit.

Kaltschmidt then hired him for $18 a week. Respa had left Germany before his term of military service came due; Kaltschmidt used this information as a club over his head, for he knew

the young man could not return to the Fatherland. On June 21 Kaltschmidt called Respa to
his office in the Kresge Building, and showed him
two elaborate time-clock devices which could be
so set as to fire bombs at any specified hour, and
Respa, at Kaltschmidt's command, carried the
clocks across the Detroit River to Windsor, Ontario, late that afternoon. His sister, Mrs.
Schmidt, went with him, and together they wan-
dered about until the hour when they knew that
William Lefler, the night watchman of the Pea-
body Overall Company factory in Walkerville,
would go on duty.

Under cover of darkness, the brother and sister met Lefler, who gave Respa two suitcases full
of dynamite which Kaltschmidt had smuggled
piecemeal into Canada under the front seat of
his automobile. Respa attached the clocks to the
charges, set one of the infernal machines near
the factory, and planted the other in the rear of
the Windsor armory, in which Canadian troops
were asleep, and near which was a Catholic girls'
school. Then he and Mrs. Schmidt scurried
back to the ferry and took the last boat to Detroit.
At three o'clock in the morning they heard a
muffled roar from the Canadian side; the factory
bomb had gone off. The other charge failed to
explode: Respa said he deliberately set the per-

cussion cap at the wrong angle, because he knew that soldiers were sleeping in the armory, and he had no stomach for murder.

One of the gang was presently arrested, and Respa was spirited away to the retirement of a mechanic's job in a West Hoboken garage. But he grew restless, and spent his money, and Kaltschmidt refused him more. He pawned his watch and his ring, bought a ticket to Detroit, and presented himself before Kaltschmidt with a demand for money, in default of which Respa proposed to "squeal." He was immediately returned to the payroll.

The Canadian provincial detectives had begun to search for the night watchman, Lefler. They found him, and from him they extracted a full confession. Respa's arrest was easy, and the United States willingly returned him, although Kaltschmidt did attempt to establish a false alibi for his underling. Respa was sentenced to life imprisonment, Lefler to ten years, for the destruction of the factory.

The dragnet closed in on Kaltschmidt. William M. Jarosch, a German-born, who later enlisted in the United States Army, had been introduced to Kaltschmidt in Chicago in 1915 by a former German consul there, Gustav Jacobsen. Jacobsen recruited two other men, and Kaltschmidt took the three to Detroit. Jarosch was directed to secure employment at the plant of the Detroit Screw Works, but he was rejected, so Kaltschmidt told him to watch the plant for a good opportunity to set a bomb there. In the course of his sojourn in Detroit he went to the Respa home in the placid little village of Romeo and returned with a generous quantity of dynamite. This he delivered to Neef, and in a conference at the magneto shop Kaltschmidt explained the operation of the time-clock, and ordered Jarosch to set the device at the Detroit Screw factory that night. He and his Chicago confederates set out for the scene, but there were guards about, and Jarosch had no desire for arrest, so he took the bomb to his hotel room, disengaged the trigger, and calmly went to sleep. Next morning Kaltschmidt reproached him, and Jarosch resigned, to return months later to show Federal officers where he had buried some 80 pounds of dynamite, nitroglycerine, and a bomb.

Kaltschmidt also conspired to destroy the Port Huron tunnel. For this enterprise he contrived a car which he proposed to load with dynamite set to explode with a time fuse. Fritz Neef, the Stuttgart graduate and expert mechanical engineer, was his able assistant and adviser in this project. The car was of standard railway gauge. It was to be set on the Grand Trunk tracks at the mouth of the Port Huron end of the tunnel and released, to roll down into the darkness under the river. At the low point in the tunnel's curve the charge would explode, bursting the walls of the tube, and completely interrupting the heavy international freight traffic at that point.

The "devil car" never was released. Kaltschmidt was arrested, and finally, in December, 1917, tried and convicted on three counts. He was given the maximum sentence, of four years' imprisonment and $20,000 fine. His sister, Mrs. Neef, who had been an active intermediary, was sentenced to three years' imprisonment and was fined $15,000; Carl Schmidt and his wife were each condemned to two years in prison, and assessed a fine of $10,000 each, and only old Franz Respa, the father of the dynamiter, was acquitted.

The activities of this group received tangible approval from the German Embassy. Even before von Papen drew the check on March 27 for Kaltschmidt, the attaché's secretary, von Igel, had transferred $2,000 to the Detroit German from the banking firm of Knauth, Nachod and Kuhne (January 23). On October 5, long after the Walkerville explosion, but while the

Port Huron venture was still a possibility, the Chase National Bank of New York transferred to Knauth, Nachod and Kuhne $25,000 from the joint account maintained there by Count von Bernstorff and Dr. Albert, and next day the money was placed to Kaltschmidt's credit.

The Port Huron tunnel was the object of German attentions from the active San Francisco consulate. Crowley, who had been von Brincken's messenger in the Van Koolbergen affair, and one Louis J. Smith, were hired by Herr Bopp to go east on a destroying mission. They ran out of money in New York, and called at the New York consulate for assistance. They were told that the New York consulate had nothing to do with Pacific coast activities, so they wired von Schack for funds. He replied, chiding them for not having called on von Papen.

Late in June Smith left New York and joined Crowley at the Normandy Hotel in Detroit. "Then we went to Port Huron," he said, "where we planned to dynamite a railroad tunnel and a horse train. We didn't do it, though.

"Then we went to Toronto, and Crowley told me to plant a bomb under a horse train in the West Toronto yards. But I saw a policeman, and I got out quick. Then we took some nitroglycerine, cotton, sawdust, and a tin pan and some other things to Grosse Isle, Ontario, and went out back of a cemetery and made some bombs.

"Well, we got back to San Francisco late in July, and Crowley and I cooked up an expense account of $1,254.80, and took it up to the consulate. Von Schack locked the door behind us, and then he said: 'I don't want any statement. Tell me how much you want?' We told him, and he said he would get it the following day. Then all of a sudden he asked: 'How do I know you fellows did any jobs in Canada?'

" 'Wire the mayor of Toronto and ask him!' Crowley answered."

On one occasion at least the Germans respected American property, for the protection America might afford. Werner Horn, a former lieutenant in the Landwehr, was in Guatemala when the war broke out. He made an attempt to return to his command, but got no farther than New York, where he placed himself at the disposal of Captain von Papen. On January 18 the military attaché paid him $700. On February 2 Horn exploded a charge of dynamite on the Canadian end of the international bridge at Vanceboro, Maine, spanning the St. Croix River to New Brunswick. The explosion caused a slight damage to the Canadian half of the bridge.

A few hours later Horn was arrested in Vanceboro, and admitted the crime.

When the Canadian authorities applied for his extradition, the warrant which Judge Hale issued was not executed, the United States Marshal for Maine having received word from Washington that a well-preserved treaty between Great Britain and the United States would cover just such a case, and Horn was indicted on a charge of having transported explosives from New York City to Vanceboro. His attorneys naïvely attempted to secure his liberty by casting a protective mantle of international law about his shoulders: Werner Horn, they said, was a First Lieutenant of the West Prussian Pioneer Battalion Number 17, and as such was sworn by His Royal Majesty of Prussia to

". . . discharge the obligations of his office in a becoming manner, . . . execute diligently and loyally whatever is made his duty to do and carry out, and whatever is commanded him, by day and by night, on land and on sea, and . . . conduct himself bravely and irreproachably in all wars and military events that may occur . . ."

Yet he was tried, and that without much delay, and convicted, and sentenced to imprisonment.

Although the destruction of railways was an attractive means of stopping the progress of munitions to the seaboard, and although it was a recognized practice during 1915, it made the Embassy at Washington uneasy. Bernstorff protested to the Foreign Office in Berlin that if a German agent should be caught in the act of dynamiting a railroad it would be exceedingly embarrassing for him, and increase the difficulties of his already ticklish rôle of apologist and explainer-extraordinary. The Foreign Office accordingly sent a telegram to von Papen:

"January 26—For Military Attaché. . . . Railway embankments and bridges must not be touched. Embassy must in no circumstances be compromised."

(Signed) "REPRESENTATIVE OF GENERAL STAFF."

And thereafter American railway bridges and embankments were safe, though their owners may not have been aware of the fact at the time.

It is no mere metaphor to say that during 1915 and 1916 the smoke of German explosions in factories in the United States was spreading across the sun, casting the deepening shadow of war over America. There was dynamite found in the coal tender of a munitions train on the Baltimore and Ohio Railroad at Callery Junction, Pa., on December 10, 1915, the day on which enormous quantities of wheat were destroyed by fire in grain elevators at Erie. A few hours earlier a two-million-dollar explosion had occurred at the Hopewell plant of the du Pont works. Shortly before Christmas a ton and a half of nitroglycerine exploded at Fayville, Illinois.

During 1916 there were a dozen major explosions in the du Pont properties alone and literally dozens of lives were lost. Two arms plants at Bridgeport, Conn., were blown up. An explosion in May wiped out a large chemical plant in Cadillac, Michigan. A munitions works of the Bethlehem Steel Company at Newcastle, Pa., was destroyed. The climax in violence came, however, in the sultry night of August 1–2. Shortly after midnight the rocky island of Manhattan trembled, and the roar of a prodigious blast burst over the harbor of New York. Two million pounds of munitions were being transported in freight trains and on barges near the island of Black Tom, a few hundred yards from the Bartholdi Statue of Liberty. Some one, somehow, supplied the spark. The loss of life was inconsiderable, for that neighborhood was not inhabited, but the confusion was complete. Heavy windows in the canyons of lower Manhattan were shivered, and for a few moments many of the streets rained broken glass. Shell-laden barges near the original explosion set up a scattering fire which continued for some time, most of the projectiles losing their power through lack of a substantial breech-block. But the immigration station on Ellis Island was in panic, and its position became more unpleasant as one of the blazing barges drifted down upon it. The shock was felt far out in Jersey, and northward in Connecticut. An estimate of damage was placed at thirty millions of dollars, probably as accurate as such an estimate need be; the event was utterly spectacular, and from the point of view of the unknown destroying agent, effective.

Exactly one year after von Papen gave up the first attempt upon the Welland Canal, a second enterprise began with the same objective. Captain von Papen felt that von der Goltz had bungled. This time he intrusted the mission to the doughty and usually reliable Paul Koenig. On September 27, 1915, Koenig, with Richard Emil Leyendecker, a "hyphenated American" who dealt during the daytime in art woods at 347 Fifth Avenue, New York, and Fred Metzler, of Jersey City, Koenig's secretary, went to Buffalo and Niagara Falls, accompanied by Mrs. Koenig. They had no trouble in crossing the border and making a thorough investigation of the canal, its vulnerable points, its guards and the patrol routes of those guards. Koenig selected men whom he detailed to watch the guards, and he fixed on satisfactory storage places for his explosives. The party then returned to Niagara Falls and later to New York.

They did not know that they were being trailed. All three men had been under surveillance for nearly a year, and after their migrations near the canal, the guard was reenforced. It became impossible to carry out the plan. A few weeks later the detectives who were shadowing Koenig noticed that George Fuchs, a relative whom he employed at a meagre salary, was seldom seen in his company. They sought Fuchs out and plied him with refreshment. A few glasses of beer drew out his story: Koenig owed him $15, and he therefore bore no affection for Koenig. The detectives turned him over to Superintendent Offley of the Department of Justice, who sympathized with Fuchs to such an extent that the latter retailed enough evidence of the Welland plot to secure Koenig's indictment on five counts. Thus did a debt of thirty pieces of silver—in this case half-dollars—rob the Hamburg-American Line of a six-foot, 200-pound detective, and the German spy system in America of one of its roughest characters, for, thanks to Fuchs' revelations, Koenig was indicted for a violation of Section 13 of the Penal Code.

Herald Square, New York, was the center of open-air oratory every evening until after America entered the war. Those who had stood and fought their verbal battles during the day about the bulletin board of the *New York Herald* remained at night to bellow to the idle passersby along Broadway, and one night Felix Galley, a leather-lunged contractor, gave an impassioned discourse justifying Germany's entrance into the war. When the meeting broke up he was followed home by one who rather passed his expectations as a convert.

The stranger was Harry Newton. He had been employed in a munitions plant in St. Catharine's, Ontario. He suggested to Galley that he would take any orders for arson which the Germans had in mind, and recommended that as proof of his ability he would oblige with a dynamiting of the Brooks Locomotive Works at Dunkirk, N. Y., for a retainer of $5,000. Or, he said, he could arrange to destroy the Federal building or Police Headquarters. This was more than the German had bargained for, and assuring Newton that he would first have to consult the "chief," he ran straightway to the police and in great agitation told what had happened. Captain Tunney, of the Bomb Squad, assigned Detective Sergeant George Barnitz to the case.

The detective, posing as a German agent, found Newton at Mills Hotel No. 3, and opened negotiations with him. After several talks, they met on the afternoon of April 19, 1916, at Grand Street and the Bowery. Barnitz said: "Now, I'm in a hurry—haven't much time to discuss all this. You say you're in the business strictly for the money. The chief is willing to pay you $5,000 if you will smash the Welland Canal or blow up the Brooks Locomotive Works or burn the McKinnon, Dash Company's plant at St. Catharine's. But how do we know you won't demand more from us after you are paid? Maybe you'll want more cash for your assistants."

Newton was quick to reply that he worked alone and wouldn't trust any assistant. He was anxious to start with the Brooks "job" at Dunkirk and told Barnitz he had left in the baggage-room of the New York Central Railroad at Buffalo a suitcase containing powerful bombs. (The suitcase actually contained a loaded 4-inch shell, with percussion cap and fuse.) It would be necessary only for him to go to Buffalo, get the suitcase, hasten to Dunkirk and blow up the locomotive works.

"Fine," said Barnitz. "You are under arrest."

Newton stared a moment, then laughed. "You New York cops are a damned sight smarter than

I ever thought you were," he said, "and you made me think you were a German!"

At Police Headquarters he described his plan for blowing up the Welland Canal. Having worked in a town located on the canal, he was familiar with the position of the locks. "It would be a simple matter," he said. "You see these buttons I am wearing on my watch chain and in my coat lapel. The plain gilt one reads 'On His Majesty's Service.' The blue and white one reads 'McKinnon, Dash Company, Munitions. On Service.' Those buttons are passes that would let me into any munitions plant in Canada or this country. They would pass me through the guards of the canal. It would be easy for me to pretend to be a workman, get a boat and, carrying a dinner pail, filled with explosives, to pick out a weak spot in the canal works and destroy the whole business.

"It would be a cinch to burn the McKinnon, Dash plant. I could go back to work there as foreman. Any Saturday night I could be the last to leave. Before going I could saturate flooring with benzine and put a lighted candle where within a half hour or so the flame would reach the benzine."

Newton also suggested his willingness to dynamite the banking house of J. P. Morgan & Co., at 23 Wall Street, or to dynamite the banker's automobile. He had a series of postcards in his own handwriting, which, in case he was hired for a dynamiting, were to be mailed from distant points every day while he was on the assignment, in order to establish an alibi.

He was an irresponsible person, and one who could not be said to be under orders from the attachés in lower Broadway. Yet he is typical of the restless and lawless floating population of which the Germans made excellent tools. When he heard Galley he promptly offered his services; his boldness would have made him a capital destroying agent, and it was fired by the speech in Herald Square, a speech inspired from Berlin. Here was his opportunity to make money. Thus, by a word of encouragement, by the whisper of "big money" to discharged, dissatisfied or disloyal employees of munitions plants, the seed of German violence was sown everywhere. Men who were well dressed and of good appearance would be remarked if they prowled about factory districts; men must be employed who would fade into the drab landscape by the very commonplaceness of their clothing and action. They could be hired cheaply and swiftly disowned, these Newtons!

The *New York Times* on November 3, 1917,

recapitulated the damage wrought by German incendiarism as follows:

"A graphic idea of what the fire losses in the United States owe to the work of war incendiaries may be gained from consideration of the fact that the total fire insurance paid in the United States in 1915, according to the figures of the National Board of Fire Underwriters, was $153,000,000. It is estimated that 60 per cent. of the loss by fires in this country is represented in insurance. Therefore, the total fire loss in the United States in 1915 was something over $200,-000,000. Of the $153,000,000 paid out by the insurance companies, $6,200,000 was represented by incendiary fires. A total of $62,000,000 was charged to fires from unknown causes.

"In 1916 the total jumped by 20 per cent., meaning an increase of about $40,000,000. The biggest items in this loss were those sustained in munition fires and explosions. Black Tom holds the record with a loss of $11,000,000; there was the Kingsland explosion, the Penn's Grove explosion, and others, all generally admitted to be the work of spies, which caused losses running into millions.

"It was estimated yesterday by an insurance official that the incendiary loss in 1916 was easily $25,000,000, or $15,000,000 above normal. And these figures take into consideration only fires where the origin was proved to be incendiary. On the books of the underwriters the Black Tom munitions fire is not listed as incendiary, because it was never legally proved that a German spy set it going.

"This increase in losses for 1916 when the big munition explosions occurred, derives significance in the discussion of losses by spy fires since this country entered the war, because the figures of fire losses in the United States for 1917 may reach $300,000,000, or a larger increase over 1916 than 1916 losses showed over 1915. An estimate made yesterday by the head of a fire insurance company shows that if the average of the losses in the first seven months of the year is maintained until Jan. 1 the total would reach well above $250,000,000, and with the increases of the past few months might easily total $300,000,000 as the cost of the American ash heaps for 1917."

How did the Germans know where munitions were being manufactured? Rumor fled swiftly through the labor districts, and the news was reported through the regular channels of espionage, cleared through the consulates and German business offices, and forwarded to the attachés and the Embassy. But the collection of information did not stop there; it was verified from another source—a serviceable factor in the general system of espionage.

The American manufacturer shared his nation's predilection for talking at meal-time. As the war contracts were distributed about the country, every machine shop worthy of the name became a "munitions plant" and the romance of having a part in the war strained the discretion of most of America's war bridegrooms; they simply "had to tell some one"; not infrequently this some one was a reliable intimate, sitting across a restaurant table at lunch.

There was in America an organization bearing a title which suggested a neutral origin, but whose officers' names, down even unto the official physician, were undeniably German. It was ostensibly for the mutual benefit of the foreign-born waiters, chefs and pantrymen who composed its membership. But its real significance was indicated by the location of its branches (its headquarters were in New York). Trenton, New Jersey, for example, was not a "good hotel town," and foreign waiters usually are to be found in a town which boasts a hotel managed by metropolitan interests, and supplied with a foreign staff; but Trenton was a munitions center, and there was a branch of this association there. Schenectady, the home of the General Electric

Company, had no first-class hotel; there was a branch of the association in Schenectady. Conversely, numerous cities whose hotels were manned by foreign waiters and cooks had no branches. The organization was founded in Dresden in 1877.

Many a confidence passed across a table was intercepted by the acute ears of a German spy. Members of the Anglo-French Loan Commission who were staying at the Biltmore in 1914 were served by a German agent in a waiter's uniform. It would have gone well for America and the preparations of supplies for her later Allies if there had been posted in every hotel dining-room the French admonition,

"Taisez-vous! Ils s'ecoutent!"

# CHAPTER X

## FRANZ VON RINTELEN

The leak in the National City Bank—The *Minnehaha*
—Von Rintelen's training—His return to America—His
aims—His funds—Smuggling oil—The Krag-Joergensen
rifles—Von Rintelen's flight and capture.

There was a suggestion in the newspapers of
dates immediately following Paul Koenig's arrest
that the authorities had been lax in allowing the
Germans to have later access to the safe in his
private office in the Hamburg-American building.
As a matter of fact the contents of the safe were
well known to the authorities—how, it is not necessary to say.  The multitudinous notes and reference data kept by the industrious "P. K." uncovered a plentiful German source of information
of munitions.

They knew the factories in which war materials
were being turned out.  They knew the numbers
of the freight cars into which the materials were
loaded for shipment to the waterfronts.  They
knew the ships into which those cargoes were
consigned.  How they knew was revealed by

Franz von Rintelen

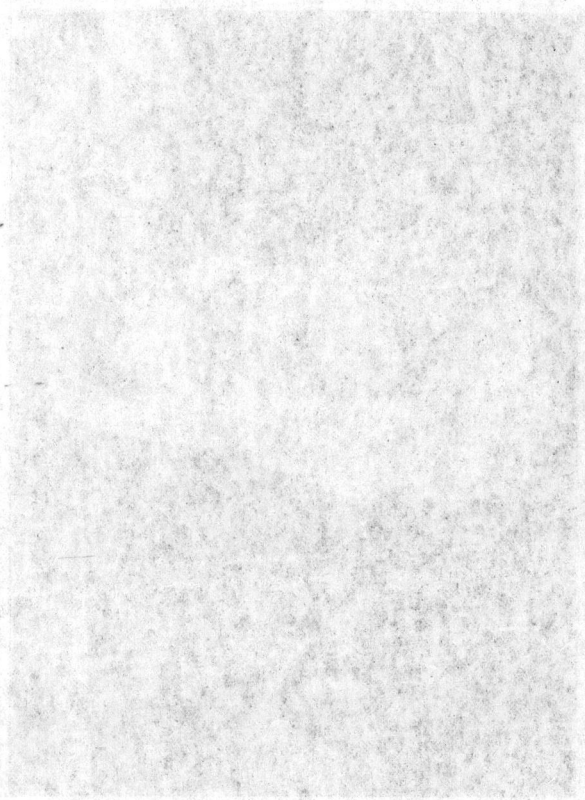

Koenig's secretary, Metzler, after he had been arrested in the second Welland episode.

Down in Wall Street, in the foreign department of the National City Bank, there was a young German named Frederick Schleindl. He had been in the United States for several years, and had been employed by various bankers, one of whom recommended him to the National City Bank shortly after the outbreak of war. In the foreign department he had access to cables from the Allies concerning the purchase of munitions. It was customary to pay manufacturers for their completed orders when the bank received a bill of lading showing their shipment by railroad or their delivery at points of departure. Close familiarity with such bills of lading and cablegrams gave Schleindl an up-to-the-minute survey of the production of supplies.

In late 1914 Schleindl registered with the German consul in New York, setting down his name and address as liable to call for special service. In May, 1915, he was directed by the consul to meet a certain person at the Hotel Manhattan; the unknown proved to be Koenig, who had been informed of Schleindl's occupation by the alert German consul. Playing on the youth's patriotism and greed, Koenig agreed to pay him $25 a week for confidential information from the bank.

From that time forward Schleindl reported regularly to Koenig. Nearly every evening a meeting occurred in the office in the Hamburg-American building, and Koenig and Metzler would spend many hours a night in copying the letters, cables and shipping documents. In the morning they would return the originals to Schleindl on his way to work—he made it his custom to arrive early at the bank—and the papers would be restored to their proper files when the business day began.

On December 17, 1915, Schleindl was arrested. In his pocket were two documents, enough to convict him of having stolen information: one a duplicate of a cablegram from the Banque Belge pour Etrangers to the National City Bank relating to a shipment of 2,000,000 rifles which was then being handled by the Hudson Trust Company; the other a cablegram from the Russian Government authorizing the City Bank to place some millions of dollars to the credit of Colonel Golejewski, the Russian naval attache and purchasing agent. From a German standpoint, of course, both were highly significant. Schleindl's arrest caused considerable uneasiness in Wall Street, and other banking houses who had been dealing in munitions "looked unto themselves" lest there be similar cracks through which information might sift to Berlin. There had been many such. Koenig was tried on the charge of having bought stolen information, and convicted, but sentence was suspended, although the United States already looked back on two years of water-front conspiracies to destroy Allied shipping.

The City Bank episode gave a clue to the source of those conspiracies, by the white light which it cast upon an explosion in hold number 2 of the steamship *Minnehaha* on July 4, 1915. Thousands of magnetos were stored there destined for automobiles at the front. The only person besides the officers of the bank and of the magneto factory who could have known of the ship in which they were transported was the man who wrote the letter to the bank enclosing the bill of lading for the shipment. Naturally the officers were not suspected of circulating the news; the leak therefore must have occurred in handling the letter. That theory was a strong scent, made no less pungent by the activities in America of one Franz von Rintelen.

Rumor has credited Franz von Rintelen with relationship to the house of Hohenzollern. Backstairs gossip called him the Kaiser's own son—a stigma which he hardly deserved, as his face bore no resemblance to the architecture of the Hohenzollern countenance. It was one of strong aquiline curves; with a coat of swarthy grease paint he would have made an acceptable Indian, except for his tight, thin lips. The muscles of his jaws were forever playing under the skin—he had a tense, nervous habit of gritting his teeth. From under his pale eyebrows came a sharp look; it contrasted strangely with the hollow, burnt-out ferocity and fright which peered out of the tired eyes of his fellow prisoners when he was finally tried. He had a wiry strength and easy carriage. If he had not been a spy, von Rintelen would have made an excellent athlete.

Like Boy-Ed he had a thorough gymnasium training. He specialized in finance and economics, entered the navy, and became captain-lieutenant. At the end of his period of service he went to London and obtained employment in a banking house. He then went to New York, where he was admitted to Ladenburg, Thalmann & Co., and found time during his first stay in America to serve as Germany's naval representative at the ceremonies commemorating John Paul Jones. The German Embassy gave him entrée wherever he turned. He was a member of the New York Yacht Club, was received at Newport and in Fifth Avenue as a polished and agreeable person who spoke English, French and Spanish as fluently as his native tongue, and he acquired a broad first-hand knowledge of American financial principles and methods. He left New York long before the war, saying he was going to open Mexican and South American branches of a German bank. When he returned to Berlin in 1909, he was well qualified to sit in council with Tirpitz and the navy group and advise them on the development of the German Secret Service in America. American acquaintances who visited Berlin he received with marked hospitality, and some he even introduced to his august friend, the Crown Prince.

In January, 1915, von Rintelen, then a director of the Deutsche Bank, and the National Bank für Deutschland, and a man of corresponding wealth, was commissioned to go to America, to buy cotton, rubber and copper, and to prevent the Allies from receiving munitions. So he went to America. And from his arrival in New York until his departure from that port, he threw sand in the smooth-running machinery of the organized German spy system.

He eluded the vigilance of the Allies by using a false passport. His sister Emily had married a Swiss named Gasche. Erasing the "y" on her passport he journeyed in safety to England as "Emil V. Gasche," a harmless Swiss, who observed a great deal about England's method of receiving munitions. Then he evaporated to Norway. His arrival in the United States was forecast by a wireless message which he addressed from his ship on April 3, 1915, asking an American friend of his to meet him at the pier. The American owned a factory in Cambrai, France, which had been closed by the German invasion on August 29, 1914. The American had hastened to Berlin in late 1914 and asked his friend Rintelen to see that the plant be opened. Rintelen had succeeded, and was come now to break the good news, knowing perfectly well that the American would be under deep obligation and would secure any introductions for him which he might need. When the ship docked, the friend was not there, for some casual reason. But Rintelen, always suspicious, hired a detective, who spent a week investigating; then the friend was discovered, and became Rintelen's grateful assistant.

So it happened that "Emil V. Gasche," the harmless Swiss, dropped out of sight for the time being, and von Rintelen assumed the parts of "Dr. Jekyll and Mr. Hyde." "Dr. Jekyll" visited the Yacht Club and called upon wealthy friends, proving a more charming, more delightful von Rintelen than ever. He met influential business men who were selling supplies to the Allies. He was presented to society matrons and débutantes whom he had use for. To these he was Herr von Rintelen, in America on an important financial mission. "Mr. Hyde" sought information from von Bernstorff, Dr. Albert, von Papen, Boy-Ed, Captain Tauscher and George Sylvester Viereck about the production of war supplies. Astounded by what he learned from them and had corroborated from other sources, he began to realize how utterly he had misjudged America's potential resources and what a blunder he had made in his predictions to the General War Staff. He saw with a chilling vividness the capacity of America to hand war materials to the Allies, and her rapidly increasing facilities to turn out greater quantities of ammunition and bullets. The facts he obtained struck him with especial force because of his knowledge of the greater strategy. It is upon a basis of the supplies of munitions in the Allied countries, particularly Russia, as von Rintelen knew them, that his acts are best judged and upon this basis only can sane motives be assigned to the rash projects which he launched.

When he arrived in New York the German drive on Paris had failed because in two months the Germans had used up ammunition they confidently expected to last three times as long; the English and French in the west could not take up the offensive because ammunition was not being turned out fast enough; the Russian drive into Germany and Austria would soon fail for lack of arms and bullets. In the winter and spring of 1915 the Russians had made a drive into Galicia and Austria, hurling the Austro-German armies back. They advanced victoriously through the first range of the Carpathian mountains until May. Meantime the German General Staff, as von Rintelen knew, was preparing for a retaliating offensive. The War Staff knew Russia's limited capacity to produce arms and ammunition, knew that during the winter, with the port of Archangel closed by ice, her only source for new supplies lay in the single-track Siberian railway bringing materials from Japan. Rintelen realized that by spring the Russian resources had been well nigh exhausted and he resolved that they must be shut off completely. He knew that England and France could not help. But spring had already come, and the ships were sailing for Archangel laden with American shells.

Von Rintelen's reputation was at stake. The work for which he had been so carefully trained was bound to fail unless he acted quickly. He exchanged many wireless communications with his superiors in Berlin—messages that looked like harmless expressions between his wife and himself, messages in which the names of American officers who had been in Berlin were used both as code words and as a means to impress their genuineness upon the American censor. He received in reply still greater authority than he had on the eve of his departure from Germany. In his quick, staccato fashion he often boasted (and there is foundation for part of what he said) that he had been sent to America by the General Staff, backed by "$50,000,000, yes $100,000,000"; that he was an agent plenipotentiary and extraordinary, ready to take any measure on land and sea to stop the making of munitions, to halt their transportation at the factory or at the seaboard. He mapped out a campaign, remarkable in its detail, scope, recklessness and utter disregard of American institutions.

Germany made her first mistake in giving him a roving commission. Germany was desperate, or she would have restricted von Rintelen to certain well-defined enterprises. Instead he ran afoul of the military and naval attachés on more than one occasion, offended them, and did more to hinder than to help their own plans.

In early April he made his financial arrangements with the Trans-Atlantic Trust Company, where he was known by his own name. Money was transferred from Berlin through large German business houses, and he deposited $800,000 in the Trans-Atlantic and millions among other banks. He rented an office in the trust company building, and had his telephone run through the trust company switchboard. He registered with the county clerk to do business as the "E. V. Gibbon Company; purchasers of supplies" and signed his name to the registry as "Francis von Rintelen." In the office of the E. V. Gibbon Company he received the forces whom he proceeded to mobilize; he was known to them as "Fred Hansen." If he wanted a naval reservist he called on Boy-Ed; if an army reservist was required von Papen sent him to "Hansen." Boy-Ed gave him data on ship sailings, von Papen on munitions plants, Koenig on secret service.

His first task was to buy supplies and ship them to Germany. He boasted that there was no such thing as a British blockade. Using his pseudonyms of Gibbon and Hansen he made large purchases and with the aid of Captain Gustave Steinberg, a naval reservist, he chartered ships and dispatched them under false manifests to Italy and Norway, where their cargoes could be readily smuggled into Germany. Through Steinberg he importuned a chemist, Dr. Walter T. Scheele, to soak fertilizer in lubricating oil for shipment to the Fatherland, where the valuable oil could be easily extracted. Through the same intermediary von Rintelen gave Dr. Scheele $20,000 to ship a cargo of munitions under a false manifest as "farm implements"; Dr. Scheele kept the $20,000 and actually shipped a cargo of farm machinery.

Rintelen's next venture attracted some unpleasant attention. The United States Government had condemned some 350,000 Krag-Joergensen rifles, which it refused to sell to any of the belligerents. Rintelen cast a fond eye in their direction. President Wilson had told a banker: "You will get those rifles only over my dead body." Rintelen heard, however, that by bribing certain officials he could obtain the guns, so he sent out agents to learn what they would cost, and found a man who said he could buy them for $17,826,000, part of which was to be used for effective bribery. "So close am I to the President," said the intermediary, "that two days after I deposit the money in the bank you can dandle his grandchild on your knee!" But just when the negotiations were growing bright, Rintelen was told that the man who proposed to sell him the rifles was a secret agent from another government. A certain "Dr. Alfred Meyer" was known to have been groping for those rifles, and the newspapers and government officials became suddenly interested in his real identity. A dowdy woman's implication reached a reporter's ears;

presently the newspapers burst out in the "discovery" that "Dr. Alfred Meyer" was none other than Dr. Meyer-Gerhardt, a German Red Cross envoy then in the United States. Like the popping of a machine gun, "correct versions of the facts" were published: "Dr. Meyer-Gerhardt denied vigorously that he was 'Dr. Alfred Meyer,'" then "'Dr. Alfred Meyer' was known to have left the United States on the same ship with Dr. Meyer-Gerhardt," then "an American citizen came forward anonymously and said that he had posed as 'Dr. Alfred Meyer' in order to test the good faith of the Government."

This last announcement may have been true. It was made to a New York *Sun* reporter by a German, Karl Schimmel, who professed his allegiance to the United States, and by the "American citizen" who said he had posed as "Dr. Alfred Meyer." It may have been made to shield Rintelen himself, for the "American citizen" was an employe of a German newspaper in New York, a friend of Rintelen's, a friend of Schimmel's and Schimmel himself was in von Rintelen's pay.

Let a pack of reporters loose on a half dozen tangents and they will probably scratch the truth. A *Tribune* man heard a whisper of the facts and set out on a hunt for "two Germans, Meyer and Hansen, who have been acting funny." He

frightened the personnel right out of the office of
the E. V. Gibbon Company. Captain Steinberg
fled to Germany with a trunkful of reports on
the necessity of concerted action to stop the shipment of munitions to the Allies, and Rintelen migrated to an office in the Woolworth Building.
Some one heard of his activities there and he was
evicted, taking final refuge in the Liberty Tower,
in the office of Andrew M. Meloy, who had been
in Germany to interest the German government
in a scheme similar to Rintelen's own. In Meloy's office Rintelen posed as "E. V. Gates"—
preserving the shadow of his identity as "Emil
V. Gasche." So effective was his disappearance
from the public view, that he was reported to
have gone abroad as a secretary, and he sat in
the tower and chuckled, and sent messages by
wireless to Berlin through Sayville, and cablegrams to Berlin through England and Holland,
and enjoyed all the sensations of a man attending
a triple funeral in his honor. "Meyer," "Hansen" and "Gasche" were all dead, and yet, here
was Rintelen!

Although his sojourn in New York covered a
period which was the peak of the curve of German atrocities in the United States, Rintelen was
a fifth wheel. No man came to America to accomplish more, and no man accomplished less.

No German agent had his boldness of project, and no German executive met a more ignominious fate. Whatever he touched with his golden wand turned to dross. He was hoodwinked here and there by his own agents, and frustrated by the vigilance of the Allied and the United States governments. He has been introduced here because of his connection with subsequent events, and yet this picturesque figure played the major part in not one successful venture.

Four months he passed in America, until it became too small for him. In August the capture of Dr. Albert's portfolio and the publication of certain of its contents frightened Rintelen, and he applied for a passport as "Edward V. Gates, an American citizen of Millersville, Pa.," but he did not dare claim it. Though he had bought tickets under the alias, and had had drafts made payable in that name, he did not occupy the "Gates" cabin on the *Noordam,* but at the last minute engaged passage under the renascent name of "Emil V. Gasche," the harmless Swiss. He eluded the Federal agents, and sailed safely to Falmouth, England, where, after a search of the ship, and an excellent attempt to bluff it through, he finally surrendered to the British authorities as a prisoner-of-war. Meloy and his secretary were captured with him.

Rintelen was returned to the United States in 1916. He was convicted in 1917 and 1918 on successive charges of conspiracy to violate the Sherman Anti-Trust law, to obtain a fraudulent passport, and to destroy merchant ships—which combined to sentence him to a year in the Tombs and nine years in a Federal prison.

# CHAPTER XI

## SHIP BOMBS

Mobilizing destroying agents—The plotters in Hoboken —Von Kleist's arrest and confession—The *Kirk Oswald* trial—Further explosions—The *Arabic*—Robert Fay— His arrest—The ship plots decrease.

The reader will recall a circular quoted in Chapter VIII, and issued November 18, 1914, from German Naval Headquarters, mobilizing all destroying agents in harbors overseas.

On January 3, 1915, there was an explosion on board the munitions ship *Orton,* lying in Erie Basin, a part of New York harbor. On February 6 a bomb was found in the cargo of the *Hannington.* On February 27 the *Carlton* caught fire at sea. On April 20 two bombs were found in the cargo of the *Lord Erne.* One week later the same discovery was made in the hold of the *Devon City.* All of which accounts for the following charge:

"George D. Barnitz, being duly sworn, deposes and says . . . on information and belief that on the first day of January, 1915, and on every day thereafter down to and including the 13th day of April, 1916, the defendants Walter T. Scheele, Charles von Kleist, Otto Wolpert, Ernst Becker, (Charles) Karbade, the first name Charles being fictitious, the true first name of defendant being unknown, (Frederick) Praedel . . . (Wilhelm) Paradis . . . Eno Bode and Carl Schmidt . . . did unlawfully, feloniously and corruptly conspire . . . to manufacture bombs filled with chemicals and explosives and to place said bombs . . . upon vessels belonging to others and laden with moneys, goods and merchandise. . . ."

Ninety-one German ships were confined to American harbors by the activities of the British fleet, ranging from the *Neptun,* of 197 tons, in San Francisco Bay, to the *Vaterland,* of 54,000 tons, the largest vessel on the seven seas, tied up to accrue barnacles at her Hoboken pier, and later, as the *Leviathan,* to transport American troops to France. Every one of the ninety-one ships was a nest of German agents. Only a moderate watch was kept on their crews, and there were many restless men among them. Every man aboard was liable to command from Captain Boy-Ed, for the German merchant marine was part of the formal naval organization. The interned sailors found shortly that they could be of distinct service to their country without stirring from their ships.

Not far from the North German Lloyd piers

in Hoboken lived Captain Charles von Kleist, 67 years old, a chemist and former German army officer. One day there came to him one who spoke the German tongue and who said he came from Wolf von Igel, in von Papen's office. Those were good credentials, especially since the gentleman was inquiring on von Igel's behalf whether Kleist needed any money in the work he was doing. The polite caller returned a few days later with another man, who spoke no German. Von Kleist asked whether he was also from the Fatherland, and was told no, but "we have to use all kinds of people in our business—that's how we fool these Yankees!" Von Kleist laughed heartily, and wagged his head, and went out in the garden and dug up a bomb-case and showed the visitors how it had been made. The visitors were Detectives Barth and Barnitz.

They assured Kleist that von Igel wanted to know precisely what he and his associates were doing, so no money might be paid to the wrong parties. The aged captain wrote out a memorandum of his activities, which he signed, and the detectives proposed a trip to Coney Island as an evidence of good faith, so the three had a pleasant afternoon at the Hotel Shelburne, and the officers then suggested: "Let's go up and see the chief." "Chief" to von Kleist meant von Igel;

he agreed, and was taken gently into the arms of the chief of detectives.

He implicated, as he sat there answering questions, Captain Eno Bode, pier superintendent of the Hamburg-American Line, Captain Otto Wolpert, pier superintendent of the Atlas Line, and Ernst Becker, an electrician on the North German Lloyd liner *Friedrich der Grosse,* tied up at Hoboken. The other conspirators were induced to come to New York, and were arrested at once. Bode and Wolpert, powerful bullies of Paul Koenig's own stamp, proved defiant in the extreme. Becker, knowing no word of English, was pathetically courteous and ready to answer. But it remained for von Kleist to supply the narrative.

Becker, working on the sunny deck of the *Friedrich der Grosse,* had made numerous bomb cases, rolling sheet lead into a cylinder, and inserting in the tube a cup-shaped aluminum partition. These containers he turned over to Dr. Walter Scheele at his "New Jersey Agricultural Company," where he filled one compartment with nitroglycerine, the other with sulphuric acid. Scheele supplied the mechanics with sheet lead for the purpose. The bombs were then sealed and packed in sand for distribution to various German gathering places, such as, for example, the Turn Verein in the Brooklyn Labor Lyceum. Wolpert appeared there at a meeting one night and berated the Germans present for talking too much and acting too little; he wanted results, he said. Eugene Reister, the proprietor of the place, said that shortly afterward Walter Uhde and one Klein (who died before the police reached him) had taken away a bundle of bombs from the Turn Verein and had placed them on the *Lusitania,* just before her last voyage, and added that Klein, when he heard of the destruction of the ship, expressed regret that he had done it. Karl Schimmel—the same who had negotiated for the Krag rifles—said later to Reister: "I really put bombs on that boat, but I don't believe that fellow Klein ever did."

Following Kleist's information, agents of the Department of Justice and New York police inspected the *Friedrich der Grosse,* and found quantities of chlorate of potash and other chemicals. They brought back with them also Garbode (mentioned in the charge as "Karbade"), Paradis and Praedel, fourth engineers on the ship, who had assisted in making the bombs, and Carl Schmidt, the chief engineer. All of the group were implicated in the plot to the complete satisfaction of a jury which concluded their cases in May, 1917, by convicting them of "conspiracy to destroy ships

through the use of fire bombs placed thereon."
Kleist and Schmidt received sentences of two
years each in Atlanta Penitentiary and were each
fined $5,000; Becker, Karbade, Praedel and Para-
dis were fined $500 apiece and sentenced to six
months in prison.  Dr. Scheele fled from justice,
and was arrested in March, 1918, in Havana.  A
liberal supply of vicious chemicals and explosives discovered in his "New Jersey Agricultural
Company" implicated him thoroughly, if the evidence given by his fellows had not already done
so.  When he was finally captured he faced two
federal indictments: one with Steinberg and von
Igel for smuggling lubricating oil out of the country as fertilizer, under false customs manifests;
the other the somewhat more criminal charge of
bombing.

On April 29, 1915, the *Cressington* caught fire
at sea.  Three days later, in the hold of the *Kirk
Oswald,* a sailor found a bomb tucked away in a
hiding place where its later explosion would have
started a serious fire.  So it came about that
when the four lesser conspirators of the fire-bomb
plot had served their six months' sentences, they
were at once rearrested on the specific charge of
having actually planted that bomb in the *Kirk
Oswald*.  The burly dock captains, Bode and
Wolpert, who had blustered their innocence in

the previous trial, and had succeeded in securing heavy bail from the Hamburg-American Line pending separate trials for themselves, were nipped this time with evidence which let none slip through. Rintelen was haled from his cell to answer to his part in the *Kirk Oswald* affair, and the jury, in January, 1918, declared the nine plotters "guilty as charged" and Judge Howe sentenced them to long terms in prison. Rintelen, alone of the group, as they sat in court, had an air of anything but wretched fanatic querulousness. He followed the proceedings closely, and once took the trial into his own hands in a flash of temper when the State kept referring to the loss of the *Lusitania*. It went hard with the nobleman to be herded into a common American court with a riff-raff of hireling crooks and treated with impartial justice. In Germany it never could have happened!

If those trials had occurred in May, 1915, the history of the transport of arms and shells would not have been marred by such entries as these:

May 8—*Bankdale;* two bombs found in cargo.

May 13—*Samland;* afire at sea.

May 21—*Anglo-Saxon;* bomb found aboard.

June 2—*Strathway;* afire at sea.

July 4—*Minnehaha;* bomb exploded at sea. (The magnetos.)

July 13—*Touraine;* afire at sea.

July 14—*Lord Downshire;* afire.

July 20—*Knutford;* afire in hold.

July 24—*Craigside;* five fires in hold.

July 27—*Arabic;* two bombs found aboard.

Aug. 9—*Asuncion de Larriñaga;* afire at sea.

Aug. 13—*Williston;* bombs in cargo.

Aug. 27—Lighter *Dixie;* fire while loading.

On August 31 the White Star liner *Arabic,* nineteen hours out of Liverpool was torpedoed by a German submarine and sank in eleven minutes, taking 39 lives, of which two were American. Germany, on September 9, declared that the U-boat commander attacked the *Arabic* without warning, contrary to his instructions, but only after he was convinced that the liner was trying to ram him; the Imperial Government expressed regret for the loss of American lives, but disclaimed any liability for indemnity, and suggested arbitration. On October 5, however, the government in Berlin had changed its tune to the extent of issuing a note expressing regret for having sunk the ship, disavowing the act of the submarine commander, and assuring the United States that new orders to submarines were so strict that a recurrence of any such action was "considered out of the question." If the cargoes could be fired at sea, no submarine issue need be raised.   And so fires and bombs continued to be discovered on ships just as consistently as before. The log, resumed, runs thus:

Sept.  1—*Rotterdam;* fire at sea.
Sept.  7—*Santa Anna;* fire at sea.
Sept. 29—*San Guglielmo;* dynamite found on pier.

Now von Rintelen's handiwork was revealed in the adventures of Robert Fay, or "Fae," as he was known in the Fatherland.   In spite of the imaginative quality of the enterprise, and the additional guilt which it heaped upon the executives of the spy system, it was not successful. There were vibrant moments, though, when only the mobilization of police from two states and special agents from the Secret Service and Department of Justice averted what would have developed into a profitable method of destroying ships.

Lieutenant Robert Fay was born in Cologne, where he lived until 1902.   In that year he migrated to Canada, where he worked on a farm, and later to Chicago, where he was employed as a bookkeeper until 1905.   He then returned to Germany for his military service, and went to work again in Cologne, in the office of Thomas Cook & Sons.   After a period in a Mannheim machine shop he went home and devoted himself to certain mechanical inventions, and was at work upon them when he was called out for war service on August 1, 1914.

His regiment went into the trenches, and the lieutenant had some success in dynamiting a French position. Conniving with a superior officer, he deserted his command, and was sent to America by a German reputed to be the head of the secret service, one Jonnersen. Jonnersen gave Fay 20,000 marks for expenses in carrying out a plan to stop shipments of munitions from America, and Fay arrived in New York April 23, 1915, on the *Rotterdam.*

Dr. Herbert Kienzle, a clock-maker, of 309 West 86th Street, had written to his father in Germany bitterly assailing the United States for shipping munitions, and enclosed in his letters information of certain American firms, such as Browne & Sharp, of Providence, and the Chalmers Motor Car Company, of Detroit, who were reputed to be manufacturing them. These letters had been turned over to Jonnersen, who showed them to Fay as suggestions. Upon his arrival in New York, then, Fay called on Kienzle, who, though he was friendly enough, was reluctant to know of the details Fay had planned. Dr. Kienzle introduced Fay to von Papen, and later to Max Breitung, from whom he purchased a quantity of potassium chlorate.

The deserter found his brother-in-law, Walter Scholz, working as a gardener on an estate near Waterford, Connecticut, and brought him to New York on a salary of $25 a week. The two crossed the Hudson to Weehawken, N. J., and set to work to make bombs. Fay had a theory that a bomb might be attached to the rudder of a ship, and so set as to explode when the rudder, swinging to port, wound a ratchet inside the device which would release a hammer upon a percussion cap. Their plan was to have the parts manufactured at machine shops, assemble and fill them themselves, and then steal up the waterfront in the small hours and attach the infernal machines to outward bound vessels. Fay even counted on disarming the police boats before setting out.

It took the two some three months to get the parts made and properly adjusted. Meanwhile they employed their spare hours in cruising about the harbor in a motor-boat. A machinist in West 42nd Street, New York, made the zinc tank which they used as a model, and the two conspirators shortly opened a garage in Weehawken where they could duplicate the bomb cases unmolested.

There came a time when the devices were satisfactory, and Fay actually attached one to the rudder of a ship to make sure that his adjustments were correct. The next move was to obtain explosives. Fay's prejudice against bombs placed in a ship's hold was that they rarely succeeded in sinking the craft; seventy or eighty pounds of high explosive detonated at the stern of a vessel, however, would blow the rudder away and not only cripple the ship but would probably burst a hole in the stern, mangle the screw, and split the shaft.

Captain Tunney, of the Bomb Squad, heard in October that two Germans were trying to buy picric acid from a man who stopped at the Hotel Breslin, and who called himself Paul Seib and Karl F. Oppegaarde, as the occasion demanded. Tunney's men located the two Germans, and some days later learned that they had placed an order for fifty-two pounds of TNT, to be delivered at the Weehawken garage. The delivery was intercepted, a similar but harmless substance substituted for the explosive, and two detective-truckmen took the package away on their truck to deliver it to Fay and Scholz. While they were in New Jersey, Detectives Coy, Sterrett and Walsh found Fay at the Breslin, and followed him back to Weehawken. As he left the garage in the evening in his automobile, the automobile of Police Commissioner Woods followed at a discreet distance.   Up the Palisades the two cars paraded, until in a grove near Grantwood, Fay and Scholz got out of their car and disappeared into the woods with a lantern.  After a time they reappeared, and returned to the garage, the police following.

Next morning Chief Flynn was called into the hunt—the morning of Saturday, October 23—and he assigned two special agents to the case.  The police department directed two detectives to watch the woods at Grantwood where the conspirators had gone the night before.  Detectives Murphy and Fennelly, each equipped with linemen's climbers, arrived at the wood-road about noon, and spent the next eleven hours in the branches of a great oak tree which commanded the road.  The perch was high and the night wind chilly, but the watchers were rewarded at last by the twin searchlights of an approaching car.  Out of it stepped Fay and Scholz.  The men in the branches saw by the light of the lantern which Scholz carried that Fay placed a package underneath a distant tree, walked to a safe distance, exploded a percussion cap, watched the tree topple over and went away, apparently satisfied with the power of his explosives.

Meanwhile other detectives were watching the rooming house at Union Hill where Fay and

Robert Fay, who made bombs with which he hoped to cripple the shipment of munitions to Europe

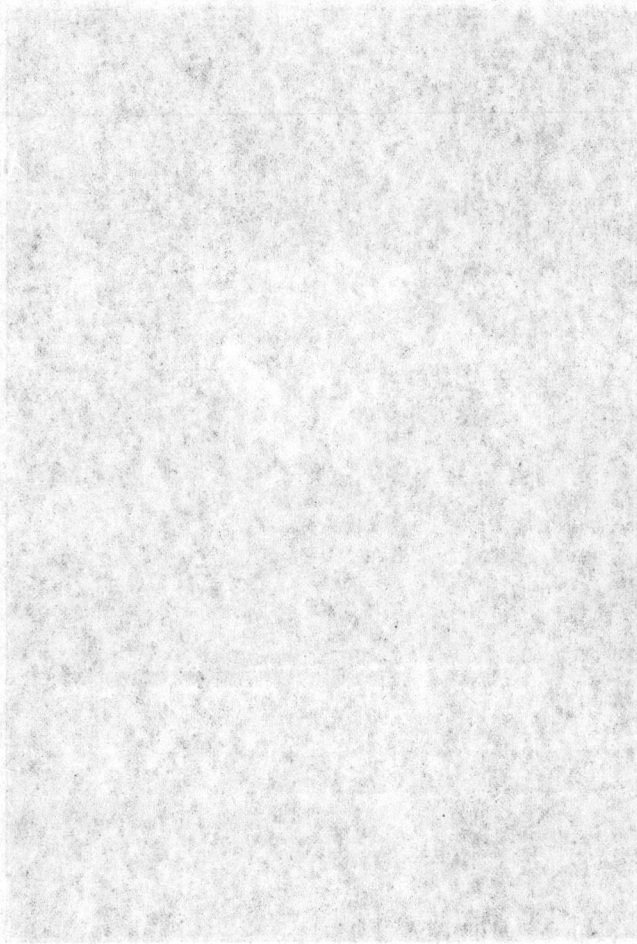

Scholz lived, and they saw the two come in about 4 o'clock in the morning. Scholz had very little sleep, for there was a ship leaving next day for Liverpool. He left the house at 7 A. M. and went to the garage. Thereupon three detectives returned to the great oak tree at Grantwood. About noon Fay and his brother-in-law drove up, and unlocking the door of a rude hut in the wood, took out a bag, from which they poured a few grains of powder on the surface of a rock. Fay struck the rock with a hammer; a loud report followed, and the hammer broke in his hand. A moment later he heard a twig snap behind him. He turned, and saw a small army of detectives with drawn revolvers closing in on him. Fay protested and pleaded, and offered to bribe the detectives for his freedom, but he was locked up with Scholz. The two had stored in a warehouse several cases containing their completed bomb mechanisms; the police confiscated from their various caches five new bombs, 25 pounds of TNT, 25 sticks of dynamite, 150 pounds of chlorate of potash, two hundred bomb cylinders, 400 percussion caps, one motor-boat, one chart of New York harbor showing all its fortifications and piers, one foreign automobile, two German automatic pistols and a long knife—a considerable arsenal.

Their confessions caused the arrest of Paul Daeche, who had furnished them with explosives, Dr. Kienzle, Breitung, and Engelbert Bronkhorst. Fay received a sentence of eight years in the penitentiary, but after America went to war, Atlanta became too confining for his adventurous spirit, and he escaped the prison, and is believed to have crossed the Mexican border to safety. Scholz was sentenced to four years, and Daeche of three. Kienzle, Breitung and Bronkhorst were not tried, their apparent ignorance of Fay's designs outweighing in the jury's mind their obvious German sympathies. Kienzle, upon the declaration of war of April 6, 1917, became an enemy alien, and was interned.

So Lieutenant Fay never qualified in active service as a destroying agent. Yet he was profligate in his intentions. He offered two men $500,000 if they could intrigue among the shippers in order that a ship laden with copper for England might wander from the path of convoy into German hands, and he even entertained the fantastic hope, with his chart and his motor-boat and his bombs, of stealing out of the harbor to the cordon of British cruisers who hung outside the three-mile limit and attaching his bombs to their rudders, that the German merchantmen might escape into the open sea.

On October 26 the *Rio Lages* caught fire at sea; fire broke out in the hold of the *Euterpe* on November 3; three days later there was fire aboard the *Rochambeau* at sea; the next day an explosion occurred aboard the *Ancona*. And so the list runs on:

Dec.   4—*Tynningham,* two fires on ship.
Dec. 24—*Alston,* dynamite found in cargo.
Dec. 26—*Inchmoor,* fire in hold.
   1916
Jan. 19—*Sygna,* fire at sea.
Jan. 19—*Ryndam,* bomb explosion at sea.
Jan. 22—*Rosebank,* two bombs in cargo.
Feb. 16—*Dalton,* fire at sea.
Feb. 21—*Tennyson,* bomb explosion at sea.
Feb. 26—*Livingston Court,* fire in Gravesend Bay.

April saw the round-up of the group who had been working under the Hamburg-American captains, and although numerous fires occurred during May, 1916, in almost every case they were traced to natural accidents. The number mounted more slowly as the year advanced. With the entrance of America into the war, and the tightening of the police cordon along the waterfront, the chance of planting bombs was still further reduced, but waterfront fires kept recurring, and until the day of ultimate judgment in Berlin, when each of Germany's arsonists in

America comes to claim his reward, none will know the total of loss at their hands. It was enormous in the damage it inflicted upon cargo, but it is improbable that it had any perceptible effect upon the whole export of shells for Flanders and France.

the United States entered the war.) He was convicted and sentenced to two years' imprisonment in Atlanta Penitentiary. He appealed the case, and while he was out on bail pending the appeal, he fell in with Rintelen.

In April, 1915, a New Yorker who dealt in publicity was introduced to Rintelen, or "Hansen," by Dr. Schimmel. Rintelen offered the publicity man $25,000 to conduct a campaign of propaganda for more friendly relations with Germany, to offset the commercial power Great Britain bade fair to have at the end of the war, and assured him that he would go to any extreme to prevent shipments of munitions to the Allies. The war, he said, would be decided not in Europe but in America. There must be strikes in the munitions factories.

When the publicity man heard also that Rintelen was trying to stir up trouble with Mexico, he wrote on May 13 to Joseph Tumulty, President Wilson's secretary, informing him of the German's intentions. He was referred to the Department of Justice, and at their dictation continued in contact with Rintelen. Shortly thereafter David Lamar and his friend Henry Martin took a trip to Minneapolis, where they met Congressman Frank Buchanan and Ex-Congressman Robert Fowler, both of Illinois. Out of that conference grew a plan for forming a labor organization the object of which was ostensibly peace, and actually an embargo upon the shipment of munitions abroad, but whether Buchanan and Fowler knew of von Rintelen's connection with the scheme remains to be proved. It can be readily seen that such a labor organization, if it had actually represented organized labor, could have forced such a stoppage, either by its collective potential voting power and influence, or by fostering a nation-wide strike of munitions workers.

The nucleus formed in Chicago, about one William F. Kramer. "Buchanan and Fowler came to me in June here in Chicago," said Kramer, "and told me about their plan to form a council. We opened headquarters, and we engaged two organizers, James Short and J. J. Cundiff, who got $50 a week apiece, a secretary, L. P. Straube, who got $50 a week, and a stenographer. I was a vice-president, but I didn't get anything. We were known then as Labor's Peace Council of Chicago, and we were supposed to be in it because of our convictions against the shipment of munitions. And I'll say that organized labor was made the goat."

Buchanan had no idea of restricting the council to one city. He called upon Samuel Gompers, head of the American Federation of Labor. at

Atlantic City on June 9 and tried to induce him to back a movement in Washington for an embargo. Gompers refused flatly and completely to have anything to do with the plan, especially when Buchanan made known his associates. Those associates were busy meanwhile lobbying in Congress, representing themselves as friends of organized labor, and pressing the embargo question. About a week later Congressman Buchanan inflated the Chicago organization into Labor's National Peace Council, with headquarters at Washington, to recommend the convocation of a special session of Congress at once to "promote universal peace," which meant simply "to promote the introduction and enactment of an embargo." Its members met frequently, and annoyed the President and other important men,—even Andrew Carnegie,—with their importunings for attention, and got exactly what they wanted— wide publicity.

About July 10 Andrew D. Meloy, whose office in New York Rintelen was sharing at the time, noticed that his German associate began to keep a clipping-file of news of the Council. Meloy learned of the project, and assured Rintelen that he was foolhardy to attempt, by bribery of labor officials, to divert common labor from earning high wages. To which Rintelen replied brusquely: "Thanks. You come into this business about 11:45 o'clock."

Rintelen sent a telegram to Lamar in Chicago on July 16, the text of which follows:

"E. Ruskay, Room 700 B, Sherman Hotel, Chicago.

"Party who receives $12,500 monthly from competitors is now interfering with business in hand. Do you know of any way and means to check him? Wire.

"F. Brown."

"Ruskay" was Lamar. Later in the day the German sent this message:

"Twelve thousand five hundred now at capitol. Conference here today plans to guarantee outsiders and settlement possible within few days. New issue urgently needed. Notify B."

The "party" mentioned in the first despatch was the code designation for Gompers, and he was indicated in the second message as "Twelve thousand five hundred." "B" was Buchanan, upon whose connection with labor Rintelen told Meloy the success of the plan rested. Lamar hurried to New York, arriving July 19, and met Rintelen in a limousine at the 100th Street entrance to Central Park; on the ride which followed the "Wolf" told Rintelen that a strike then going on among the munitions workers at Bridgeport was "only a beginning of his efforts," and that within thirty days the industry would be paralyzed throughout the country. Meloy advanced the information that Gompers had just gone to Bridgeport to stop the strike, to which Lamar replied:

"Buchanan will settle Gompers within twenty-four hours!"

The clippings kept coming in as testimony to the vigorous work being done by the organization's press bureau: the Council attacked the Federal Reserve Banks as "munitions trusts," it cited on July 8 nine ships lying in port awaiting munitions cargoes, and attacked Dudley Field Malone, then Collector of the Port of New York, for permitting such ships to clear; it claimed to represent a million labor votes, and four million and a half farmers; it listened eagerly to an address by Hannis Taylor, a disciple of the late warm-hearted Secretary of State, Mr. Bryan, in which Taylor criticized President Wilson and was roundly cheered by the German-American element in the audience. Semi-occasionally during the midsummer heat Charles Oberwager, attorney for the Council (whose firm had received handsome fees from von Papen), rose to deny any German connection with the organization. The Council assailed Secretary Lansing as a man "whose radicalism was liable to plunge this nation into war." The Council assailed, in fact, any project which furthered the interests of the Allies. Rintelen began to have his doubts of the effectiveness of Lamar's work. The bank account in the Trans-Atlantic Trust Company had dwindled from $800,000 to $40,000, and Rintelen admitted that his transactions with Lamar cost him several hundred thousand dollars. Labor's National Peace Conference died quietly, Lamar flitted away to a country estate at Pittsfield, Mass., and Rintelen started across the Atlantic Ocean.

August wore on. The Council was getting ready for a second gaseous session, when Milton Snelling, a representative of the Washington Central Labor Union, who had been elected a first vice-president of the Council, withdrew from its membership, because he "discovered persons participating in the meetings who have been hanging on the fringe of the labor movement for their own personal aggrandizement, men who have been discarded . . . others never having been members of any organization of labor," and because Jacob C. Taylor, the cigar-making delegate from East Orange, N. J., said, in answer to a query as to the Council's purpose: "We want to stop the export of munitions to the Allies. You see Germany can make all the munitions she wants."

Then—and it may be coincidence—about one week later the *New York World* began its publication of certain of the papers found in the brief case which Dr. Heinrich Albert, of the German Embassy, allowed to escape him on a New York elevated train; on August 19 Buchanan resigned the Council, and Taylor was elected to succeed him.

Indictments were returned against Rintelen, as well as against Lamar, Martin, Buchanan and their associates, on December 28, 1915. Buchanan at once exploded with a retaliatory demand for the impeachment of United States District Attorney Marshall, upon which Congress dared not take action. Marshall gracefully retired from the trial in May, 1916, lest he prejudice the Government's case, and Lamar, Martin and Rintelen were convicted of infraction of the Sherman Anti-Trust Law and sentenced to one year each in a New Jersey prison. Thus ended Labor's National Peace Council, thanks to David Lamar.

The project for an embargo looked attractive to the Embassy, however—so attractive that while the Council was at the height of its activity, Baron Kurt von Reiswitz wrote on July 22, 1915, from Chicago to Dr. Albert:

"Everything else concerning the proposed embargo conference you will find in the enclosed copy of the report to the Ambassador. A change has, however, come up, as the mass meeting will have to be postponed on account of there being insufficient time for the necessary preparations. It will probably be held there in about two weeks.

"Among others the following have agreed to coöperate: Senator Hitchcock, Congressman Buchanan, William Bayard Hale of New York and the well known pulpit orator, Dr. Aked (born an Englishman), from San Francisco.

"Hitchcock seemed to be very strong for the plan. He told our representative at a conference in Omaha: 'If this matter is organized in the right way you will sweep the United States.'

"For your confidential information I would further inform you that the leadership of the movement thus far lies in the hands of two gentlemen (one in Detroit and one in Chicago) who are firmly resolved to work toward the end that the German community, which, of course, will be with us without further urging, shall above all things remain in the background, and that the movement, to all outward appearances, shall have a purely American character. I have known both the gentlemen very well for a long time and know that personal interest does not count with them; the results will bring their own reward.

"For the purposes of the inner organization, to which we attribute particular importance, we have assured ourselves of the coöperation of the local Democratic boss, Roger C. Sullivan, as also Messrs. Sparman, Lewis and McDonald, the latter of the *Chicago American*. Sullivan was formerly leader of the Wilson campaign and is a deadly enemy of Wilson, as the latter did not keep his word to make him a Senator; therefore, principally, the sympathy of our cause."

One is inclined to wonder where Rintelen's vast credits went, during his short visits in 1915. Lamar took a goodly sum, as we have seen; the negotiations for the purchase of the Krag rifles cost him no small amount; his ship bomb activities required a considerable payroll. But as further evidence of the high cost of causing trouble, we must consider briefly the profligate methods he employed in other attempts to inflame and seduce labor.

A walkout by the longshoremen of the Atlantic coast would cripple the supply of munitions to Europe, and might be successful enough to cause a shell famine in France of which the Central Powers could readily take advantage. There were 23,000 dock-workers in American ports; they must be guaranteed a certain wage for five weeks of strike; the cost in wages alone would therefore amount to about $1,635,000, besides service fees to intermediaries. He had the money, and the first step was taken in the otherwise placid city of Boston.

On May 7, 1915, the day the *Lusitania* sank, William P. Dempsey, the secretary-treasurer of the Atlantic Coast International Longshoremen's Union, met Dennis Driscoll, a Boston labor leader and former city office-holder, at the old Quincy House in Hanover Street. Driscoll said that Matthew Cummings, a wealthy Boston grocer, had outlined to him the plan for the strike, and said he was acting for parties who were willing to pay a million dollars. Dempsey maintained his poise when the startling information was recited, but he was frightened, and at the conclusion of the interview he telegraphed at once to T. V. O'Connor, the president of the union, requesting an interview. The two union men met in Albany and discussed the affair pro and con, arriving at the conclusion that they had best reveal the plot to the Government. O'Connor accordingly told of the negotiations to Secretary Wilson of the Department of Labor, and then in connivance with the Secret Service, went on dealing with the grocer, constantly pressing him for the identity of the principals who, he said, were prepared to supply all the necessary money. He implicated George Sylvestor Viereck, the editor of a subsidized German propaganda-weekly called *The Fatherland,* and said that he had been introduced to him by Edmund von Mach. Neither of those men figured except as intermediaries, and Cummings suggested that Dr. Bernhard Dernburg, a loyal propagandist then in the United States, was the director of the enterprises. Owing to the high pitch of public feeling over the *Lusitania,* Cummings could not receive permission from his superiors to go ahead with O'Connor, but he did his best to keep O'Connor interested. The latter, fearing that German agents were at work on the Pacific coast, took a trip to the far West, and during his absence Cummings telegraphed him twice. There the affair ended, for O'Connor ignored the message, and on July 14 returned to New York to find that a German attempt to force a walkout on the New York waterfront had failed, and that Cummings had stopped playing with fire and had gone back to his grocery in Boston.

When the Government turned the story over to a newspaper to publish on September 13, the time was not ripe to fix the responsibility for the attempt. Dr. Dernburg was a popular scapegoat at the time, and the implication of his authority in the attempt was allowed to stand. Rintelen was in Donington Hall, a prison camp in England, and it was months thereafter before the United States and British Secret Services had fully compared notes on him. By that time there were other charges lying against him which promised better cases than an abortive attempt to promote a strike 'longshore.

We have witnessed the cumulative influence of newspaper reports in surrounding Labor's National Peace Council with an almost genuine atmosphere of national interest; we have been able to picture the hostility which the publication of the longshoremen's strike story aroused in legitimately organized labor; and although as a typical instance of newspaper influence we should postpone the following incident, it is a temptation too great to resist. It is the story of The Story That Cost an Ambassador, and if any further plea for its introduction be needed, let it be that it is another subtle attempt upon labor in the summer of 1915.

James F. J. Archibald, an American correspondent who had seen most of the wars of recent years, and who wanted to see more, set sail from New York on August 21, 1915, for Amsterdam, with his wife, his campaign clothes, and a portfolio. At Falmouth, England, the usual

Copyright, International Film Service

Dr. Constantin Dumba, Austrian ambassador to the United States, recalled after the disclosures of the correspondence captured on the war correspondent, Archibald

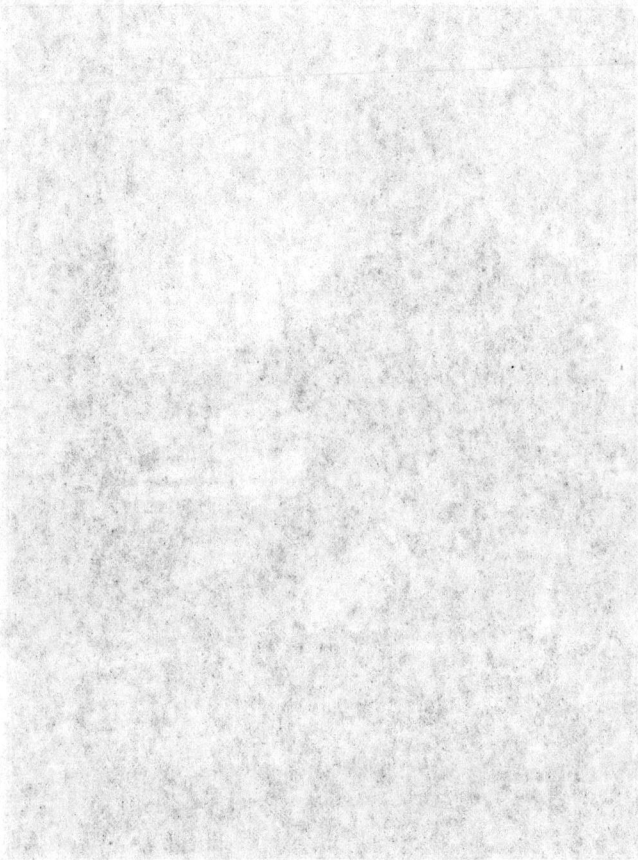

search party came aboard, and inspected the papers in the portfolio. Archibald proved to be an unofficial despatch-bearer, upon whom his German and Austrian acquaintances in the United States placed great reliance—such men as Papen, Bernstorff, and Dr. Constantine Dumba sent reports to their governments in his care.

On September 5 the *New York World* burst forth with the text of one of the letters—one from Dr. Dumba, the Austro-Hungarian ambassador at Washington, to his chief in the foreign office at Vienna, Baron Burian. It is worth reproducing here intact:

"New York, August 20."

"Your Excellency:

"Yesterday evening Consul-General von Nuber received the enclosed aide memoire from the chief editor of the local influential paper *Szabadsag,* after a previous conversation with me in pursuance of his verbal proposals to arrange for strikes at Bethlehem in Schwab's steel and munitions factory and also in the middle West.

"Archibald, who is well known to your Excellency, leaves today at 12 o'clock on board the *Rotterdam* for Berlin and Vienna. I take this rare and safe opportunity of warmly recommending these proposals to your Excellency's favorable consideration. It is my impression that we can disorganize and hold up for months, if not entirely prevent, the manufacture of munitions in Bethlehem and the middle West, which, in the opinion of the

German military attaché, is of great importance and amply outweighs the comparatively small expenditure of money involved.

"But even if strikes do not occur it is probable that we should extort under pressure more favorable conditions of labor for our poor downtrodden fellow countrymen in Bethlehem. These white slaves are now working twelve hours a day, seven days a week. All weak persons succumb and become consumptive. So far as German workmen are found among the skilled hands means of leaving will be provided immediately for them.

"Besides this, a private German registry office has been established which provides employment for persons who voluntarily have given up their places. It already is working well. We shall also join in and the widest support is assured us.

"I beg your Excellency to be so good as to inform me with reference to this letter by wireless. Reply whether you agree. I remain, with great haste and respect,

"DUMBA."

The aide memoire, written by the editor of a Hungarian weekly, proposed to create unrest by a campaign in foreign language newspapers circulated free to labor, muck-raking labor conditions in Bethlehem, Youngstown, Cleveland, Pittsburg, and Bridgeport, where there were great numbers of foreign workmen, Hungarians, Austrians, and Germans. This was to be supplemented by a "horror novel" similar to the bloody effort of Upton Sinclair to describe the

Chicago stockyards. Special agents of unrest, roll-turners, steel workers, soapbox orators, picnic organizers, were all to be insinuated into the plants to stir up the workmen. This editor had stirred them up a few weeks before at Bridgeport—the strike which Lamar claimed as his own accomplishment—and he presented to Baron Burian a really comprehensive plan for creating unrest through his well-subsidized foreign-language press. And in passing it on, Dr. Dumba stood sponsor for it.

The British government saw in the discovery of the letter and the cool impudence of it, a rare chance for propaganda in America. So, as has been said, the *World* published the story, and at once the wrath of the truly American people justified President Wilson in doing what he and Secretary Lansing had already determined to do—to send Dr. Dumba home. Perhaps Dumba's reference to the "self-willed temperament of the President" in another note found on Archibald had something to do with the haste with which the Ambassador's recall was demanded; it followed on the heels of the publication of the letter:

"By reason of the admitted purpose and intent of Mr. Dumba to conspire to cripple legitimate industries of the United States and to interrupt their legitimate trade, and by reason of the flagrant violation of diplomatic propriety in employing an American citizen protected by an American passport as a secret bearer of official despatches through the lines of the enemy of Austria-Hungary, the President directs us to inform your Excellency that Mr. Dumba is no longer acceptable to the Government of the United States as the Ambassador of his Imperial Majesty at Washington."

So went Dumba.

After his departure Baron Zwiedinek, his chargé d'affaires, and Consul von Nuber advertised widely in Hungarian newspapers calling on Austrians and Hungarians at work in munitions plants to leave. If they wrote the Embassy on the subject, the reply they received read:

"It is demanded that patriotism, no less than fear of punishment, should cause every one to quit his work immediately."

But neither threats, nor walking delegates, nor German spies could check the output of shells and guns. An attempt made by Dr. Albert to buy, for $50,000, a strike in Detroit motor factories failed. The factories were making money as they had never made money before, and labor was buying luxuries. To the American munitions-worker a comfortable supply of money meant much more than the shrill bleat of the Central Powers. And what was more, he was not entirely satisfied that the right was all on Ger-

many's side. (Our space does not permit, nor
is definite information at present available, to discuss the anarchist, socialist, and I. W. W. elements of labor, and their relations to Germany.
These three factors, especially the last named, effected in the years 1914–1918 a sufficient amount
of industrial unrest to qualify them as allies, if
not actual servants, of the Kaiser. Whether
they were employed by Germany will be brought
out in a trial which began in Chicago in April,
1918.)

# CHAPTER XIII

## THE SINKING OF THE LUSITANIA

The mistress of the seas—Plotting in New York—The *Lusitania's* escape in February, 1915—The advertised warning—The plot—May 7, 1915—Diplomatic correspondence—Gustave Stahl—The results.

In the eyes of the German Admiralty the *Lusitania* was the symbol of British supremacy on the seas. There were larger ships flying the Prussian flag, but one of them lay in her German harbor, the other at her Little-German pier in Hoboken, while the *Lusitania* swept gracefully over the Western Ocean as she regally saw fit, leaving only a thin trail of smoke for the sluggish undersea enemy to follow. Time and again during the early months of war the plotters in Berlin had attempted her destruction, and every time she had slipped away—until the last, when the plot was developed on American soil.

Her destruction would carry home to Germany news of heartening influence out of all proportion to the mere sinking of a large single tonnage. The German visible navy had, with the exception of scattering excursions into the North Sea, and

The *Lusitania* leaving the Hudson River on her last voyage

the swiftly quenched efforts of the South Atlantic fleet, been of negligible—and irksome—consequence. To sink the mistress of the British merchant fleet would be to inform all the world that Britain was incapable of protecting her cargo and passenger vessels, to puncture the comfortable British boast of the moment that business was being performed "as usual," and to gratify the blood-letting instincts of the Junkers. So von Tirpitz, with his colleagues, undertook to sink the *Lusitania,* and to warn neutrals to travel in their own ships or stay ashore.

Early in December, 1914, the German agents who met nightly at the Deutscher Verein in Central Park South speculated on ways and means of bringing down this attractive quarry. Communication between Berlin and New York at that time was as facile as a telephone conversation from the Battery to Harlem. There were new 110-kilowatt transmitters in the German-owned Sayville wireless station, imported through Holland and installed under the expert supervision of Captain Boy-Ed, and memoranda issued in Berlin to the naval attaché were frequently the subject of guarded conversation in the German Club within a few hours after they had left the Wilhelmstrasse. Occasionally the conspirators found it more tactful to drive through the Park in a limousine during the evening, to discuss the project. Spies had made several trips to Liverpool and back again aboard the ship, under false passports, and Paul Koenig's waterfront henchmen supplied all necessary information of the guard maintained at the piers. All this was passed up to the clearing-house of executives, and their plans began to take shape.

Boy-Ed possessed a copy of the secret British Admiralty code, which explained his frequent trips to Sayville. He knew—and Tirpitz's staff therefore knew—the position of any British vessel at sea which had occasion to utter any message into the air. But before he conceived a use for this code other than as a source of information, he decided to try out a code of his own.

He arranged with Berlin a word-system whose theory was popular with Germany throughout the earlier years of her secret war communication: under the guise of apparently harmless expressions of friendship, or grief, or simple business, were transmitted quite definite and specific secret meanings. A message addressed by wireless from the *Lusitania* to a friend in England which read for example "Eager to see you. Much love" would scarcely arouse suspicion, especially as there was no word in it which might suggest military information. Yet in February, 1915, a message of that type was despatched from the eastward-bound *Lusitania* to a British station; it was intercepted and interpreted by a German submarine commander in the "zone" nearby, who presently popped up in the ship's wake and fired a torpedo. His information was better than his aim. The *Lusitania* dodged the steel shark, and fled to safety, her wireless informing the British naval world meanwhile of the presence of the U-boat.

The plotters had to reckon with her unequalled speed. The *Lusitania* and her sister ship, the *Mauretania,* had each rather prided herself in the past on reducing the other's fresh, bright passage-record from Queenstown to New York—a record of four days and a few hours! The submarine of 1915 knew no such speed, and it was necessary, if the liner was to be torpedoed, to select out of the vastness of the ocean one little radius in which the submarine might lie in wait for a pot-shot. But just how?

Spies had reported that it was customary as the *Lusitania* neared the Irish coast on her homeward voyage for her captain to query the British Admiralty for instructions as to where her convoy might be expected. They reported that under certain conditions German agents might be placed on board. And they reported that the wireless operator was susceptible to bribery. Those three facts formed the nucleus of the final plan.

Audacious as they were in their use of American soil as the base for their plans, the German Embassy had certain obligations to the United States Government, which they felt must be observed. The unspeakable falsifying which is sometimes called expediency, sometimes diplomacy, required that official America must know nothing of the intentions of which the Embassy itself was fully conversant and approving. Further, a palliative must be supplied to the American people in advance. Consequently Count von Bernstorff, under orders from Berlin, inserted in the *New York Times* of April 23, 1915, the following advertisement:

## NOTICE

Travelers intending to embark on the Atlantic voyage are reminded that a state of war exists between Germany and her Allies and Great Britain and her Allies; that the zone of war includes the waters adjacent to the British Isles; that in accordance with formal notice given by the German Imperial Government, vessels flying the flag of Great Britain or any of her Allies are liable to destruction in these waters and that travelers sailing in the war zone on ships of Great Britain or her Allies do so at their own risk.

IMPERIAL GERMAN EMBASSY.

Washington, D. C., April 22d, 1915.

# NOTICE!

TRAVELLERS intending to embark on the Atlantic voyage are reminded that a state of war exists between Germany and her allies and Great Britain and her allies; that the zone of war includes the waters adjacent to the British Isles; that, in accordance with formal notice given by the Imperial German Government, vessels flying the flag of Great Britain, or of any of her allies, are liable to destruction in those waters and that travellers sailing in the war zone on ships of Great Britain or her allies do so at their own risk.

**IMPERIAL GERMAN EMBASSY**

WASHINGTON, D. C., APRIL 22, 1915.

The newspaper advertisement inserted among
"ocean travel" advertising by the Imperial German Embassy prior to
the *Lusitania's* departure on
what proved to be her
last voyage

Germans in New York who knew of the plot dropped hints to their friends; anonymous warnings were received by several passengers who had booked their accommodations; Alfred Gwynne Vanderbilt received such a message, signed "Morte." But such whispers were common, the *Lusitania* had outrun the submarines before and could presumably do it again; further, most Americans at that moment had some confidence left in civilization.

The plot was substantially this: when Captain Turner, on the last day of the voyage, should send his wireless query to the Admiralty, inquiring for his convoy of destroyers, a wireless reply in the British code directing his course must be sent to him from Sayville. His query would be heard and answered by the Admiralty, of course, but the genuine reply must not reach him.

Berlin assigned two submarines to a point ten miles south by west of the Old Head of Kinsale, near the entrance to St. George's Channel. She selected an experienced commander for the especial duty, and with him went a secret agent to shadow him as he opened his sealed instructions, and shoot him if he balked. And about the time when the U-boats slipped out of the Kiel Canal, and threaded their way through the mine-fields into the North Sea, submerging as they picked up the smoke of British ships on the western horizon, the *Lusitania* warped out of her pier in the Hudson River and set her prow for Sandy Hook, the Grand Banks, and Ireland.

She carried 1,254 passengers and a crew of eight hundred, a total of more than 2,000 souls, of whom 1,214 were sailing to their death. Germany had selected their graves; von Rintelen had two friends aboard who were detailed to flash lights from the portholes in case the ship made the submarine rendezvous at night. The *Lusitania* carried bombs which Dr. Karl Schimmel placed on board; she carried bombs which wretched little Klein placed on board; she carried, too, the creature who was to betray her. Her company was gay enough, and interesting; besides Mr. Vanderbilt her passenger list included Charles Frohman, the most important of theatrical managers; Elbert Hubbard, a quaint and lovable writer-artisan; Charles Klein, a playwright; Justus Miles Forman, a novelist; and numerous others of more or less celebrity, among them an actress who lived to reënact her part in the tragedy for the benefit of herself and a motion picture company. Ruthless as it was, the *Lusitania* also carried Lindon W. Bates, Jr., a youth whose family had befriended von Rintelen. And there were the women and children.

Meanwhile, Sayville was in readiness, a trained wireless operator prepared at any moment to hear Captain Turner's inquiry, and to flash a false reply with a perfect British Admiralty touch. On May 5 Captain Boy-Ed received word from Berlin that he had been awarded the Iron Cross. On May 7 the *Lusitania* spoke: Captain Turner's request for instructions. Presently the reply came, and was hurried to his cabin. From his code book he deciphered directions to "proceed to a point ten miles south of Old Head of Kinsale and thence run into St. George's Channel, arriving at the Liverpool bar at midnight." He carefully calculated the distance and his running time on the assumption that he was protected on every side by the British fleet, and set his course for the Old Head of Kinsale.

The British Admiralty also received Captain Turner's inquiry, just as the Sayville operator had snatched it from the air, and despatched an answer: orders that the *Lusitania* proceed to a point some 70 or 80 miles south of the Old Head of Kinsale, there to meet her convoy. *Captain Turner never received that message.* The British Government knows why the message was not delivered, though the fact has not, at this date, been made public.

The *Lusitania* headed northeast all morning.

At 1:20 o'clock she ran the gauntlet of two submarines; a torpedo was released, and found its
target. The ghastly details of what followed
have been told so fully, so vividly, and so appeal-
ingly that they need not be repeated here. They
made themselves heard around a world that was
already vibrant with uproar. The first sodden
tremor of the ship told Captain Turner that he
had been betrayed. He described later at the Cor-
oner's inquest how he had received orders sup-
posedly from the Admiralty, and had set out to
obey them. He produced the copy of those orders, but of the genuine message from the Admiralty he knew nothing. Asked if he had made
special application for a convoy, he said: "No,
I left that to them. It is their business, not mine.
I simply had to carry out my orders to go, and I
would do it again."

America was in a turmoil. Germany had
presumed too far; she—it is almost incongruous
to call Germany "she"—had believed that her
warning declaration that the waters about the
British isles were a war zone would be respected,
or if not respected, would serve as an excuse, and
that the torpedoing would be accepted calmly by
America. She was not prepared for Colonel
Roosevelt's burning denunciation of this act of
common piracy, nor for the angry editorial re-

monstrance of a people outraged at the loss of one hundred and fourteen American lives. But Germany recovered her presumptuous poise swiftly, and while ugly medals were being struck off commemorating the German triumph over the ship, and while destroyers were still searching British waters for the bodies of the dead, she sent a note of commiseration and sympathy to Washington. Three days later—on May 13—the United States conveyed to Berlin a strong protest against the submarine policy which had culminated in the sinking of the *Lusitania*. Three days before Germany replied on May 28, a submarine attacked an American steamer, the *Nebraska,* and the Imperial government followed up its first reply with a supplementary note justifying its previous attacks upon the American vessels *Gulflight* and *Cushing*. Germany's fat was in the fire.

A German editor in the United States had the effrontery to announce that American ships would be sunk as readily as the *Lusitania*. Secretary Bryan, of the Department of State, at that time a confirmed pacifist, resigned his post on June 8, thus drawing the sting of a second and sharper protest which went forward to Germany the next day. To this the Foreign Office replied on July 8 that American ships would be safe in the submarine zone under certain conditions, and the

President on July 21 rejected this diplomatic sop as "very unsatisfactory." Count von Bernstorff finally announced, on September 1, that German submarines would sink no more liners without warning, and his government ratified his promise a fortnight later. The promise was at best a quibble, and it in no way restricted undersea depredations upon commerce and human life. After the *Lusitania* affair followed the *Leelanaw*, the *Arabic*, and the *Hesperian* and on February 16, 1916, Germany acknowledged her liability for the *Lusitania's* destruction—the day after Secretary Lansing declared the right of commercial vessels to arm themselves in self-defense, and five days before the Crown Prince began the ten-months' battle of Verdun.

The published correspondence of the State Department gives in detail the negotiations regarding maritime relations, a record of Imperial hypocrisy which indicates clearly the desire and intention of the Germans to retain their submarine warfare at any cost. There is not space here to brief the papers, nor any great need, for it was the *Lusitania* which dictated the tone and outcome of the correspondence, and which brought the United States rudely face to face with the cruel facts of war.

In spite of these facts, Germany employed her

agents in desperate, devious and futile attempts to gloss over the crime.   Relatives of those who had drowned were persuaded by agents (one of them was "a lawyer named Fowler, now under Federal indictment on another count") to sue the Cunard Line for damages for having mounted guns on the liner, thus making her liable to attack.   Paul Koenig paid a German, Gustave Stahl, of Hoboken, to swear to an affidavit that he had seen guns on the ship; this affidavit was forwarded by Captain Boy-Ed on June 1, to Washington, and had a wide temporary effect upon public sentiment until Stahl was convicted of perjury and sentenced to 18 months in Atlanta.   It was Koenig who hid Stahl where neither the police nor the press could find him after he made his statement, and it was Koenig who, at the command of the Federal authorities, produced him. It was Rintelen who dined on the night of the tragedy at the home of one of the victims; it was Rintelen who received the news with a mild expression of regret because "he had two good men aboard."

Tactically Germany had attained her objectives; her submarines had obeyed orders and sunk a liner.   Strategically Germany had made a gross miscalculation; recruiting in England took a pronounced rise, the Admiralty was shocked into re-

doubled vigilance, the United States instead of
swallowing the affront complicated the question
of the freedom of the seas beyond all untangling
except by force of arms, and beside the word
"Belgium" on the calendar of crime the world
wrote the word *"Lusitania,"* as equally typical
of the warfare of the Hun.

# CHAPTER XIV

## COMMERCIAL VENTURES

German law in America—Waetzoldt's reports—The British blockade—A report from Washington—Stopping the chlorine supply—Speculation in wool—Dyestuffs and the *Deutschland*—Purchasing phenol—The Bridgeport Projectile Company—The lost portfolio—The recall of the attachés—A summary of Dr. Albert's efforts.

In addition to the exercise of its diplomatic functions, now more important than they had ever been before, the German Embassy had assumed the burden of large commercial enterprises. Their execution was entrusted to Dr. Albert, the privy councillor and fiscal agent for the Empire. There was apparently no limit, either financial or territorial, to the scope of his efforts, and the fact that he was able to administrate such a volume of work is no small tribute to his zeal. But that very zeal outran his regard for American law, so in one of his earlier ventures he set out to substitute the law of the Empire for that of the nation to which he was accredited.

Dr. Albert was informed on March 10, 1915, by

a German lawyer, S. Walter Kaufmann of 60 Wall Street, that his clients, the Orenstein-Arthur Keppel Company, had an order for 9,000 tons of steel rails to be shipped to Russia, despite instructions from the company's home office in Berlin that "no orders should be accepted for shipment to any country at war with Germany, because of Paragraph 89 of the Gesetz Buch." The Gesetz Buch is the German Penal Code. (One of Kaufmann's law partners was Norvin R. Lindheim, legal adviser to Germany's agents in the United States.) The manufacturers begged the permission of the Embassy to accept the order and pass the actual manufacture on to the United States Steel Company, in order to evade the letter of Paragraph 89, and in order "to delay the order, if that would in any way be desirable." The matter was neglected in the Embassy, and on July 13 the Orenstein-Arthur Keppel Company wrote from Keppel, Pa., to the German consul, Philadelphia, Dr. George Stobbe, again asking permission to accept the order. The consul replied, denying permission, on the ground that the shipment would facilitate the Russian transport of troops, and that such action would be within the meaning of Paragraph 89 of the Gesetz Buch. "That you are in position to delay the delivery of the order, to the prejudice of the hostile country

ordering, in no way makes you less punishable,"
he continued. He forwarded a copy of his ruling
to the Ambassador for approval, and it in turn
was forwarded to Dr. Albert. The order was not
taken; the fear of punishment by Germany was
greater than the protection afforded by American
Law.

The foregoing episode reveals the nature of Dr.
Albert's chief problem—the financial blocking of
supplies for the Allies. Let Boy-Ed destroy the
ships, von Papen dynamite the factories and railways, Rintelen run his mad course of indiscrim-
inate violence—the smooth financial agent would
undertake only those great business ventures in
which his shrewdness and experience could have
play. He was receiving reports constantly on the
economic status, and the following extract from a
report from G. D. Waetzoldt, a trade investigator
in the Consulate in New York, will illustrate the
German frame of mind about midsummer of
1915:

"The large war orders, as the professional
journals also print, have become the great means
of saving American business institutions from
idleness and financial ruin.

"The fact that institutions of the size and international influence of those mentioned could not
find sufficient regular business to keep them to

some extent occupied, half at least, throws a harsh light upon the sad condition in which American business would have found itself had it not been for the war orders. The ground which induced these large interests to accept war orders rests entirely upon an economical basis and can be explained by the above-mentioned conditions which were produced by the lack of regular business. These difficulties, resulting from the dividing up of the contracts, are held to have been augmented, as stated in business circles, by the fact that certain agents working in the German interest succeeded in further delaying and disturbing American deliveries. . . .

"So many contracts for the production of picric acid have been placed that they can only be filled to a very small part."

Dr. Albert also received a report from another trade expert, who had had a long conference with ex-Senator John C. Spooner of Wisconsin as to whether or not there could be prosecutions under the Sherman Anti-Trust Law against British representatives because of the restrictions placed by the British Government upon dealings by Americans in certain copper, cotton and rubber.

Naturally one of the most vital problems that stirred Dr. Albert was the British Orders in Council blockading Germany, from which resulted the seizure of meat and food supplies and cotton by British war vessels. He was always on the alert for information of the attitude of the Administration and the people of the United States toward the blockade. In another report dated June 3, 1915, Waetzoldt said:

"There can be no doubt that the British Government will bring into play all power and pressure possible in order to complete the total blockade of Germany from her foreign markets, and that the Government of the United States will not make a strenuous effort to maintain its trade with Germany. . . .

"It has been positively demonstrated during this time that the falling off of imports caused by the war in Europe will in the future be principally covered by American industry. . . .

"The complete stopping importation of German products will, in truth, to a limited extent, especially in the first part of the blockade, help the sale of English or French products, but the damage which will be done to us in this way will not be great. . . .

"The *Lusitania* case did, in fact, give the English efforts in this direction a new and powerful impetus, and at first the vehemence with which the Anti-German movement began anew awakened serious misgivings, but this case also will

have a lasting effect, which, unless fresh compli-
cations arise, we may be able to turn to the advantage of the sales of German goods. . . .

"The war will certainly have this effect, that
the American business world will devote all its
energy toward making itself independent of the
importation of foreign products as far as possible. . . .

"If the decision is again brought home to German industry it should not be forgotten what position the United States took with reference to
Germany in this war. Above all, it should not
be forgotten that the 'ultimate ratio' of the United
States is not the war with arms, but a complete
prohibition of trade with Germany, and in fact,
through legislation. That was brought out very
clearly and sharply in connection with the still
pending negotiations regarding the *Lusitania*
case."

That Dr. Albert used secret and perhaps devious means to secure his information is revealed
by an unsigned confidential report which he received under most mysterious circumstances concerning an interview by a man referred to as "M.
P." with President Wilson and Secretary Lansing. The person who wrote of "the conversation" on July 23, 1915, with "Legal Agent" Levy

and Mr. John Simon does not give his name. A striking part of this conversation follows:

"Levy advises regarding a conference with M. P. Thereafter M. P. saw Lansing as well as Wilson. He informed both of them that an American syndicate had approached him which had strong German relations. This syndicate wishes to buy up cotton for Germany in great style, thereby to relieve the cotton situation, and at the same time to provide Germany with cotton." (Dr. Albert attempted, with a suitable campaign of press and political propaganda, to inflame the Southern planters over the British embargo on cotton.) "The relations of the American syndicate with Germany are very strong, so that they might even possibly be able to influence the position of Germany in the general political question. M. P. therefore asked for a candid, confidential statement in order to make clear not only his own position, but also necessarily the political opportunity. The result of the conversation was as follows:

"1. The note of protest to England will go in any event whether Germany answers satisfactorily or not.

"2. Should it be possible to settle satisfactorily the *Lusitania* case, the President will bind himself to carry the protest against England through to the uttermost.

"3. The continuance of the difference with Germany over the *Lusitania* case is 'embarrassing' for the President in carrying out the protest against England. . . .

"4. A contemplated English proposal to buy cotton in great style and invest the proceeds in America would not satisfy the President as an answer to the protest. . . .

"5. The President, in order to ascertain from Mr. M. P. how strong the German influence of this syndicate is, would like to have the trend of the German note before the note is officially sent, and declares himself ready, before the answer is drafted, to discuss it with M. P., and eventually to so influence it that there will be an agreement for its reception, and also to be ready to influence the press through a wink.

"6. As far as the note itself is concerned, which he awaits, so he awaits another expression of regret, which was not followed in the last note. Regret together with the statement that nobody had expected that human lives would be lost and that the ship would sink so quickly.

"7. The President is said to have openly declared that he could hardly hope for a positive statement that the submarine warfare would be discontinued."

Dr. Albert conferred with Captains Boy-Ed and von Papen on all military and naval matters having a commercial phase. Captain von Papen, on July 7, 1915, submitted to Dr. Albert a memorandum for his consideration and further recommendation, headed "Steps Taken to Prevent the Exportation of Liquid Chlorine." He told of the efforts made by England and France to buy that chemical in America, estimated the output here, and cited the manufacturers. He also enclosed a plan for checkmating the Allies and concluded with the following paragraph:

"It will be impossible, however, for this to go on any length of time, as the shareholders wish the profits to be derived therefrom. Dr. Orenstein therefore suggests that an agreement be consummated with the Electro Bleaching Company, through the President, Kingsley, whereby the delivery of liquid chlorine by this country to France and England will be stopped. A suggested plan is enclosed herewith.

"From a military standpoint I deem it very desirable to consummate such an agreement, in order to stop thereby the further exportation of about fifty-two tons of liquid chlorine monthly, especially in view of the fact that in France there is only one factory (Rouen) which can produce this stuff in small amounts, while it is only produced in very small quantities, in England."

During 1914 and 1915 German speculation in wool was active. Early in the war von Bernstorff summoned a German-American wool merchant recommended by a business friend in Berlin and directed him to buy all the wool he could secure. He did so, using Deutsches Bank credits for the purchases made for Germany, and making his purchases of wool for Germany even in Cape Town and Australia. The German-American, after following this practice for some months, decided that his financial allegiance belonged to America, so he tried, through Hugo Schmidt, to induce the German interests in his firm to sell out to him. On August 9, 1915, Schmidt wrote to Keswig, the Berlin principal:

"Your friend here has inquired in London, and he offers no matter what price may be realizable in London at that time to take over the wool from you at the original price, in which case you would naturally pay all the expenses, which are estimated to be about 6 per cent. As you see, it is not so simple to deal with your friends."

The German-American's offer meant a good profit to him, as the London price of wool at that time had advanced nearly 15 per cent. Yet he apparently fell into no ill favor with Berlin, for in June, 1916, the German Foreign office wrote von Bernstorff:

"Interested parties here have repeatedly made representations for preferential treatment of the firm of Forstmann & Huffman in Passaic, N. J., in connection with shipment of coal tar dyes to the United States of America. Since this pure German firm, as is well known on your side, undertook last year the wool supply for Germany, and therefore claim it has been especially badly treated by England, it is most respectfully recommended to Your Excellency, should there be no reason to the contrary, to arrange for the greatest possible consideration for this firm in the later distribution of the shipments to consumers which now are in prospect."

Necessity, the mother of invention, had forced America's production of coal-tar derivatives and dyestuffs upward enormously during the first year of war. As the British blockade tightened, the German supply, which had long constituted the world supply, was cut off completely. The value of dyestuffs in America increased enormously from 1914 to 1915. Germany witnessed this growth with apprehension, and realized gravely that export expansion would follow increased and perfected production in America, which it promptly did. German chemical interests involved in a drug house familiar with the German market, have testified that their firm "paid three times the value" of a cargo of dyestuffs shipped from Bremen to Baltimore in 1916 in the huge undersea-boat *Deutschland,* "which paid for the ship and cargo." Her sister ship, the *Bremen,* which set forth for America, but never arrived, was also "built with money furnished by the dyestuff manufacturers," according to Ambassador Gerard.

The *Deutschland* herself was 300 feet long, with a cargo capacity of some 800 tons. She docked at the North German Lloyd piers in Baltimore, and after loading a cargo of rubber and nickel, took an opportune moment one foggy twilight to cast off and slip out to sea. She not only returned safely to Germany but made another round trip to America, putting in the second time at New London. She was at sea about three weeks on each crossing of the Atlantic.

Dr. Albert made plans for buying up carbolic acid to prevent it from reaching the Allies. Dr. Hugo Schweitzer, a German-American chemist of New York, paid down $100,000 cash on June 3, 1915, to the American Oil & Supply Company in New Jersey as part payment of $1,400,000 for

1,212,000 pounds of carbolic acid, of which the American Oil & Supply Company had directed the purchase from Thomas A. Edison. Dr. Schweitzer said that he bought the liquid not to prevent it from falling into the hands of the Allies but to use in the manufacture of medical supplies.

Not the least interesting of Dr. Albert's financial experiences is that which conceived and bore the Bridgeport Projectile Company. In a conference early in 1915 in the offices of G. Amsinck & Co., in New York, Count von Bernstorff came to the conclusion that one way to prevent the shipment of munitions to the enemy was to monopolize the industry, or at least to control it financially as far as possible. Dr. Albert made an unsuccessful attempt to buy the Union Metallic Cartridge plant for $17,000,000. He chose as his lieutenants for his next task Hugo Schmidt, the New York representative of the Deutsches Bank, and Karl Heynen, whose past record had been auspicious, as agent for Mexico of the Hamburg-American Line. Heynen it was who had smuggled a cargo of arms ashore for Huerta at Vera Cruz, under the nose of the American fleet; he had received some 40,000 pesos (Mexican) for the coup, and he was regarded as a capable individual. On March 31, 1915, the Bridgeport Projectile Company was incorporated for $2,000,000, paid in, with Walter Knight as president, Heynen as treasurer, and Karl Foster as secretary and counsel.

Schmidt drew up a contract with the new-born company calling for a large order of shells. On May 17 Heynen reported to Albert that 534 hydraulic presses for making shells of calibres 2.95 to 4.8 had been ordered, and would cost $417,550. These orders, with all others for tools and machinery which the Bridgeport company placed, were so well concealed about the business world that as late as August the impression was current that Great Britain was financing the company. On June 30 Heynen reported to Albert through Schmidt that the first shell cases would be manufactured under United States government inspection, in order to create the impression that the company was anxious for American contracts, and so that immediate delivery could be made in case such contracts were actually secured. "The most important buildings, forges, and machine shops, are almost under roof; the other buildings are fairly under way; presses, machinery and all other materials are being promptly assembled, and there is every indication that deliveries will commence as provided in the contract; i. e., on Sept. 1st, 1915."

The Bridgeport Projectile Company contracted with the Ætna Powder Company, one of the largest producers of explosives in America, for its entire output up to January, 1916, and then turned round and offered the Spanish government a million pounds of powder.   The Spanish representatives may have suspected the identity of the company, for they raised certain objections to the contract, to which Heynen refused to listen, and he also reported to his superiors that British and Russian purchasing agents were going to call on him within a few days.   He made a contract with Henry Disston & Co. for two million pieces of steel, most of them tools, for which Schmidt advanced the money.   He contracted with the Camden Iron Works of Camden, N. J., for presses, and posted a forfeit of $165,000 in case the contract should be cancelled; the contract was signed and cancelled the next day by the Bridgeport company, causing the Camden concern great business difficulty.

Thus, by the manipulation of contracts, Dr. Albert and his associates were accomplishing the following ends:

1. Arranging to supply Germany with shells and powder (as soon as smuggling could be effected) at a time when official Germany was attempting to persuade the United States to place

an embargo on the shipment of war materials to the Allies.

2. Securing a monopoly on all powder available.

3. So tying up the machinery and tool manufacturers that all their production for months to come was under contract to the Bridgeport Projectile Company, yet so wielding the cancellation clauses in its contracts that delivery could be delayed and the date further postponed when the manufacturers of machinery and tools could be free to take Allied orders.

4. Arranging to accept contracts for the United States and the Allies under such provisions that there would be no impossible forfeit if the contracts could not be fulfilled. This would have the effect of making the Allies believe that they were going to receive supplies which the Bridgeport Projectile Company had no intention of furnishing them.

5. Heynen, by the contract with the munitions industry, which his work afforded, knew where Allied orders for shells were placed, and he learned to his pleasure that the Allies were being forced to contract for shrapnel which was forged — a less satisfactory process than pressing. He also learned that the first two orders for forged

shrapnel placed by the Allies had been rejected because the product was inferior.

6. Paying abnormal wages with the unlimited funds at its disposal, stealing labor from the Union Metallic Cartridge Company in Bridgeport, and generally unsettling the labor situation.

7. Offering powder to Spain, a neutral with strong German affiliations.

The project was glorious in its forecast. But we may well let a German hand describe how it failed; among the papers captured by the British on the war correspondent and secret messenger Archibald at Falmouth in late August was a letter from Captain von Papen to his wife in Germany, in which he said:

"Our good friend Albert has been robbed of a thick portfolio of papers on the elevated road. English secret service men of course." (Papen was not altogether correct in this statement.) "Unfortunately, some very important matters from my report are among the papers, such as the purchase of liquid chlorine, the correspondence with the Bridgeport Projectile Company, as well as documents relating to the purchase of phenol, from which explosives are manufactured, and the acquisition of Wright's aeroplane patents. I send you also the reply of Albert, in order that you may see how we protect ourselves. This we compounded last night in collaboration." [1]

Dr. Albert could hardly have chosen a more unfortunate set of documents to carry about with him and lose. "Pitiless publicity" was his reward, and the statement which he and von Papen prepared in refutation and denial was received by those in authority as precisely the sort of denial which any unscrupulous and able master of intrigue might be expected to issue under the circumstances—and no more. If there had been any doubt of the perniciousness of his activities —and there was none—it would have been dispelled by the seizure of the Archibald letters, but the result of the exposures of German activity which made the *New York World,* a newspaper worth watching during August and September, 1915, was not the expulsion of Dr. Albert, but of the military and naval attachés. Albert, while he had been magnificently busy attempting to disturb America's calm, had been cunning enough to keep his hands free of blood and powder smoke;

[1] The captain added: "The sinking of the *Adriatic*" (by which he meant the *Arabic,* which had been sunk without warning on August 19, with a loss of sixteen lives, two of them American), "may be the last straw for the sake of our cause. I hope the matter will blow over." On October 5 the German Government, consistent with its assurance of September 1 that no more ships would be sunk without warning, disavowed the sinking of the *Arabic,* and offered to pay indemnities. So the matter "blew over."

Boy-Ed and von Papen had to answer for the origination of so many crimes that it is almost incredible in the light of later events that they escaped with nothing more than a dismissal.   On December 4, Secretary Lansing demanded their recall on account of their connection "with the illegal and questionable acts of certain persons within the United States"; Bernstorff made no reply for ten days, and received a sharp reminder for his delay; he then replied that the Kaiser agreed to the recall.   Four days before Christmas von Papen sailed for England and Holland. On January 2 and 3, 1916, his effects were searched by the British at Falmouth and two documents among others found may be cited here. Boy-Ed sailed on New Year's Day, but with no incriminating documents, for he had been warned.

The first document found on von Papen was a letter from President Knight of the Bridgeport Projectile Company, dated Sept. 11, 1915, addressed to Heynen at 60 Wall Street—the building in which von Papen had his office—giving certain specifications for shells that were being made in the new Bridgeport plant; the second was a memorandum of an interview on December 21, between Papen, Heynen, G. W. Hoadley of the affiliated American-British Manufacturing Company, and Captain Hans Tauscher. The four men had discussed specifications for a time, and had agreed that firing tests of the projectiles could be made "in a bomb-proof place by electrical explosion." Delays in production at Bridgeport are evident in the last sentence of the memorandum:

"It was agreed that Mr. Hoadley, till date, has complied with all the conditions of the contracts of the 1st April, with the exception of the commencement of the delivery of the shells, which is due to *force majeure*, i. e., to failure to timely obtain the delivery of machinery and tools occasioned by strikes in the machine factories."

A letter to von Papen from Dr. Albert, then in San Francisco, undated but obviously written in December, 1915, contained these farewell sentiments:

"Dear Herr von Papen,
"Well, then! How I wish I were in New York and could discuss the situation with you and B. E. . . . So we shall not see each other for the present. Shall we at all before you leave? It would be my most anxious wish; but my hope is small. From this time, I suppose, matters will move more quickly than in Dumba's case. I wonder whether our Government will respond in a suitable manner! In my opinion it need no longer take public opinion so much into consideration, in spite of it being artificially and intentionally agitated by the press and the legal proceedings, so that a somewhat 'stiffer' at-

titude would be desirable, naturally quiet and dignified!
. . . Please remember me to your chief personally. I
assume that he still remembers me from the time of the
'experimental establishment for aircraft,' and give my
best wishes to Mr. Scheuch, and tell him that the struggle
on the American front is sometimes very hard. . . .
When I think of your and Boy-Ed's departure, and that
I alone remain behind in New York, I could—well,
better not!"

Perhaps Dr. Albert would have accompanied
the attachés had not the submarine situation been
so acute. For while the Government had in its
possession sufficient provocation for his dismissal,
and that of Count von Bernstorff as well, the
Government's desire at that time was peace, and
stubbornly, patiently, it clung to its ideal in a
dogged attempt to preserve its neutrality. Dr.
Albert had run the British blockade with his supplies for Germany, and had roared protest when
Great Britain seized cargoes of meat intended for
Germany, although she paid the packers for them
in full. He had floated a German loan through
Chandler & Company, a New York house of
which Rudolph Hecht, one of his agents, was a
member; he had sold $500,000,000 worth of Ger-
man securities; to sum up his financial activities,
he had played every trick he knew, and his last
year in America was unfruitful of result, for he

was watched.   He returned to Germany personally enriched, for time and again, prompted by
stock tips from his German friends on stocks or
"September lard," and by diplomatic information
which he knew would influence the stock market,
he made handsome winnings for von Bernstorff
and himself.

# CHAPTER XV

## THE PUBLIC MIND

Dr. Bertling—The *Staats-Zeitung*—George Sylvester Viereck and *The Fatherland*—Efforts to buy a press association—Bernhardi's articles—Marcus Braun and *Fair Play*—Plans for a German news syndicate—Sander, Wunnenberg, Bacon and motion pictures—The German-American Alliance—Its purposes—Political activities—Colquitt of Texas—The "Wisconsin Plan"—Lobbying—Misappropriation of German Red Cross funds—Friends of Peace—The American Truth Society.

Some one has said that America will emerge from this war a gigantic national entity, a colossus wrought of the fused metal of her scores of mixed nationalities. That is naturally desirable, and historically probable. If such is the result, Germany will have lost for all time one of her most powerful allies—the German population in the United States. Nearly one-tenth of the population of the United States in 1914 was of either German birth or parentage. Ethnic lines are not erased in a generation except by some great emergency, such as war affords. Germany is doomed to a deserved disappointment in the loss of her

American stock—deserved because she tried so hard to Germanize America.

She wasted no time in injecting her verbal propagandists into the struggle on the American front. On August 20, 1914, Dr. Karl Oskar Bertling, assistant director of the Amerika Institut in Berlin, landed in New York, and went at once to report to von Bernstorff. The Amerika Institut had of recent years made considerable progress in familiarizing Germany with American affairs; its chief director, Dr. Walther Drechsler, had been master of German in Middlesex, a prominent boys' school in Massachusetts; he returned to Berlin in 1913 and was attached, upon the outbreak of war, to the press office. All who were associated with it knew something of America. It is characteristic of the convertibility of German institutions to war that another executive of this organization, employed in peace times to cement the friendship between the two nations, should be sent on the day war was declared to America to establish a German press bureau.

Dr. Bertling went about delivering pro-German speeches, and prepared articles for the press on international questions. These he submitted to Bernstorff himself for approval—one such story was to be published in a Sunday magazine supplement to a long "string" of American news-papers. Although every editor was on the look-out for any "war stuff" which was written with any apparent background of European politics, he found small market for his wares among the New York newspapers, and some of his speaking dates were cancelled. He proposed to publish, with one of his stories, a set of German military maps of Belgium, but to this von Papen wrote him on November 21: "I entirely agree with you in your opinion in regard to the maps—it is a two-edged sword," and he added: "One observes how very ill-informed the average American is." Bert-ling's lack of accomplishment drew censure, how-ever, from several sources: the head of the Ger-man-American Chamber of Commerce in Berlin chided him for not having carried out his "spe-cial mission to supply a cable service to South America and China," and the late Professor Hugo Muensterberg of Harvard waxed righteously in-dignant over the fact that Bertling opened and read a letter entrusted by the psychologist to him for safe delivery to Dr. Dernburg. Bertling ap-plied to the Embassy for special employment, and on March 19, 1915, the ambassador's private sec-retary wrote him:

"His Excellency is entirely agreeable to giving you the desired employment, but he considers the present conditions too uncertain, as his departure for Germany in the near future is not impossible."

Excellent testimony to the subtle iniquity of his task lies in the names of the men whose pro-Ally utterances he was striving to counteract. In a letter written December 20, 1914, to Bertling by C. W. Ernst, a Bostonian of German birth and American naturalization, appears this passage:

"Is it prudent to defend the German cause against such men as C. W. Eliot and other Americans who consider themselves artistocratic and important? . . . Who, apparently, was of more importance than Roosevelt, to whom now even the dogs pay no attention? . . . The feeling of men like Eliot, C. F. Adams, etc., is well understood. German they know not. They understand neither Luther nor Kant, nor the history of Germany. . . . Tactically it is a mistake to be easy going with England, or in discussion with her American toadies. By curtness, defiance, irony one can get much further. . . ."

His friend in the German-American Chamber of Commerce wrote again to Berlin in a vein which showed how closely Germany herself was watching publicity in America. "Viereck has sent me a letter," he said, "and *Harper's* printed some matter by way of Italy. . . . The Foreign Office and the War Department urgently want more reports sent here. If cables through neutral countries are not feasible, could not Americans travelling be called upon? More steam, please. . . . The exchange professors should get busy. . . . One is quite surprised here that with the exception of Burgess and possibly Sloan, nobody seems to be doing anything. . . . Nasmith's article, 'The Case for Germany,' in the *Outlook* is very good—inspired by me. The same of Mead's in *Everybody's*."

And again: "We will dog Uncle Sam's footsteps with painful accuracy—his sloppy, obstinate, pro-English neutrality we utterly repudiate. When God wishes to punish a country he gives it a W. J. B. as Secretary of State."

(When Bryan resigned, German rumors were circulated from time to time that Secretary Lansing, who succeeded him, had had a falling out with President Wilson, and was himself on the point of resigning. What Herr Walther thought of "W. J. B." 's successor is a matter of conjecture.)

The documents found in Dr. Bertling's possession, and the method of securing them, brought forth a sharp editorial from Bernard Ridder of the *New Yorker Staats-Zeitung,* then one of the stanch members of the foreign language press engaged in defending Germany. Dr. Bertling remained unmolested in the United States until

April, 1918, when he was arrested as an enemy alien in Lexington, Mass., and interned. Dr. Bernhardt Dernburg, to quote the words of a German associate, "had some propaganda and wrote some articles for the newspapers" . . . and was "certainly in connection with the German Government," gave Adolph Pavenstedt $15,000 in early October, 1914. To this Pavenstedt added $5,000, and on October 12 paid the sum of $20,000 to the *Staats-Zeitung*, to tide the newspaper over a rough financial period. "I expected," said Pavenstedt, "that if the business were bankrupt it would be lost to the Ridders, who have always followed a very good course for the German interests here."

Soon after the war began George Sylvester Viereck brought out his publication, *The Fatherland*, a moderately clever attempt to appeal to intelligent readers in Germany's behalf. On July 1, 1915, the publication having stumbled along a rocky financial path—for no publication distributed gratis can make money—Dr. Albert wrote Viereck:

"Your account for the $1,500—bonus, after deducting the $250 received, for the month of June, 1915, has been received. I hope in the course of the next week to be able to make payment. In the meantime, I request the proposal

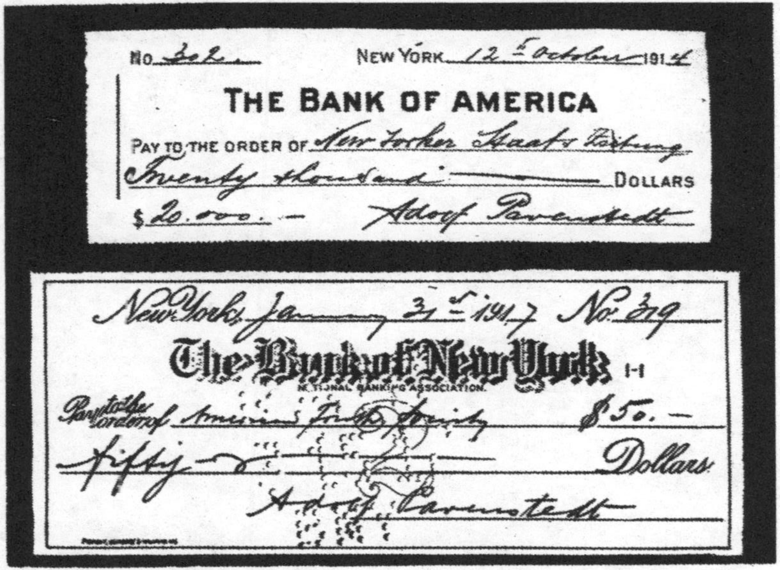


Photographs of checks signed by Adolf Pavenstedt

of a suitable person who can ascertain accurately
and prove the financial condition of your paper.
From the moment when we guarantee you a
regular advance, I must

"1. Have a new statement of the condition of
your paper.

"2. Practise a control over the financial management.

"In addition to this we must have an understanding regarding the course in politics which
you will pursue, which we have not asked hereto-
fore. Perhaps you will be kind enough to talk
the matter over on the basis of this letter, with
Mr. Fuehr." Fuehr's office was across the hall
from Viereck.

Viereck had assembled about him among others a staff of contributors which included Dr.
Dernburg, Frank Koester, Rudolph Kronau, J.
Bernard Rethey, a writer who affects the *nom
de plume* of "Oliver Ames," Edmund von Mach
(whose brother is an official of some prominence
in Germany), and Ram Chandra (the editor of
a revolutionary Hindu newspaper published in
California). Viereck, in his paper, forecasted
the sinking of the *Lusitania* and later gloated
over it as well as over the murder of Edith Ca-
vell. His father is the Berlin correspondent of
his paper. They are both "naturalized" citizens

of the United States. One of his contributors, as late as 1918, wrote for Viereck a peculiarly suspicious essay on his conversion to Americanism, setting forth in exhaustive detail the pro-German convictions which he had previously held, and the justification for them, and winding up with a pallid renunciation of them, the document as a whole intended ostensibly to stimulate patriotism, while in reality it would have rekindled the dying German apology. The pernicious Viereck, whose mental stature may be judged by the fact that he treasured a violet from the grave of Oscar Wilde, sought to interest the Embassy in his merits as a publisher of German books, and was supported, as pro-German volumes were issued from the Jackson Press which he controlled. He suggested, too, to Dr. Albert names of American publishing houses as excellent media for bringing out propaganda books on account of their obvious innocence of German sympathies.

A more patent attempt to influence the public originated in the German Embassy itself. Dr. Albert, through intermediaries, schemed to obtain for $900,000 control of a press association. The sale was not made. One of Dr. Albert's agents, M. B. Claussen, formerly publicity agent for the Hamburg-American Line, established in the Hotel Astor, New York, the "German Information Bureau" for disseminating "impartial news about the war" and "keeping the American mind from becoming prejudiced," and he issued many a red-white-and-black statement to the newspapers.

The German interests also had designs on buying an important New York evening newspaper, the *Mail*. One of von Papen's assistants, George von Skal, a former reporter (and the predecessor as commissioner of accounts of John Purroy Mitchel, New York's "fighting mayor"), entered the negotiations in a letter written by Paul T. Davis to Dr. Albert at the embassy. This letter, dated, June 21, 1915, set forth that—

"In November, 1914, my father, George H. Davis, conceived the idea that Germany ought to be represented in New York by one of the papers printed in English. He spoke to a number of German-Americans about the scheme and finally through Mr. George von Skal got in touch with Ambassador Count von Bernstorff. Mr. Percival Kuhne acted as the head of the movement until it was found that he could not devote the necessary time to the matter in hand and at father's suggestion Mr. Ludwig Nissen was substituted. . . . We decided upon the *Mail* as the only paper that was not too expensive. . . . We opened negotiations with the proprietors of the *Mail* and proceeded until Ambassador Count von Bernstorff notified both Mr. Kuhne and Mr. Nissen that at that time nothing further should be done in the matter. . . ."

The *Mail* was sold, however, to Dr. Rumely.

Dr. Albert collected for General Franz Bernhardi the proceeds of the publication in American newspapers of the latter's famous "Germany and the Next War." Bernhardi wrote von Papen on April 9, 1915:

"I have now written two further series of articles for America. The Foreign Office wanted to have the first of these, entitled 'Germany and England,' distributed in the American press; the other, entitled 'Pan-Germanism,' was to appear in the Chicago *Tribune*. They will certainly have some sort of effect, this is evident from the inexpressible rage with which the British and French press have attacked those *Sun* articles."

Bernstorff and Papen, under orders from Chancellor von Bethmann-Hollweg, in May, 1915, had under consideration the payment of from $1,000 to $1,200 for the expenses of a trip to Germany for Edward Lyell Fox, a newspaper writer, who "at the time of his last sojourn in Germany" (in 1914)" was of great benefit to us by reason of his good despatches."

George Sylvester Viereck, founder and Editor of *The Father-land* a pro-German propaganda weekly known later as *Viereck's Weekly*

Von Bernstorff himself wrote on March 15, 1915, to Marcus Braun, a Hungarian, and editor of a review called *Fair Play*:

*"My dear Mr. Braun:*

"In answer to your favor of the 12th instant, I beg to say that I have read the monthly review *Fair Play* for the last 3 years, and I can state that this publication is living up to its name, and that it has always taken the American point of view. During the last 7 months *Fair Play* has, in its editorial policy, treated all belligerents justly and thereby rendered great services to the millions of foreign born citizens in this country, especially to those of German and Austro-Hungarian origin. *Fair Play* has fought for the rights of the latter and for truth, always maintaining an American attitude and showing true American spirit.

"You are at liberty to show this letter to anybody who is interested in the matter, but I beg you not to publish it, as to (do) this would be contrary to the instructions of my government, who does not wish me to publicly advertise any review or newspaper.

"Very sincerely yours,
"J. BERNSTORFF."

On May 28, 1915, J. Bernstorff signed another gratifying document for the same Braun—a check for $5,000 payable to the Fair Play Printing & Publishing Company. Such was the reward of "true American spirit."

When Germany embarked upon an enterprise

she usually followed charts prepared by trained surveyors. Her attempts at newspaper and magazine propaganda in the first ten months of war had been hastily conceived and not altogether successful. One of the most comprehensive reports which have come to light is a recommendation, dated July, 1915, in which the investigator discusses the feasibility of a strong German news-syndicate in America.

It was to be operated by two bureaus, one in Berlin as headquarters for all news and pictures from Germany, Austria-Hungary, Turkey and the Balkans, one in New York for distribution of the matter to the American press. Correspondents from America were to be given the privileges of both Eastern and Western fronts, from 3,000 to 4,000 words a day were to be sent by wireless from Nauen to Sayville, secret codes were to be arranged so that the cable news might be smuggled past the enemy in the guise of commercial messages. The bureau in New York was to gather American news for Germany, and the service was eventually to extend over the whole world.

"In fact," said the report, "it will be particularly desirable to inaugurate the Chinese service at once, so that the American public is informed about that which really happens in order to create

GERMAN EMBASSY
WASHINGTON, D.C.

Washington, D.C., March 15, 1915.

J. No 4344

My dear Mr. Braun,

In answer to your favor of 12th instant I beg to say that I have read the monthly review „Fair Play" for the last 3 years, and I can state that this publication has been living up to its name and that it has always taken the American point of view. During the last 7 months „Fair Play" has, in its editorial policy, treated all belligerents justly and thereby rendered great services to the millions of foreign born citizens of this country, especially to those of German and Austro-Hungarian origin. „Fair Play" has fought for the rights of the latter and for truth, always maintaining an American attitude and showing true American spirit.

You are at liberty to show this letter to anybody who is interested in the matter, but I beg you not to publish it, as to this would be contrary to the instructions of my Government, who does not wish me to publicly advertize any reviews or newspaper.

Very sincerely yours,

*J. Bernstorff*

Marcus Braun, Esq.,
Editor of „Fair Play"
            New York City.


Fac-simile of a letter from Count von Bernstorff
to the editor of "Fair Play"

an effective counter-weight against the Japanese propaganda in the American press."

The New York bureau was estimated to cost $6,640 per month, the bureau in Berlin about half that sum; two years' effort would have cost about $200,000. The writer proposed to establish a lecture service as auxiliary, the total expenses of which, covering the Chautauquas of one summer, he estimated at $75,000. The investigator concluded:

"Hoping that my proposals will lead to a successful result, I will take the liberty of advising in the interest of the German cause—aside from the fact whether my proposals will be carried out or not—that the following should be avoided on the part of Germany in the future:

"1. The Belgian neutrality question as well as the question of the Belgian atrocities should not be mentioned any more in the future.

"2. It should not be tried any more in America to put the blame for the world war and its consequences alone on England, as a considerable English element still exists in America, and the American people hold to the view that all parties, as usual, are partly guilty for the war.

"3. The pride and imagination of the Americans with regard to their culture should not continually be offended by the assertion that German culture is the only real culture and surpasses everything else.

"4. The publication of purely scientific pamphlets should be avoided in the future as far as the American people are concerned, as their dry reading annoys the American and is incomprehensible to him.

"5. Finally it is of the utmost importance that the authorities as well as the German people cease continually to discuss publicly the delivery of American arms and ammunition, as well as to let every American feel their displeasure about it."

The Foreign Office never saw fit to act upon the investigator's proposals, for less than a month after he had written his report, it appeared, verbatim, in the columns of a New York newspaper. Axiom: The most effective means of fighting enemy propaganda is by propaganda for which the enemy unwittingly supplies the material.

Motion pictures appealed to the Germans as a practical and graphic means of spreading through America visual proof of their kindness to prisoners, their prodigious success with new engines of war, and their brutal reception at the hands of the nations they were forced in self-defence to invade. So Dr. Albert financed the American Correspondent Film Company, two of whose

No _____

New York, May 28th 1915

**Kuhn, Loeb & Co.**
WILLIAM & PINE STREETS.

Pay to the order of Fair Play Printing & Publishing Company

Five Thousand _____ 00/100 Dollars

$ 5000 00/100

J. Bernstorff

Copy of a check from Count von Bernstorff to the Fair Play Printing
and Publishing Company

stockholders were Claussen and Dr. Karl A. Fuehr, a translator in Viereck's office. As late as August, 1916, Karl Wunnenberg and Albert A. Sander, of the "Central Powers Film Company," which was also subsidized to circulate German-made moving pictures, engaged George Vaux Bacon, a free-lance theatrical press agent, to go to England at a salary of $100 a week, obtain valuable information, and transmit it in writing in invisible ink to Holland, where it would be forwarded to Germany. The two principals were later indicted on a charge of having set afoot a military enterprise against Great Britain, and were sentenced to two years in prison; Bacon, the cat's-paw, received a year's sentence. (Sander, a German, had been involved in secret-agent work on a previous occasion when he assaulted Richard Stegler for not disavowing an affidavit explaining his acquisition of a false passport.) The secret ink they gave Bacon was invisible under all conditions unless a certain chemical preparation, which could be compounded only with distilled water, was applied to it.

At the start of the war there began in Congress a vehement debate over the question of imposing a legislative embargo on the shipment of arms and ammunition to the Allies. In these debates participated men who undoubtedly were sincere in the convictions they expressed. Nevertheless, in the late winter and early spring of 1915, a hireling of the Germans began to seek secret conferences with congressmen in a Washington hotel and to outline to them plans for compelling an embargo on munitions. His activities bring us to the affairs of the National German-American Alliance, Germany's most powerful and least tangible factor of general propaganda in the United States.

The organization had a large membership among Germans in America; it has been estimated that there were three million members, who constituted a great majority of the adult German-American population. It received a Federal charter in 1907. The Alliance, to quote Professor John William Scholl, of the University of Michigan, (in the New York *Times* of March 2, 1918), "strives to awaken a sense of unity among the people of German origin in America; to 'centralize' their powers for the 'energetic defense of such justified wishes and interests' as are not contrary to the rights and duties of good citizens; to defend its class against 'nativistic encroachments'; to 'foster and assure good, friendly relations of America to the old German fatherland.' Such are its declared objects.

"All petty quibbling aside, this programme can

mean nothing else than the maintenance of a Germanized body of citizens among us, conscious of their separateness, resistent to all forces of absorption. It is mere camouflage to state in a later paragraph that this body does not intend to found a 'State within the State,' but merely sees in this centralization the 'best means of attaining and maintaining the aims' set forth above.

"All existing societies of Germans are called upon as 'organized representatives of Deutschtum' to make it a point of honor to form a national alliance, to foster formation of new societies in all States of the Union, so that the whole mass of Germans in America can be used as a unit for political action. This league pledges itself 'with all legal means at hand unswervingly and at all times to enter the lists for the maintenance and propagation of its principles for their vigorous defense wherever and whenever in danger.'"

Professor Scholl, himself a teacher of German, continues: "A little attention to the context of the sentences quoted shows that these Germans demand the privilege of coming to America, getting citizenship on the easiest terms possible, while maintaining intact their alien speech, alien customs, and alien loyalties. That is 'assimilation,' the granting of equal political rights and commercial opportunities, without exacting any alteration in modes of life or 'Sittlichkeit.' 'Absorption' means Americanization, a fusing with the whole mass of American life, an adoption of the language and ideals of the country, a spiritual rebirth into Anglo-Saxon civilization, and this has great terrors for the members of a German alliance.

"A glance back over the whole scheme will show how cleverly it was made to unite the average recent comeoverer with his beer-drinking proclivities, with the professor of German, who had visions of increased interest in his specialty, and the professor of history, who hoped for larger journal space and ampler funds, and the readily flattered wealthy German of some attainments, into a close league of interests, which could be used at the proper time for almost any nefarious purpose which a few men might dictate.

"Add to this the emphatic moral and financial support of the German-language press as one of the most powerful agencies of the organization, and we have the stage set for just what happened a little over three years ago."

The Alliance, long before the war, had been active in extending German influence. Among other affairs, it had arranged the visit of Prince Henry of Prussia. Its president, Dr. C. J. Hexamer, whose headquarters were in Philadelphia, had received special recognition from the Kaiser for his efforts—efforts which may be briefly set forth in a speech addressed to Germans in Milwaukee by Hexamer himself:

"You have been long-suffering under the preachment that you must be assimilated, but we shall never descend to an inferior culture. We are giving to these people the benefits of German culture."

The outbreak of war made the Alliance an exceedingly important, if unwieldy, instrument for shaping public opinion. It promoted and sponsored a so-called National Embargo Conference in Chicago in 1915, working hand-in-glove with Labor's National Peace Council in an attempt to persuade Congress to pass a law forbidding the export of munitions. At every congressional election, particularly in such cities as Chicago, Cincinnati, Milwaukee, and St. Louis, the hand of Prussia was stirring about. When O. B. Colquitt, a former governor of Texas, decided to run for the Senate in late 1915, he corresponded with the editors of the *Staats-Zeitung* and a New York member of the Alliance for support from the German press and the German vote in his state.

The next year saw the approach of a presidential campaign, and the Alliance established a campaign headquarters in New York to dictate which candidates for United States offices should receive the solid German-American vote. Such candidates had to record themselves as opposed to the policies of the Administration. An effort was made to further the nomination of Champ Clark as the Democratic candidate, succeeding Wilson. A German professor, Leo Stern, superintendent of schools in Milwaukee, after a conference with Hexamer there, wrote to the New York headquarters approving the "Wisconsin plan" (Hexamer's) for swaying the Republican national convention. This plan set forth that "it is necessary that a portion of the delegations to the . . . convention—a quarter to a third—shall consist of approved, distinguished German-Americans." The Alliance was bitterly opposed to Wilson, it hated the lashing tongue and the keen nose of Theodore Roosevelt, it distrusted Elihu Root, and deriving much of its income from the liquor business, it feared prohibition.

Politically the Alliance was constantly active. It supported in early 1916, through its friendly congressmen, the McLemore and Gore resolutions, the latter of which, according to Hexamer, deserved passage because it would—

"1. Refuse passports to Americans travelling on ships, of the belligerents.

"2. Place an embargo on contraband of war.

"3. Prohibit Federal Reserve Banks from subscribing to foreign loans." The Alliance's lobbyist called on Senators Stone, Gore, O'Gorman, Hitchcock (all of whom he reported as "opposed to Lansing"), Senator Smith of Arizona, Senators Kern, Martine, Lewis ("our friend"), Smith of Georgia, Works, Jones, Chamberlain, McCumber, Cummins, Borah and Clapp. Borah, he said, had "a fool idea about Americans going everywhere." In the House of Representatives he canvassed the Democratic and Republican leaders, Kitchin and Mann, and a group "all of whom want the freedom of the seas," which included Dillon of South Dakota, Bennett of New York, Smith of Buffalo, Kinchloe of New York, Shackleford of Missouri, and Staley and Decker of Kentucky. "I saw Padgett, chairman of the house naval affairs committee," he continued, "he will fall in line after a while. . . . I am working with Stephens of the House and Gore of the Senate to put their bills in one bill as a joint resolution. I have told them that my league would aid them in getting members of the House and the Senate, as well as helping them with propaganda (this was their suggestion)."

The resolutions failed.

All these activities cost money. The German

Embassy through Dr. Albert furnished the headquarters of the Alliance with sufficient funds for
its many purposes.   Count von Bernstorff is alleged to have handled a large fund for bribery of
American legislators, but the fact has never been
established, beyond his request in January, 1917,
for $50,000, for such purposes.   It is a fact, how-
ever, that the National German-American Alliance collected a sum of $886,670 during the
years 1914-1917 for the German Red Cross; this
was turned over to von Bernstorff for transmission to Germany, and officers of the Alliance have
admitted that of this sum about $700,000 was
probably employed in propaganda by Dr. Dernburg and Dr. Meyer-Gerhardt, who posed as the
head of the German Red Cross in America.
Contributions to the German and Austrian relief
funds came in as late as October, 1917, although
no part of them were forwarded to Europe after
the entrance of America into the war.

This last event occasioned further activity on
the part of the Alliance; during the period which
followed the break in diplomatic relaxations, and
while Congress was debating the question of war,
members of Congress were deluged with an
extraordinary flood of telegrams from German-
Americans cautioning them against taking such
a step.   These telegrams were prepared by the

Alliance and the "American Neutrality League" and circulated among their members and sympathizers, to be sent to Washington. The Alliance then issued to its branches throughout the states a resolution of loyalty to be adopted in case war was declared. This resolution, after making a hearty declaration of loyalty to the United States, went on to belie its promise with such pacifist utterances as this:

"Our duty before the war was to keep out of it. Our duty now is to get out of it."

So earnest were the efforts of the Alliance to keep out of war that some ten months after its declaration of loyalty was promulgated, Congress decided to investigate the organization, with a view to revoking its charter. The investigation wrote into the archives certain characteristics of the Alliance which had long been obvious to the truly American public; its deep-rooted Teutonism, its persistent zeal, and its dangerous scope of activity. The courageous legislators who initiated and pursued the investigation, in the face of constant opposition of the most tortuous variety, had their reward, for on April 11, 1918, the executive committee of the National Alliance met in Philadelphia and dissolved the organization, turned the $30,000 in its coffers over to the American Red Cross, and uttered a swan song of loyalty to the

United States. The body of the octopus was dead. One by one, first in Brooklyn, then in San Francisco, then elsewhere, its tentacles sloughed away.

A word for the pacifists. One pacifist constitutes a quorum in any society. There were in America at the outbreak of war one hundred million people who disliked war. As the injustices of Germany multiplied, the patriotic war-haters became militarists, and there sprang up little groups of malcontents who resented, usually by German consent, any tendency on the part of the Government to avenge the insult to its independence. Social and industrial fanatics of all descriptions flocked to the standard of "Peace at Any Price," and for want of a dissenting audience soon convinced themselves that they had something to say.

Many of the peace movements which were set going during the first three years of the war were sincere, many were not. A mass meeting held at Madison Square Garden in 1915 at which Bryan was the chief speaker, was inspired by Germany. In the insincere class falls also the "Friends of Peace," organized in 1915. Its letterhead bore the invitation: "Attend the National Peace Convention, Chicago, Sept. 5 and 6," and incidentally betrayed the origin of the society. The letterhead stated that the society represented the American Truth Society (an offshoot of the National German-American Alliance), The American Women of German Descent, the American Fair Play Society, the German-American Alliance of Greater New York, the German Catholic Federation of New York, the United Irish-American Societies and the United Austrian and Hungarian-American Societies. Among the "honorable vice-chairmen" were listed Edmund von Mach, John Devoy, Justices Goff and Cohalan (a trinity of Britonophobes), Colquitt of Texas, Ex-Congressman Buchanan (of Labor's National Peace Council fame), Jeremiah O'Leary (a Sinn Feiner, mentioned in official cables from Zimmermann to Bernstorff as a good intermediary for sabotage), Judge John T. Hylan, Richard Bartholdt (a congressman active in the German political lobby), and divers officers of the Alliance.

The American Truth Society, Inc., the parent of the Friends of Peace, was founded in 1912 by Jeremiah O'Leary, a Tammany lawyer later indicted for violation of the Espionage Act, who disappeared when his case came up for trial in May, 1918; Alphonse Koelble, who conducted the German-American Alliance's New York political clearing house; Gustav Dopslaff, a German-

American banker, and others interested in the German cause. In 1915 the Society, whose executives were well and favorably known to German embassy, began issuing and circulating noisy pamphlets, with such captions as "Fair Play for Germany," and "A German-American War." O'Leary and his friends also conducted a mail questionnaire of Congress in an effort to catalogue the convictions of each member on the blockade and embargo questions. Their most insidious campaign was an effort to frighten the smaller banks of the country from participating in Allied loans, by threats of a German "blacklist" after the war, to organize a "gold protest" to embarrass American banking operations, and in general to harass the Administration in its international relations.

So with their newspapers, rumor-mongers, lecturers, peace societies, alliances, bunds, vereins, lobbyists, war relief workers, motion picture operators and syndicates, the Germans wrought hard to avert war. For two years they nearly succeeded. America was under the narcotic influence of generally comfortable neutrality, and a comfortable nation likes to wag its head and say "there are two sides to every question." But whatever these German agents might have accomplished in the public mind—and certainly they

# THE·FRIENDS·OF·PEACE

## Attend the National Peace Convention, Chicago, Sept. 5 and 6, 1915

### Representing

American Truth Society
American Independence Union
American Humanity League
American Women of German Descent
American Fair Play Society
Continental League
German-American Alliance of Greater N.Y.
German Catholic Federation of New York
United Irish-American Societies
United Austrian & Hungarian-American Soc's
Upholsterers' International Union
and other American Societies.

### National Convention Committee

JOHN BRISBEN WALKER,
of New York, Chairman

ALEXANDER P. MOORE,
of Pittsburgh, Pa., Secretary

### Publicity Committee

RUTLEDGE RUTHERFORD, Chairman
HENRY SCHAEFFER, ⎫
RICHARD M. McCANN, ⎬ Secretaries
HUGH MASTERSON, ⎭

GENERAL OFFICES: 150 NASSAU ST., NEW YORK, N. Y.
Tel. 2168 Beekman

New York,_____1915

Hon. Vice-Chairmen
of
Convention Committee

Michael J. Ryan
Robert E. Ford
Edmund von Mach
John Devoy
Jeremiah R. Murphy
Henry Weismann
Horace L. Brand
Paul Mueller
Prof. Wm. I. Shepherd
Joseph Frey
Judge T. O'Neill Ryan
Richard Bartholdt
Jeremiah O'Leary
Judge John J. Rooney
Ferd Timm
E. K. Victor
Hon. John W. Goff
Hon. Daniel Cohalan
Joseph P. McLaughlin
Judge John T. Hylan
Judge J. Harry Tiernan
Patrick O'Donnell
James T. Clarke
Hugh H. O'Neill
Frank Buchanan
O. B. Colquitt
Daniel O'Connell
Col. Wm. Hoynes
Stephen E. Folan
John F. Kelly
Hon. James K. McGuire
A. L. Morrison
Miss Annie C. Malia
Ellen Ryan Jolly
Thomas O'Brien
J. B. Murphy
Thomas H. Maloney
T. J. Corrigan
Marry F. McWhorter
P. J. Reynolds
Frank J. Ryan
J. P. O'Mahony
Thomas F. Anderson

were sowing their seed in fertile ground—was nullified by acts of violence, ruthlessness at sea, and impudence in diplomacy. The left hand found out what the right hand was about.

# CHAPTER XVI

## HINDU-GERMAN CONSPIRACIES

The Society for Advancement in India—"Gaekwar
Scholarships"—Har Dyal and *Gadhr*—India in 1914—
Papen's report—German and Hindu agents sent to the
Orient—Gupta in Japan—The raid on von Igel's office—
Chakravarty replaces Gupta—The *Annie Larsen* and
*Maverick* filibuster—Von Igel's memoranda—Har Dyal
in Berlin—A request for anarchist agents—Ram Chandra
—Plots against the East and West Indies—Correspond-
ence between Bernstorff and Berlin, 1916—Designs on
China, Japan and Africa—Chakravarty arrested—The
conspirators indicted.

As far back as 1907 a plot was hatched in the
United States to promote sedition and unrest in
British India. The chief agitators had the effrontery in the following year to make their headquarters in rooms in the New York Bar Association, and to issue from that address numerous
circulars asking for money. The late John L.
Cadwallader, of the distinguished law firm of
Cadwallader, Wickersham and Taft, was then
president of the Bar Association, and when he
learned of the Hindu activities under the roof of

the association he swiftly evicted the ringleaders. Their organization, chartered in November, 1907, was called The Society for the Advancement of India. One of its officers was a New York man to whom the British have since refused permission to visit India. Its members included several college professors.

The presence of several educators in the list may be accounted for by the fact that the society existed apparently for the purpose of supplying American college training to selected Hindu youths. Many of them were sent to the United States at the expense of the Gaekwar of Baroda, one of the richest and most influential of the Indian princes; the Gaekwar's own son was a student in Harvard College in the years 1908–1912. Considerable sums of money were solicited from worthy folk who believed that they were furthering the cause of enlightenment in India; others who sincerely believed that British rule was tyrannical gave frankly to the society to help an Indian nationalist movement for home rule; others contributed freely for the promotion of any and every anti-British propaganda in India. The source of the latter funds may be suggested by the understanding which long existed between the Society for the Advancement of India and the Clan-na-Gael, an understanding

witnessed by the frequent quotation in the dis-
affected press of India of articles from the *Gae-
lic-American*. Another successful solicitor was
a contemptible Swami, Vivekahanda, who discussed soul matters to New York's gullible-rich to
his great profit until the police gathered him in
for a very earthly and material offense. But the
students were the best material for revolt,
whether it was to be social or military, and we
shall see presently how they were made use of.

The Gaekwar of Baroda came to America in
the first decade of the new century and expressed
freely at that time his dislike for the British. At
the time of the Muzaffarpur bomb outrage, in
which the wife and daughter of an English official were killed, the police found in the outskirts
of Calcutta a Hindu who had been educated at an
American college at the Gaekwar's expense and
who was at that time conducting a school of in-
struction in the use of explosives and small arms;
he even had considerable quantities of American
arms and ammunition stored in his house. The
youths who held "Gaekwar scholarships" in
America were under the general oversight of a
professor attached to the American Museum of
Natural History, and the accumulation of evidence of the activities of the students finally
caused his removal.

The Society established branches in Chicago, Denver, Seattle, and even in St. John, New Brunswick, and it thrived on the Pacific Coast. Within the purlieus of the University of California, there lived in 1913 one Har Dyal, a graduate of St. John's college at Oxford. Har Dyal in that year founded a publication called *Gadhr,* which being translated means "mutiny," its main edition published in Urdu, other editions published in other vernaculars, and appealing not only to Hindus, but to Sikhs and Moslems. The publication and the chief exponents of its thought formed the nucleus of a considerable system of anti-British activity.

Whatever was anti-British found a warm reception in Berlin. England, in August and September, 1914, was wrestling heroically with the problem of supplying men to the Continent before the German drive should reach the Channel. Her regulars went, and the training of that gallant "first hundred thousand" followed. She combed her colonies for troops, and having an appreciable force of well-trained native soldiers under arms in India, she brought them to France, and the chronicles of the war are already full of stories of the splendid fighting they did, and the annoyance they caused to the grey troops of Germany. From the German standpoint it was good strategy to incite discontent in India, both as tending to remove the Hindu and Sikh regiments from the fighting zone, and as distracting England's attention from the main issue by making her look to the preservation of one of her richest treasure lands; there was the further possibility, after the expected elimination of Russia, of German conquest of India, and a German trade route from the Baltic to the Bay of Bengal, through the Himalayan passes. Germany seized upon the opportunity. The Amir of Afghanistan had trained his army under Turkish officers, themselves instructed by Germany through the forces of Enver Pasha. The Afghans were told that the Kaiser was Mohammedan, and by the faith prepared to smite down the wicked unbeliever, England. The Amir himself spoiled Germany's designs among his people, however, for upon the outbreak of the war he pledged his neutrality to the British Government, and he kept his word.

A report found on the war correspondent Archibald and written by Captain von Papen to the Foreign Office in the summer of 1915, outlines the German version of the situation in India:

"That a grave unrest reigns at the present time throughout India is shown by the various following reports:

"Since October, 1914, there have been various local mutinies of Mohammedan native troops, one practically succeeding the other. From the last reports, it appears that the Hindu troops are going to join the mutineers.

"The Afghan army is ready to attack India. The army holds the position on one side of the Utak (?) River. The British army is reported to hold the other side of the said river. The three bridges connecting both sides have been blown up by the British.

"In the garrison located on the Kathiawar Peninsula Indian mutineers stormed the arsenal. Railroads and wireless station have been destroyed. The Sikh troops have been removed from Beluchistan; only English, Mohammedans and Hindu troops remain there.

"The Twenty-third Cavalry Regiment at Lahore revolted, the police station and Town House were stormed. The Indian troops in Somaliland in Labakoran are trying to effect a junction with the Senussi. All Burma is ready to revolt.

"In Calcutta unrest (is reported) with street fighting. In Lahore a bank was robbed; every week at least two Englishmen killed; in the north-western district many Englishmen killed; munitions and other material taken, railroads destroyed; a relief train was repulsed.

"Everywhere great unrest. In Benares a bank has been stormed.

"Revolts in Chitral very serious, barracks and Government buildings destroyed. The Hurti Mardin Brigade, under Gen. Sir E. Wood, has been ordered there. Deputy Commissioner of Lahore wounded through a bomb in the Anakali Bazaar.

"Mohammedan squadron of the cavalry regiment in Nowschera deserted over Chang, southwest Peshawar. Soldiers threw bombs against the family of the Maharajah of Mysore. One child and two servants killed, his wife mortally wounded.

"In Ceylon a state of war has been declared."

In February, 1915, Jodh Singh, a former student of engineering in the United States, was in Rio de Janeiro. He was directed by a fellow Hindu to call upon the German Consul, and the latter gave him $300 and instructions to proceed to the German consul in Genoa, Italy, for orders. Thence he was forwarded to Berlin, where he attended the meetings of the newly formed Indian Revolutionary Society and absorbed many ideas for procedure in America. Supplied with more German money he came to New York and was joined by Heramba Lal Gupta, a Hindu who had been a student at Columbia, and Albert H. Wehde, an art collector. The three went to Chicago, and Singh called at once upon Gustav Jacobsen, the real estate dealer who will be recalled in the Kaltschmidt bomb plots in Detroit. Jacobsen assembled a group of German sympathizers which included Baron Kurt von Reiswitz, the consul, George Paul Boehm (mentioned in instructions to von Papen to attack the Canadian Pacific Railway) and one Sterneck. At the conference Jodh Singh, Boehm, Sterneck and Gupta were detailed to go to the far East: Singh to Siam, to recruit Hindus for revolutionary service, Gupta to China and Japan to secure arms; Boehm to the Himalayas, to attack the exploring party of Dr. Frederick A. Cook, the notorious, to impersonate Dr. Cook, and thus travel about the hills spreading sedition. Wehde, with $20,000 of von Reiswitz's money, Boehm and Sterneck sailed for Manila, and apparently escaped thence to Java, to meet two officers from the *Emden*, for the three are at this writing fugitives from justice; Jodh Singh was arrested in Bangkok and turned over to the British authorities.

In the diary of Captain Grasshof of the German cruiser *Geier*, interned in Honolulu, appears the following entry, establishing Wehde's call in Hawaii, and the complicity of the Consulate there in his plans:

"At the Consulate I met Mr. A. Wehde from Chicago, who is on way to Orient on business.

"One of the Hindoos sent over by Knorr (naval attaché of German Embassy at Tokio) left for Shanghai on the 6th. In Hongkong there are 500 Hindoos, 200 officers and volunteers, besides one torpedo boat and two Japanese cruisers.

"K-17 (A. V. Kircheisen) was almost captured in Kobe. The first officer of the *China* warned him and he immediately got on board again as soon as possible. K-17 informed me that the Japs have sold back to the Russians all the old guns taken from the latter during the Russo-Japanese war."

Reiswitz in June added $20,000 more to the fund for revolution in India. Gupta, to whom von Papen had paid $16,000 in New York, went on to Japan with Dhirendra Sarkar, a fellow conspirator.

The presence of the two plotters in Japan became known to the authorities and soon thereafter to the public. They were shadowed everywhere, and a complete record was kept of their activities; the newspapers discussed them, and it was common property that they gave a banquet on the night of November 9, 1915, to ten other Hindus, to toast a plot for revolution in India. On November 28 they were ordered by the chief of police to leave Japan before December 2, which was tantamount to a delivery into the hands of the British, as the only two steamers available were leaving for Shanghai and Hong Kong, both ports well supplied with British officers. On the afternoon of December 1 the two plotters escaped in an automobile to the residence of a prominent pro-Chinese politician (a friend of Sun Yat Sen) and were concealed there, between false walls, until May, 1916, when they stowed away on a ship bound for Honolulu. Sarkar returned to India, Gupta to America. When the round-up came, in 1917, Jacobsen, Wehde and Boehm were each convicted of violation of section 13 of the Federal Penal Code, and sentenced to serve five years in prison and pay $13,000 fines; Gupta's sentence was three years, his fine $200.

The scene shifts for a moment from the Orient to the Occident, and the twenty-fifth floor of the building at 60 Wall Street, New York, on the morning of April 19, 1916. There von Papen had had his office; there when he was sent home in December, 1915, he had left in charge a sharp-eyed youth named Wolf von Igel as his successor. Von Igel, at eleven o'clock, was surveying the result of several hours' work in sorting and arranging neat stacks of official papers for shipment to the German Embassy at Washington, for he had got word that trouble was brewing, and that the documents would be safer there. An attendant entered. "A man wants to see you, Herr von Igel," he announced. "He won't tell his business, except that he says it is important."

Von Igel was gruffly directing the attendant to make the stranger specify his mission when the door burst open, and in dashed Joseph A. Baker, of the Department of Justice, and Federal Agents Storck, Underhill and Grgurevich.

"I have a warrant for your arrest!" shouted Baker. Von Igel jumped for the doors of the safe, which stood open. Baker sprang simultaneously for von Igel, and the two went to the floor in battle. The German was overpowered, and the attendant cowed by a flash of revolvers.

"This means war!" yelled von Igel. "This is part of the German Embassy and you've no right here."

"You're under arrest," said Baker.

"You shoot and there'll be war," said von Igel, and made another frantic attempt to close the safe doors. A second skirmish ended in von Igel's removal to a cell, while the agents took charge of the documents. The collection was a rare catch. It contained evidence which supplied the missing links in numerous chains of suspected German guilt, and the matter was at once placed in the safe keeping of the Government.

One letter was dated Berlin, February 4, 1916, and addressed to the German Embassy in Washington. It reads:

"In future all Indian affairs are to be exclusively handled by the committee to be formed by Dr. Chakravarty. Dhirendra Sarkar, and Heramba Lal Gupta, which latter person has meantime been expelled from Japan," . . .

(Gupta was at that moment between the walls of the Japanese politician's house.)

. . ."thus cease to be independent representatives of the Indian Independence Committee existing here.
"(Signed)  ZIMMERMANN."

The Embassy on March 21, 1916, wrote von Igel as follows:

"The Imperial German Consul at Manila writes me:

"'Unfortunately the captured Hindus include Gupta, who last was active at Tokio. The following have also been captured: John Mohammed Aptoler, Rulerhammete, Sharmasler, No-Mar, C. Bandysi, Rassanala. Apparently the English are thoroughly informed of all individual movements and the whereabouts at various times of the Hindu revolutionists.'

"Please inform Chakravarty."

The name "Chakravarty" occurring in these two memoranda makes it necessary here to turn back the calendar to 1915, in order to outline another conspicuous Hindu-German activity. Not only were the East Indian students and sympathetic educators in America prolific in their verbal advocacy of revolt in India, but with German assistance they attempted at least one clearly defined bit of filibustering, which if it had been successful would have supplied the would-be mutineers in the Land of Hind with the arms they so longed to employ against the British.

The reader will recall the mention of a large quantity of weapons and cartridges which Captain Hans Tauscher had stored in a building in 200 West Houston Street, New York, and which he said he had purchased for "speculation." The speculation was apparently the project of Indian mutiny, which in the eyes of the Indian Nationalist party was to equal in grandeur the infamous mutiny of 1857. For those arms were shipped to San Diego, California, secretly loaded aboard the steamer *Annie Larsen,* and moved to sea. The plan provided for their transshipment off the island of Socorro to the hold of the steamship *Maverick,* which was to carry them to India. The two ships failed to effect a rendezvous, and after some wandering the *Annie Larsen* put in at Hoquiam, Washington, where the cargo was at once seized by the authorities. The *Maverick* sailed to San Diego, Hilo, Johnson Island, and finally to Batavia.

Count von Bernstorff had sufficient courage, on July 2, to inform the Secretary of State "confidentially that the arms and ammunition . . . had been purchased by my government months ago through the Krupp agency in New York for shipment to German East Africa." On July 22, he wrote again, asking that the arms be returned as the property of the German Government, and offering to give the Department of Justice "such further information on the subject as I may have" if they cared to push an examination of the cargo. On October 5 he threw all responsibility for the movements of the *Maverick* upon Captain Fred Jebsen, her skipper—by this time a fugitive from justice—and stating "the German Government did not make the shipment, and knows nothing of the details of how they were shipped"—which was a rather shabby way of discrediting his subordinates.

It developed later that the arms were purchased

—sixteen carloads of them—by Henry Muck, Tauscher's manager, for $300,000, made payable by von Papen through G. Amsinck & Co. to Tauscher. A part of the shipment was sent to San Diego; the balance was to have gone to India via Java and China, but never left on acount of the protests of the British Consul. Instead, a number of machine guns and 1,500,000 rounds of ammunition were sold to a San Francisco broker who was acting as agent for Adolphi Stahl, financial agent in the United States for the Republic of Guatemala. When Zimmermann cabled to von Bernstorff on April 30, 1916 (through Count von Luxburg in Buenos Aires), "Please wire whether von Igel's report on March 27, Journal A, No. 257, has been seized, and warn Chakravarty," he had grave concern over the betrayal of German influences in the Hindu conspiracies. This was fully justified when a correspondence notebook of von Igel's disclosed, among other entries, the following transactions:

August 12, 1915—Captain Herman Othmer inclosed documents about the *Annie Larsen* and von Igel forwarded charter to Consul at San Francisco.

September 2—The embassy forwarded papers from San Francisco about the *Annie Larsen* and von Igel returned them.

September 7—The embassy sent a telegram from San Francisco about the *Maverick*.

September 9—The consulate, San Francisco, sent a letter for information and von Igel replied with a telegram about *Maverick* repairs.

September 9, 1915—The Embassy sent a letter from the consulate at San Francisco about shipment and von Igel replied to embassy that the proposals were impracticable.

October 1—The embassy sent a cipher message to Berlin about the *Maverick*.

October 9—The Consulate, San Francisco, sent a letter about the *Maverick* negotiations.

October 20, 1915—Von Igel received a report about a shipment of arms from Manila.

January 27, 1916—The embassy forwarded copies of telegrams to San Francisco in the matter of the *Maverick*.

August 28—The Consulate, Manila, sent a cipher letter about the transport of arms.

November 8, 1915—AAA 100 sent a report from or concerning Ispahan arms.

The peaceful Har Dyal, Oxford graduate, lecturer at Leland Stanford, denizen of the University of California, and editor of *Gadhr*, had laid down the following rules for the guidance of members of the group of revolutionaries which he headed: each candidate for membership must

undergo a six months' probationary period before
his admission; any member who exposed the
secrets of the organization should suffer death;
members wishing to marry could do so without
any ceremony, as they were above the law.   Under such amiable rules of conduct he accumulated
a number of followers of the faith, and more
swarmed to the tinkle of German money.   In
August, 1914, the "first expeditionary force" of
revolutionists set sail for India in the *Korea*.   A
few months later, Har Dyal left for Berlin, where
he organized the Indian Revolutionary Society,
leaving Ram Chandra as his successor to edit
*Gadhr* in Berkeley.

The avowed object of this society was to establish a Republican government in India with the
help of Germany.   They held regular meetings
attended by German officials and civilians who
knew India, among them former teachers in India.   At these meetings the Germans were advised as to the line of conduct to be adopted.
The deliberations were of a secret nature.   Har
Dyal and Chattopadhay had considerable influence with the German Government and were the
only two Indians privileged to take part in the
deliberations of the German Foreign Office.

Besides these societies there were in Berlin

two other associations known as the Persian and
Turkish societies. The object of the first named
was to free Persia from European influences in
general, and create ill feeling against the British
in particular, and to assist the natives to form a
republic. The object of the Turkish society was
practically the same. They established an
Oriental translating bureau which translated
German news and other literature selected by the
Indian Revolutionary Society into various
Oriental languages and distributed the transla-
tions among the Hindu prisoners of war.

Har Dyal continued in close touch with American affairs. On October 20 and 26, 1915, he
wrote to Alexander Berkman, a notorious
anarchist imprisoned in 1918 for violation of the
draft law, urging Berkman to send to Germany
through Holland comrades who would be valuable
in Indian propaganda, and asking for letters of
introduction "from Emma or yourself" (Emma
Goldman) to important anarchists in Europe;
these communications are unimportant except as
they betray the Prussian policy of making an ally
of anarchy, although anarchy as a social factor
is the force from which Germany has most to
fear. "Perhaps you can find them," wrote Dyal,
"in New York or at Paterson. They should be

real fighters, I. W. W.'s or anarchists. Our Indian party will make all the necessary arrangements."

Ram Chandra went on with the work until he was stopped by the Foreign Office. He printed anti-Britannic pamphlets quoting Bryan for circulation in India; he printed and delivered to Lieutenant von Brincken at the German Consulate in San Francisco some 5,000 leaflets, which were to be shipped to Germany and dropped by the Boche aviators over the Hindu lines in France: the handbills read, "Do not fight with the Germans. They are our friends. Lay down your arms and run to the Germans." Chandra and his crew supplied the *Maverick* with quantities of literature, but most of it was burned when the Hindu agents aboard feared that there were British warships near Socorro Island. In the same group were G. B. Lal and Taraknath Das, two former students at the University of California, the latter a protégé of a German professor there himself engaged in propaganda work.

Throughout the fall of 1915 the Hindus in America awaited word of Gupta's success in Japan. They heard nothing but news of his disappearance. Accordingly in December, Dr. Chakravarty, a frail little Hindu of light chocolate complexion, sailed from Hoboken for Germany, traveling as a Persian merchant, on a false passport. He made a good impression on the Foreign Office, as may be judged by the following letter, dated January 21, 1916, addressed to L. Sachse, Rotterdam:

"Dr. Chakravarty will return to the United States and form a working committee of only five members, one of whom should be himself and another, Ram Chandra. In addition to sending more Indians home the new American committee will undertake the following:

"1—An agent will be sent to the West India islands, where there are nearly 100,000 Indians, and will organize the sending home of as many as possible.

"They have not yet been approached by us and there are no such difficulties in the way of their going to India as are encountered by our countrymen from the United States.

"2—An agent will be sent to British Guiana with the same object.

"3—A very reliable man will be sent to Java and Sumatra.

"4—It is proposed to have pamphlets printed and circulated in and from America. The literature will be printed secretly and propaganda will be carried on with great vigor.

"5—An effort will be made to carry out the plan of the secret Oriental mission to Japan. Dr. Chakravarty is in a position to get letters of introduction to important persons in Japan, as well as a safe-conduct for himself and other members of mission."

After conferring with Dyal, Zimmermann, and Under secretary Wesendonk of the Foreign Office, he was given money and sent back to the United States, arriving in February, 1916. He at once sent H. A. Chen to China to purchase arms and ship them to India. He then reported to Wolf von Igel, who paid him $40,000 for the purchase of a house in 120th Street and one in 17th Street. There he held forth for more than a year, working in conjunction with von Igel, and the latter with the Embassy in Washington. His activities may be indicated, and the complicity of the German Government again established, in the following communications:

*From von Igel to von Bernstorff*

"New York, April 7, 1916—A report has been received here that Dr. Chakravarty was taken Monday, the 3d of April, to the Providence Hospital with concussion of the brain in consequence of an automobile accident. His convalescence is making good progress. A certain Ernest J. Euphrat has been here and he came from the Foreign Office and had orders with respect to the India propaganda. He could not identify himself, but made a very good impression. He told us Herr von Wesendonk told him to say that Ram Chandra's activity in San Francisco was not satisfactory. This person should for the time being suspend his propaganda activities."

"In re No. 303: Euphrat was sent by me to India in October of last year, and is so far as known here reliable.

He was, indeed, recommended at the time by Marcus Braun. Please intimate to him cautiously that he should not speak too much about his orders he received in Berlin. San Francisco is being informed."

"For Prince Hatzfeld."

### *From New York to von Bernstorff*

"New York, April 15, 1916—Mr. E. J. Euphrat has asked that the inclosed documents be forwarded to his excellency in a safe way. He asks for a reply as quickly as possible, because if he does not receive the desired allowance he will have to change the plans for his journey.

"(Signed) K. N. St."

### *To H. Eisenhuth, Copenhagen, from New York, and unsigned*

"May 2, 1916. We have also organized a Pan-Asiatic League, so that some of our members can travel without arousing any suspicion. Also everything has been arranged for the 'mission to Japan.' Please let me know when your men can come, so that we can approach the party more definitely. I had talks with one of the directors of the *Yamato Shimbun* of Tokio and *Chinvai Dempo* of Kyoto. It would not be necessary to buy off these papers, as they understand it is to mutual interest. But they ask for certain considerations to help their financial status. They are also decided to attack Anglo-Japanese treaty as antagonistic to national interest. To carry on work it will be necessary to place at the disposal of the committee here $25,000."

*Cablegram from Zimmermann, Berlin, to von Bernstorff, via von Luxburg, Buenos Aires*

"To Bernstorff, May 19, 1916:  Berlin telegraphs No. 28 of May 19.  Answer to telegram 23.  Your excellency is empowered to give the Indians $20,000.  No. 29 of May 19 in continuation of telegram No. 16.  Please, in making direct payments to Tarak Nath Das, avoid receipts.  Das will receipt own payment through a third party as Edward Schuster.

"(Signed)  ZIMMERMANN."

*Zimmermann to Peking, transmitted by Luxburg, to Bernstorff for Peking legation*

"The confidential agent of the Nationalists here, the Indian, Tarak Nath Das, an American citizen, is leaving for Peking by the Siberian Railway.  Please give him up to 10,000 marks.  Das will arrange the rest.

"ZIMMERMANN."

"Ambassador at Washington:  Please advise Chakravarty.

"LUXBURG."

*From Bernstorff, mailed at Mt. Vernon, N. Y., to Z. N. G. Olifiers, a German agent in Amsterdam*

"June 16, 1916—Referring to my letter A275 of June 8, Chakravarty reports:  Organization has been almost completed, and many of our old members are active and free.  Only they are afraid if arms are not available soon there may be premature uprising in Madras and the Punjab as well as in Bengal.  The work in Japan is going unusually well, more than our expectations."

### From Berlin to Chakravarty

"July 13, 1916—In organizing work in the United States and outside, remember our primary object is to produce revolutions at home during this war. Trinidad, British Guiana and East Africa, including Zanzibar, should be particularly tapped for men.

"We wired your name to Francis E. M. Hussain, Bachelor of Arts, Barr. at Law, Port of Spain, Trinidad. Through messenger communicate full programme desired in Trinidad to him, and mention the name 'Binniechatto.' He can be trusted. If, after some secret work, you think revolution can be organized in island itself, then we may try to smuggle arms, and our men will seize Government and set up independent Hindustani Republic. Do not let such plan be carried out if our prospects for work at home are likely to be ruined."

### A report from Chakravarty, written July 26, 1916

"I am going to Vancouver next week to see Bhai Balwant Singh and Nano Singh Sihra, who have asked me to go there to arrange definite plan of action for group of workers there, and then to San Francisco to induce Ram Chandra to plan our committee here, and to include him and his nominees in the said committee, so that our work does not suffer in the East by placing enemies on their guard and right track by his thoughtless, enthusiastic writings. . . . Gupta is back in New York and has seen me, but has not submitted any report. We need $15,000 more for the next six months to carry out the new plan and to continue the previous work undertaken."

*From von Bernstorff, at Rye, N. Y., to Olifiers, trans-
mitting Chakravarty's report*

"August 5, 1916—Our organization has been well perfected in the West Indies and Houssain has been approached. We have also enlisted the sympathy of the
Gongoles party, a strong fighting body of colored people,
who have ramifications all over Central America, including British Guiana and Guatemala. Arms can be easily
smuggled there and if we can get some of the German
officers in this country to go there and lead them there
is every possibility that we can hold quite a while. But
the question is—ask the Foreign Secretary whether it is
desirable, for it might simply create a sensation and nothing more. As soon as we hold there the Governmental
power the island would be isolated by the British navy,
and the attitude of the United States is uncertain, and
we may be compelled to surrender sooner or later; but if
it serves any purpose either as a blind or otherwise, and
after due consideration of its advantages and disadvan-
tages, wire at once the authorities here to give us a few
officers, as we need them badly, and other help necessary
to carry out the plan, and it can be done without much
difficulty. I believe if a sensation is desired something
also can be done in London, at least should be tried. If
we can get a few men from the Pacific Coast we can send
them easily as a crew with a Dutch passport.

"We are sending arms in small quantities through
Chinese coolies over the border in Burmah, but in big
quantities we do not find possibility. However, we are
on the lookout. We have been trying our best with a
Japanese firm who have a business affiliation in Calcutta,

whether they will undertake to transmit some arms through their goods.

"To complete the chain we are sending Mr. Chandra to London as a medical student in the university, and he will send men and other informations to you via Switzerland. We are also sending a few Chinese students to China to help us in the work, and if you want it can also be arranged they give you a personal report through Russia and Sweden.

"We need $15,000 more, as I return from the Pacific Coast, to carry out these plans, excepting that of Trinidad operations, which, if you approve, wire at once the military agent here to arrange to buy and ship arms to us, before the enemy can be on guard."

### To H. Eisenhuth, Copenhagen, in cipher

"September 5, 1916—Arms can no more be safely sent to India through Pacific, except through Japanese merchandise or through China merchants, shipped to Chinese ports and then to our border. Responsible men are willing to take the risk and they are willing to send their confidential agents to Turaulleur."

### Chakravarty to Berlin, Foreign Office

"September 5, 1916—Li Yuan Hung is now President of China. He was formerly the southern revolutionary leader. W. T. Wang was then his private secretary. He is now in America and starting for China. He says Li Yuan Hung is in sympathy with the Indian revolution and would like English power weakened. Some of the prominent people are quite eager to help India directly, and Germany indirectly, without exposing themselves to any great risk, on three conditions:

"The first—Germany to make a secret treaty with China, that in case China is attacked by any power or powers, Germany will give her military aid. It will be obligatory for five years after the discontinuance of the present war and there will be an understanding that China shall get one-tenth of all arms and ammunition she will receive for and deliver to the Indian revolutionaries and the Indian border.

"In return, China shall prohibit the delivery of arms and ammunition in the name of the Chinese Government and from China through private sailing boats and by coolies to any nearby point or any border place as directed. She will help Indian revolutionaries as she can, secretly and in accord with her own safety.

"But this is to be regarded as a feeler through a third party, and, if it is acceptable to the German Government, then they will send one of their trusted representatives to Berlin to discuss the details and plan of operations, and if it is settled, then negotiations should take place officially and papers signed through the embassies in Berlin and Peking. They want to know the attitude of the German Foreign Office as soon as possible so that they can set the ball rolling for necessary arrangements."

### *Von Bernstorff to Zimmermann*

"October 13, 1916—Chakravarty's reply is not sent; too long. Require at end of October a further $15,000. According to news which has arrived here Okechi has not received the $2000 and in the meantime left Copenhagen.

Please withhold payment until Polish National Committee provides therefor.

"BERNSTORFF."

### To Olifiers, Amsterdam, postmarked Washington

"November 21, 1916—Rabindranath Tagore has come at our suggestion and saw Count Okuma, Baron Shimpei Goto, Masaburo Suzuki, Marquis Yamanouchi, Count Terauchi and others; Terauchi is favorable and others are sympathetic. Rash Behari Bose is still there to see whether they can be persuaded to do something positive for our cause. S. Sekunna and G. Marsushita are doing their best. Yamatashimbun is strongly advocating our cause. D. Pal has not come. Benoy Sarkar is still in China. Lala is willing to go, but this passage could not be arranged. As soon as Tilak arrives he will be approached. Bapat is still free and writes that he has been trying his best, but for want of arms they have not been able to do anything. Received a note from Abdul Kadir and Shamshar Singh from Termes-Buchare that they are proceeding on slowly to their destination. Barkatullah is in Kabul; well received, lacks funds. Mintironakaono is here. Isam Uhiroi is in Pekin. Tarak has safely reached there. Our publication work is going on well. We have brought out seven pamphlets and one in the press. We are waiting for definite instructions as to the work in Trinidad and Damrara.

"Wu Ting Fang has been now made the Foreign Minister. He has always been sympathetic with our cause. But the influence of Sun Yat Sen still persists in opposing us in that direction."

### Zimmermann to Bernstorff

"December 20, 1916—According to Chakravarty, the Indians were paid up to September 30 $30,000. Total credit for Indians, $65,000.

"ZIMMERMANN."

### Zimmermann to Bernstorff

"January 4, 1917—very secret. The Japanese, Hideo Nakao, is traveling to America with important instructions from the Indian Committee. He is to deal exclusively with Chakravarty. Please, after consultation with Chakravarty, inform Imperial Minister at Peking and the Imperial Consulate at Shanghai that they are to send in Nakao's reports regularly. I advise giving Nakao in installments up to fifty thousand dollars in all for the execution of his plans in America and Eastern Asia. Decision as to the utility of the separate payments is left to your excellency and the Imperial Legation at Peking. Despatch follows.

"(Signed)  ZIMMERMANN."

On March 7, 1917, Guy Scull, deputy police commissioner in New York, with eight detectives, called at 364 West 120th Street, found Dr. Chakravarty clad in a loin cloth, and arrested him on a charge of setting afoot a military enterprise against the Emperor of India. With Sekunna, a German who had been writing tracts for him, he was later transferred to San Francisco to stand trial. The typewriter in the 120th Street house, whose characteristics—all typewriters are as in-

dividual and as identifiable as finger-prints—had
betrayed the conspirators, lay idle for many
months, but as late as March 18, 1918, a Hindu,
Sailandra Nath Ghose, who had collaborated with
Taraknath Das in writing a propaganda work
called "The Isolation of Japan in world politics,"
was arrested there in company with a German
woman, Agnes Smedley. The two were accused
of violating the espionage act by representing
themselves to be diplomatic agents of the Indian
Nationalist Party, and of having sent an appeal
for aid in the establishment of a democratic fed-
erated republic in India to the Brazilian Embassy
in Washington, to Leon Trotzky in Russia, and to
the Governments of Panama, Paraguay, Chile
and other neutral nations.

In the course of the years 1916 and 1917 the
Government built up an unusually exhaustive and
troublesome case for nearly one hundred defendants, including the personnel of the San Francisco consulate, the German consul at Honolulu
(who had supplied the *Maverick* in Hilo Harbor [1]), a large group of Hindu students, a smaller
group of war brokers, and numerous lesser intermediaries. Their trial was one of the most
cumbersome and interesting cases ever heard in

---

[1] The *Maverick* was lost in a typhoon off the Philippines in
August, 1917.

an American court. It began on November 19,
1917, in San Francisco, with Judge Van Fleet on
the bench. Witness after witness recited his
story of adventure, each stranger than the last,
and all stranger than fiction. Lieutenant von
Brincken, one of the San Francisco consulate,
pleaded guilty within a few weeks; his sentence
was long deferred by the prosecution on account, presumabably, of evidence which he supplied the Government. George Rodiek, the German consul in Honolulu, followed suit and was
fined heavily; Jodh Singh turned state's evidence
and presently his mind became diseased and he
was committed to an asylum; the procedure
was interrupted from time to time with wran-
gles among the defendants, and on one occasion Franz Bopp, the San Francisco consul,
shouted to one of his fellows, "You are spoiling
the whole case!" When the Government,
through United States Attorney Preston, introduced evidence from the Department of State,
the Hindus attempted to subpœna Secretary Lansing; when Bryan's pacifist tracts were introduced
the defendants sought Bryan. On April 18,
1918, Chakravarty confessed, to the irritation of
the other defendants. The climax in melodrama
occurred on the afternoon of April 23, 1918,
when, with the case all but concluded, Ram Singh

shot and killed Ram Chandra in the courtroom. A moment later Ram Singh lay dead, his neck broken by a bullet fired over the heads of the attorneys by United States Marshal Holohan. That afternoon Judge Van Fleet delivered his charge to the jury; that night a verdict of guilty was returned against twenty-nine of the thirty-two defendants who had not been dismissed as the trial proceeded.

Judge Van Fleet, on April 30, 1918, pronounced the following sentences:

Franz Bopp, German consul in San Francisco, two years in the penitentiary and $10,000 fine; F. H. von Schack, vice-consul, the same punishment; Lieutenant von Brincken, military attaché of the consulate, two years' imprisonment without fine; Walter Sauerbeck, lieutenant commander in the German navy, an officer of the *Geier* interned in Honolulu, one year's imprisonment and $2,000 fine; Charles Lattendorf, von Brincken's secretary, one year in jail; Edwin Deinat, master of the German ship *Holsatia,* interned in Honolulu, a term of ten months in jail and a fine of $1,500; Heinrich Felbo, master of the German ship *Ahlers,* interned in Hilo, Hawaii, six months in jail and a fine of $1,000. These men may be described as the loyal German group.

Robert Capelle, agent in San Francisco of the

North German Lloyd line, fifteen months' imprisonment and a fine of $7,500; Harry J. Hart, a San Francisco shipping man, six months in jail and a fine of $5,000; Joseph Bley of the firm of C. D. Bunker & Co., customs brokers, fifteen months in prison and a fine of $5,000; Moritz Stack von Goltzheim, a real estate and insurance broker, six months in jail and $1,000 fine; Louis T. Hengstler, an admiralty lawyer and professor in the University of California and in Hastings Law College, a fine of $5,000; Bernard Manning, a real estate, insurance and employment agent in San Diego, nine months in jail and a fine of $1,000; and J. Clyde Hizar, a former city attorney in Coronado and assistant paymaster in the United States Navy, one year's imprisonment and a fine of $5,000. These gentlemen constituted the so-called "shipping group" which was intimately concerned with the affairs of the *Annie Larsen* and the *Maverick*.

Dr. Chakravarty, who had been delegated by no less a personage than Zimmermann of Berlin to handle all Indian intrigue in America, received a crushing sentence of sixty days in jail and a fine of $5,000. Bhagwan Singh, the "poet of the revolution," was sentenced to eighteen months in the penitentiary; Taraknath Das, the author and lecturer, to twenty-two months' imprisonment;

Dr. Chakravarty (on the right), the accredited agent of Germany in the Hindu-German intrigues in America. With him is Ernest Sekunna, also a German agent, arrested with Chakravarty

Gobind Behari Lal, the University of California student, to ten months in jail. The smaller fry of the University of California-*Ghadr* group were disposed of as follows: Nandekar to three months in jail, Ghoda Ram to eleven months, Sarkar, who had been in Japan with Gupta, to four months, Munshi Ram (of the *Ghadr* staff) to sixty days, Imam Din to four months, Nerajan Das to six months, Singh Hindi to nine months, Santokh Singh to twenty-one months in the penitentiary, Gopalm Singh to one year and a day, and Nidhan Singh to four months.

Those defendants who remained had not been allowed at large on bail, thanks to the vigilance of Preston. Yet in spite of all precautions, the proceedings frequently threatened to get out of control. The United States had been at war for a year; the Federal Court was trying both alien enemies of military status and alien enemies who had engaged in and stood convicted of conspiracy, as well as conspirators against the rule of Britain in India who had revolution quite definitely in mind. Great Britain, for six months before the trial began, had been our ally and, in spirit at least, a traitor to Great Britain was a traitor to the United States. In spirit, but not in the letter of the law: the worst punishment which any existing statutes could impose on any single defendant found wholly and completely guilty of the charge was *two years' imprisonment and a fine of $10,000*. For such conviction, and for such punishment of the United States' military enemies, the prosecution clambered about through the tangle of civil procedure; we had been six months at war and laws had not been supplied to facilitate the swift justice due such enemies, nor have laws been supplied as this is written. More than eighty "court days" were consumed, the shorthand reporting alone cost more than $35,000. A court commissioner released four important witnesses "for want of evidence." (One of them was indicted in New York and the commissioner was himself dismissed.) Gupta, arrested in New York, was released on bail and swiftly fled across the Mexican border to continue his propaganda. Trying as the case was to all who were concerned in it, expeditiously as it was handled by the authorities, and informative as it proved to be, it was monumental in its confession that civil courts cannot act with the warning vigor and speed made necessary by war conditions.

The evidence introduced pointed clearly to the conclusion that the German-Hindu plot, complex as it is to us as critics, was unfruitful even to Berlin. Perhaps its very breadth made it awkward to manage. Nearly four years of war passed, and there was no mutiny in India. The stewards of the Indian domain knew anxious moments, but they found some solace in the realization that half way around the world, in the United States, there was a pair of eyes to watch every pair of mischievous hands, and that the conspiracy directed against the Orient could not take effect while those eyes were open.

It requires no special gift of prophecy to predict that secret conspiracies will continue unless those eyes are more vigilant than ever. The United States Attorney announced as the conspirators were being sentenced that he felt that the court might well instruct their dark associates to "cut out their propaganda," and that their *Gahdr* presses were even then turning out "barrels and bales of seditious literature." To this Judge Van Fleet gravely responded:

"The people are going to take the law into their own hands, as much as we regret it. The citizens of this country are going to suppress manifestations hostile to our allies."

# CHAPTER XVII

## MEXICO, IRELAND, AND BOLO

Huerta arrives in New York—The restoration plot—German intrigue in Central America—The Zimmermann note—Sinn Fein—Sir Roger Casement and the Easter Rebellion—Bolo Pacha in America and France—A warning.

Germany learned during President Roosevelt's administration that the Monroe Doctrine was not to be tampered with. The United States stood squarely upon a policy of "hands off Latin America." But both commercial and diplomatic Germany were attracted by the bright colors of the somewhat kaleidoscopic political condition of the Central and South American nations. In political confusion, Mexico, at the outbreak of war, led all the rest. This suited Germany's purpose perfectly—provided that at least one faction in Mexico might be susceptible to her influence. The first three years of war proved to the satisfaction of the most skeptical that Mexican unrest would trouble the United States, and it was upon this theory that Germany long before 1914 baited her hook for Mexico.

Propagandists in our neighbor republic added fuel to the already brisk flame of native hostility to the Yankee. A considerable German commercial colony grew up, assimilated the language and customs of Mexico, and bade fair to be a strong competitor in the development of the huge natural resources waiting there for foreign capital. By 1914 Germany had evidently expected to be in a position sufficiently strong to enlist Mexico on her side in case the United States gave trouble. The reader will recall that Admiral von Hintze in the summer of 1914 had recommended Captain von Papen for a decoration for having organized a fair military unit of the Germans in Mexico. That same summer, however, saw Mexico with troubles of her own, and German efforts against the United States through Mexico had to be postponed.

Early in 1914 General Huerta, an unscrupulous, powerful and dissolute factionist, had executed a *coup d'etat* which placed him in the president's chair. He at once advertised for bids. The United States had no intention of protecting him, and in order to stop at its source any trouble which might prove too attractive to a foreign power, placed an embargo upon the shipment

of American arms into Mexico. The American
fleet was despatched to Vera Cruz to see that the
order was carried out. The steamship *Ypiranga,*
with a cargo of arms, succeeded in eluding the
fleet, and under orders from the German admiral,
and the direction of Karl Heynen, the arms were
landed.

Huerta had promised the presidency to Felix
Diaz. In order to get him out of the way he sent
Diaz to negotiate a Japanese understanding.
The United States gently diverted Señor Diaz
from his mission. Huerta began to lose the grip
he held; three other factionists, Villa, Carranza
and Zapata, each at the head of an army, were
aiming at his head, and shortly before the world
went to war the old rogue fled to Barcelona.

There Rintelen negotiated with him in February, 1915, and out of their conferences grew a
plan to restore him to the Mexican presidency.
This plan would have meant war between Mexico
and the United States, which was precisely what
von Rintelen and his Wilhelmstrasse friends desired: American forces would have to be mobilized at the Rio Grande, and American munitions,
destined for the Allies, would have to be commandeered and diverted to Mexico.

The aged general arrived in New York in
April, and was interviewed and photographed.

He told the public through the newspapers that he proposed to acquire an estate on Long Island and the public considered it not inauspicious that the veteran warrior should have come to pass the remainder of his stormy life in the world's most peaceful country. Fortunately for the peace of the United States not every one believed him.

Within a week of his arrival von Rintelen slipped into New York. He placed in the Havana branch of the Deutsches Bank and in banks in Mexico City some $800,000 to Huerta's credit, and within a short time the political jackals who lived on foreign subsidy began to prick up their ears. Von Papen and Boy-Ed had made trips to the Mexican border, arranging through their consular agents in the Mexican towns across the river the mobilization of Germans in Mexico, the storing of supplies and ammunition, and the deposit of funds in banks at Brownsville, El Paso, San Antonio and Douglas. Not all Mexicans in the United States were Huertistas, however, and one Raphael Nieto, Assistant-Secretary of Finance to Carranza, was quite as eager to follow Huerta's activities as were the agents of the United States. The Carranzistas joined forces with the Secret Service and found out that the plot had already begun to develop.

During the month of May, Huerta frequently

met a member of the German Embassy at the Hotel McAlpin. Von Rintelen was clever enough not to negotiate in person, but he dined frequently with the Embassy member. Much of what had occurred at these conferences in the McAlpin was known to government agents, who had been concealed where they could take notes on the conversation. On June 1, 1915, General Huerta, with Jose Ratner, his "financial adviser," held a conference in the Holland House with a former Huertista cabinet minister, a son of the Mexican general, Angeles, and certain other personages who purposed to take part in the revolution for the sake of this world. One of the men present was a Carranza spy, and through him it became known that Huerta outlined that he had ten millions of dollars for immediate use in a plot to restore him to his former position, twice that sum in reserve, and that more would be forthcoming if necessary. Arms and ammunition, he said, would be shipped into Mexico secretly, supplies would be accumulated at certain border towns, and envoys had already been sent to incite desertion from the armies of Carranza and Villa.

Rintelen did not know that the Carranzistas had sold out to the authorities. Rintelen had already purchased some $3,000,000 worth of arms and cartridges, and he was prepared to see the enterprise to a successful conclusion. Incidentally he was quietly supplying six other Mexican factions with funds in case Huerta's measure of success should prove too intoxicating.

Because he was a figure of considerable international notoriety and indisputable news interest, the press had been following Huerta's movements with strict attention. Affairs at the border were not reassuring and there persisted the feeling that Huerta in the United States held promise of Huerta once more in Mexico. In July, his agent, Ratner, issued the following frank though apparently ingenious statement:

"General Huerta and those of us associated with him are confident that the whole Mexican situation will be cleared up within ninety days. We believe that to rule the country is a one-man job. And in that time we expect that one man to come forward and unite the country. General Huerta does not care to indicate the man he has in mind, but he is from our viewpoint a true patriot, and naturally that excludes both Carranza and Villa.

"General Huerta may or may not return to Mexico some day, and may or may not hold office there again. At present he is giving himself up wholly to an agreeable and home life in this city (New York)."

Whether or not General Huerta was to "return to Mexico some day" depended upon the temper of the United States. He knew that when he authorized the statement. He did not know—or else he was incredibly bold—that the Government was in possession of the whole story, and that orders had been issued from the highest source in the country not to let him return. One day in the late summer he slipped away, ostensibly to visit the San Francisco Exposition. Government agents shadowed him and let him make his own pace. He took the southern route, and traveled so quietly that his flight was not publicly marked until he had passed through Kansas City. As he approached the border he became as eager as a boy at the prospect of his 'return from Elba'; then, as he was almost in sight of the soil from which he had been exiled, he was arrested on a technical charge and jailed.

In August Rintelen fled the country. The *Providence Journal* had just published an irritating charge that Boy-Ed was carrying on negotiations with Mexico; the German Embassy denied the charge, although Boy-Ed with his knowledge of Mexico had assisted ably in the plot; and the excitement of official interest in Huerta's recent connections made von Rintelen nervous. When he was captured at Falmouth by the British, his man-Friday, Andrew V. Meloy, confessed that he had inadvertently tipped over the plot when he had innocently telephoned a Carranzista to find out, for safety sake, whether the Carranza party suspected Huerta. It was this Carranzista who made a few inquiries of his own, and succeeded in planting the spy in the Holland House meeting.

The aged general, although he was transferred to a more comfortable prison, took his confinement bitterly. His dream had been bright indeed, and it had been bluntly interrupted. As the autumn came on his health showed signs of failing, and his career of dissipation began to total the final reckoning. The illness became grave, and after two surgical attempts to save his life, he died in January, 1916, heartbroken.

Von Eckhart, the minister to Mexico City, was to Mexico what Bernstorff was to the United States and he employed faithfully the familiar tactics of his superior: revolution, editorial propaganda, filibustering and double dealing. In the fall of 1916 the fine German hand could be seen prompting a note sent by Mexico to the United States urging an embargo on the shipment on munitions and foodstuffs to the warring nations (Mexico had neither foodstuffs nor munitions to supply). And in December, 1916, Eckhart was robbed of the achievement of a conspiracy of fantastic proportions.

In order to appreciate the fantasy, one must bear in mind the temperament of a Central American. Eckhart and his colleague, Lehmann, German minister to Guatemala, proposed to harness that temperament to a German wagon and drive the Latin republics to the formation of "the United States of Central America," which presumably would have borne a Prussian eagle in the field of its ensign.

Carranza disliked Cabrera of Guatemala; so, too, did Dr. Irias, a Nicaraguan liberal. Certain factions in Honduras disapproved of their president; certain factions in Guatemala could be counted on to support revolution against Cabrera; Dr. Irias, the defeated candidate, disliked Emiliano Chammorra, the President of Nicaragua, enormously. What more natural than that they combine forces and with German money and arms kindle not one revolution but a series of them, with an invasion thrown in for good measure? Accordingly they conferred with a Salvadorean politician, a Cuban revolutionist, and an associate of the Costa Rican minister of war. The cast complete, they planned to assemble revolutionary forces, with German military advisers, on the coast of Salvador. Using Salvador as a base, attacks were to be made upon Nicaragua and Guatemala, and at the proper time Carranza was to invade Guatemala from the north. Colombia's services were to be enlisted by the promise of restoration of the Republic of Panama—originally a Colombian province. As soon as the combined revolutionaries had succeeded in overthrowing their governments, they were to form the United States of Central America, with Irias as president, and William of Hohenzollern as counsel.

Our levity is pointed not at the Central American temperament and political instability, but rather towards the grotesquely serious objective of the German plotters. If their military forces had been Prussian shock troops they would certainly have succeeded. The use of a Mexican gunboat to transport German officers with an airplane and wireless apparatus from Mexico to Salvador exposed the plan. President Cabrera of Guatemala had a small but effective force of thirty thousand men, and a well-equipped artillery, armed—and he was prepared for attack from either frontier. He also enjoyed the confidence of Washington, and he informed Washington at once what was afoot. The answer arrived presently in the shape of the American fleet, on a peaceful expedition to survey the Gulf of Fonseca, its newly acquired Nicaraguan naval base. The revolutions failed for want of revolutionists, the German enterprise failed for want of revolutions, and of the conspirators only one, Tinoco of Costa Rica, succeeded in capitalizing the unrest by a *coup d'etat* which made him president. The plot never reached maturity in Colombia or Panama.

Before dismissing it from consideration, however, it is worth a moment's analysis. With any degree of success it would have distracted the United States, and perhaps have involved her marine corps as well as her navy. It contained possibilities of war between Mexico and the United States. It projected a blow at the Panama Canal. It concerned a territory in which commercially as well diplomatically the United States had definite concern and in which Germany had already shown a greedy interest. Incidentally it reveals—in its offer to Colombia—the same diplomatic technique as that which was shortly to startle the United States into the last step towards war, the so-called "Zimmermann note."

At 3 A. M. (Berlin time) on January 19, 1917, the following message was sent by wireless to Count von Bernstorff from the Foreign Office:

"BERLIN, January 19, 1917.

"On the first of February we intend to begin submarine warfare unrestricted.  In spite of this it is our endeavor to keep neutral the United States of America.

"If this is not successful we propose an alliance on the following basis with Mexico:  That we shall make war together and together shall make peace.  We shall give general financial support and it is understood that Mexico is to recover the lost territory in New Mexico, Texas and Arizona.  The details are left to you for settlement.

"You are also instructed to inform the president of Mexico of the above in the greatest confidence as soon as it is certain there will be an outbreak of war with the United States and suggest that the President of Mexico on his own initiative should communicate with Japan suggesting adherence at once to this plan; at the same time offer to mediate between Germany and Japan.

"Please call to the attention of the President of Mexico that the employment of ruthless submarine warfare now promises to compel England to make peace in a few months.

"(Signed)  ZIMMERMANN."

This document was decoded from the official dictionary cipher and laid in the hands of President Wilson almost immediately following the rupture of diplomatic relations.  It was made public on February 28, when the public temper was at whitest heat.  Mexico did not repudiate the note at once, and four days later despatched a denial of having received any such proposal as Zimmermann had suggested.  Eckhart was forcing Carranza's hand with the lure of the projected Central American enterprise already outlined.   (Eckhart had had Carranza so completely under his influence at one time that when the United States despatched to Mexico a friendly note warning her of the presence of German submarines in the Gulf, Mexico retorted—at Eckhart's literal dictation—that the United States might do well to ask the British Navy why it did not prevent German undersea craft from approaching the Americas.)   The month of March fled by, and America went to war; since that date no official expression except one of praise for Mexico's attitude of amiable neutrality has issued from Washington.

Just as the proximity of Mexico to the United States had for a number of years past carried with it the possibility, almost the certainty, of differences between the two countries, rising out of the temperamental differences of their peoples, so for a longer period had Ireland and England suffered for their contiguity.  It is a truism to remark that the Irishman cherishes his national grievances, but that characteristic accounts for a further phase of German intrigue on American soil.  Hatred of England sent many thousands of Irish to the United States in the past fifty years. They found it a country to their liking, which England was not, and although they had become indissolubly attached to their adopted land, there were in America in 1914 (and there are in 1918) numerous Irish who had no dearer wish than that England come off second best in the great war. Allies after Germany's own heart they were, therefore. They had been cultivated long since: in 1909, when plans were being made for a centenary celebration in 1914 of the peace that had reigned between the United States and England, German-American and Irish-American interests began to raise a structure of their own, exploiting the prominence which certain Germans, such as Franz Sigel and Carl Schurz, had enjoyed in the construction of the nation. The programme of these interests included the erection of elaborate memorials over the graves of prominent German Americans, the dissemination of legends of German heroes in America, and more practically the frustrating of the projected Peace Centenary.

Many of the organizations thus united for a practical purpose found a clearing-house in the American Truth Society, of which Jeremiah O'Leary was the head. Although the Centennial Celebration itself was rudely interrupted by the advent of war, the German-Irish acquaintanceship was nourished by the German propagandists in America. They observed with pleasure the circulation by the Clan-na-Gael of cards informing the Irish in America that troops from Erin were being assigned to the most dangerous posts and the bloodiest attacks and subjected to the most severe enemy fire in France, and that the hated British were dragging Irish boys from their homes to fill up the ranks. Between September, 1914, and April, 1915, funds amounting to $80,-000 for the purchase of arms and the printing of seditious papers and leaflets were forwarded from America to Dublin banks, and then mysteriously were withdrawn. An inflammatory publication known as *Bull,* published by O'Leary, and not barred from the mails until September, 1917, went broadcast over the United States, inciting bitterness against England, and found a greedy circle of readers in the German-American population. John Devoy, a Sinn Feiner of standing in America, fanned the flame with a newspaper known as the *Gaelic American,* published in New York, and it is this American-printed sheet which furnished the Irish revolutionists with material for a part of the plot which they were preparing for fruition in the year 1916.

In 1916 Sir Roger Casement, an Irish knight, made his way into Germany. He was permitted

Jeremiah A. O'Leary

to visit the prison camp at Limburg where some 3,000 Irish prisoners of war were quartered, and he moved about among them attempting to obtain enlistments in an army which was to effect a coup in Dublin to overthrow the British government in the Castle and to proclaim an Irish Republic. He circulated numerous copies of the *Gaelic American* to arouse the men. He was variously received. Some of the prisoners held their release worth treason—but only fifty-odd. The greater majority rejected Sir Roger's offer, and some even chose to curse and spit at the suggestion that they break their oaths of allegiance to Great Britain. He succeeded, however, in enlisting German financial assistance, and in early April, 1916, a cargo of captured Russian arms and ammunition was forwarded to Kiel and loaded into the German auxiliary steamship *Aud*.

Some 11,000 revolutionists were in a state of mental if not martial mobilization in Ireland by this time. There were in Dublin some 825 rifles. But so cleverly were the volunteers' orders passed from member to member, that Sir Matthew Nathan, Under-secretary of State for Ireland, testified later that he did not know until three days before the outbreak occurred that German interests were coöperating. Evidently, however, sympathizers in America knew it full well, for in the von Igel papers captured in von Papen's office in New York was found the following message to von Bernstorff:

"NEW YORK, April 17, 1916.

"Judge Cohalan requests the transmission of the following remarks:

"The revolution in Ireland can only be successful if supported from Germany, otherwise England will be able to suppress it, even though it be only after hard struggles. Therefore, help is necessary. This should consist primarily of aerial attacks in England and a diversion of the fleet simultaneously with Irish revolution. Then, if possible, a landing of troops, arms, and ammunition in Ireland, and possibly some officers from Zeppelins. This would enable the Irish ports to be closed against England and the establishment of stations for submarines on the Irish coast and the cutting off of the supply of food for England. The services of the revolution may therefore decide the war.

"He asks that a telegram to this effect be sent to Berlin."

Presumably such a telegram was sent, although on April 17 Sir Roger, with his recruits, was at Kiel. Three days before the Berlin press bureau had authorized the issuance of a despatch through the semi-official Overseas News Agency that "political rioting in Ireland is increasing." On the same day a news item was published in Copenhagen stating that Sir Roger had been arrested in

Germany to allay any suggestion that he was engaged in any other enterprise. On the afternoon of Thursday, April 20, a German submarine stuck its conning tower out of water off Tralee, on the Irish coast. Three men presently emerged, unfolded a collapsible boat, and rowed ashore in it. The three were Casement and two of his henchmen, come home to Ireland to spread the news that German arms and German aid were at hand. Off the southwest coast the patrol ship *Bluebell* of the British Navy sighted, on Good Friday morning, a ship flying the Norwegian flag, and calling herself, in answer to the *Bluebell's* hail, the *Aud,* out of Bergen for Genoa. Under the persuasive effect of a warning shot from the *Bluebell* the *Aud* followed her as far as Daunt's Rock, where her crew of German sailors set fire to her, hoisted the German naval ensign, abandoned ship, and then surrendered under fire. The *Aud* sank, carrying the arms for Irish revolution with her. Sir Roger was arrested in hiding, and on Easter Sunday Dublin broke out in revolt. On Monday a cipher message reached O'Leary, telling him of the uprising hours before the British censor permitted the news story to cross the ocean. John Devoy burst out in a heated charge in the *Gaelic American* that—

"The sinking of the German ship loaded with

arms and ammunition . . . was the direct result of information treacherously given to the British Government by a member of the Washington Administration . . . Wilson's officials obtained the information by an act of lawlessness, a violation of international law and of American law, committed with the deliberate purpose of helping England, and it was promptly put at the disposal of the British Government . . ."

This charge was denied at once from Washington. The specific "violation of international law and of American law" to which Devoy referred was generally supposed to be the seizure of the von Igel papers, for the accusation is the same as that which von Igel made when his office was raided. How Devoy knew that the von Igel papers contained information of the proposed expedition from Kiel to Ireland is a question which Devoy has no doubt had to answer to the Government of the United States since then. He and O'Leary, with Dennis Spellisy, who had collected large sums of money for the Sinn Fein cause, were loud in their protests against the execution of the ringleaders of the revolt on May 3rd, which put a sharp end to the endeavors of the revolutionists. That O'Leary was known to the German system of secret agents in America needs no further substantiation. To credit him

with generalship, however, would be doing
him too great honor and the Irish-American
population injustice; O'Leary was bitterly pro-
German, but so were hundreds of more prominent and influential Irish-Americans: one could
find the names of several New York Justices
upon the roster of the Friends of Peace. Sir
Roger Casement petitioned for a Philadelphia
lawyer at his trial for treason, and Sir Roger's
sister attempted unsuccessfully to reach President
Wilson, through his secretary, Joseph P. Tumulty, in an effort to bring about intercession
in the doomed knight's favor. (Mr. Tumulty
was approached more than once by persons
whom he had reason to suspect of alloyed motives
who desired to "set forth a case to the President.") The link between the old country
and the new is close, the future of Ireland is one
of more than usual interest and concern to the
United States, and the fact that the great majority of Irish-Americans have subordinated their
insular convictions to the greater conviction of
loyalty to their adopted land is at once a fine
augury of ultimate solution of the Irish question,
and a dignified rebuke to the efforts which Germany has made through America to exploit Ireland.

On Washington's Birthday, 1916, there came to

New York one who posed as a French publisher and publicist. He brought excellent letters of recommendation, and was well supplied with money. He was personable, and well sponsored, and he was correspondingly well received. Within a month he left the United States for France, with appropriate expressions of his appreciation of American hospitality.

In April, 1918, that same man faced a French firing squad, guilty of having attempted to betray his country, and of having traded with the enemy.

He was Paul Bolo Pacha, Paul Bolo by common usage, Pacha by whatever right is vested in a deposed Khedive to confer titles. Born somewhere in the obscurity of the Levant, he came as a boy to Marseilles. He was successively barber's-boy, lobster-monger, husband of a rich woman who left him her estate, then café-owner and wine-agent. Then he drifted to Cairo, and into the good graces of Abbas Hilmi, the Khedive. Abbas was deposed by the British in 1914 as pro-German, and went to Geneva; Bolo followed.

Charles F. Bertelli, the correspondent in Paris of the Hearst newspapers, naïvely related before Captain Bouchardon, a French prosecutor, the circumstances of his acquaintanceship with Bolo, which led to the latter's cordial reception at the hands of Hearst when he arrived in New York. ". . . Jean Finot, Directeur of *La Revue, . . .* had sent him a letter of introduction to Mr. Hearst and had requested me to accredit him with Mr. Hearst. He had said to me: 'Occupy yourself with the matter, Bolo has very great political power; he is the proprietor of *Le Journal* and it would be well that Hearst should know him.' . . . I made the voyage with Bolo. . . . I spoke of Bolo to Hearst and the latter said to me, 'If he is a great proprietor of French newspapers, I should be very glad to. . . .' As a compliment to Hearst, Bolo gave a grand dinner at Sherry's. . . . Bolo had two personal guests: Jules Bois and the German, Pavenstedt. . . ." We need draw on Bertelli no further than to introduce the same Adolph Pavenstedt in whose offices Papen and Boy-Ed had sought refuge at the outbreak of war in 1914; Adolph Pavenstedt, head of the banking house of G. Amsinck & Co., through which the attachés paid their henchmen for attempts at the Welland Canal, the Vanceboro bridge, and at America's peace in general. Bolo had made Pavenstedt's acquaintance in Havana in 1913.

Four days after he landed in New York, and before the Hearst dinner (which was incidental to the plot) Bolo had progressed with his negotiations to betray France to a point where von Bernstorff sent the following message to the Foreign Office in Berlin:

"Number 679, February twenty-sixth.

"I have received direct information from an entirely trustworthy source concerning a political action in one of the enemy countries which would bring about peace. One of the leading political personalities of the country in question is seeking a loan of one million seven hundred thousand dollars in New York, for which security will be given. I was forbidden to give his name in writing. The affair seems to me to be of the greatest possible importance. Can the money be provided at once in New York? That the intermediary will keep the matter secret is entirely certain. Request answer by telegram. A verbal report will follow as soon as a trustworthy person can be found to bring it to Germany.

"BERNSTORFF."

Herr von Jagow felt that even at that date peace with any belligerent was worth $1,700,000. He cabled back:

"No. 150, February twenty-ninth.

"Answer to telegram No. 679:

"Agree to the loan, but only if peace action seems to you a really serious project, as the provision of money in New York is for us at present extraordinarily difficult. If the enemy country is Russia have nothing to do with the business, as the sum of money is too small to have

Paul Bolo Pacha (on the right)

any serious effect in that country. So too in the case of Italy, for it would not be worth while, to spend so much.

"(Signed) JAGOW."

The plan approved, the next step was to pay Bolo. Bernstorff's cablegram of March 5, Number 685, pleaded for the money.

"Please instruct Deutsches Bank to hold 9,000,000 marks at disposal of Hugo Schmidt. The affair is very promising. Further particulars follow."

The next day Hugo Schmidt, American representative of the Deutsches Bank, sent the following wireless through the station at Sayville to the Deutsches Bank Direktion, Berlin:

"Communicate with William Foxley (the Foreign Office) and telegraph whether he has placed money at my disposal for Charles Gladhill (Count von Bernstorff)."

The reply came three days later. It read:

"Replying your cable about Charles Gladhill (von Bernstorff) Fred Hooven (the Guaranty Trust Company of New York) will receive money for our account. You may dispose according to our letter of November 24, 1914, to Fred Hooven."

On March 11, Schmidt, who was working night and day to consummate the deal, wirelessed again to Berlin:

"Your wireless received. Paid Charles Gladhill (von Bernstorff) $500 (which signified $500,000) through Fred Hooven (the Guaranty Trust Company). Gladhill requires further $1,100 ($1,100,000) which shall pay gradually."

Bolo's affairs were promising well. He had brought with him from Paris a letter of introduction to the New York manager of the Royal Bank of Canada, stating that he was the publisher of *Le Journal*, which required a large quantity of news print paper every day, and that he had been commissioned by all of the other large newspaper publishers in Paris to arrange a contract for 20,000 tons monthly. Bolo confirmed his intention to perform this mission when he deposited in the Royal Bank of Canada $500,-000 which Hugo Schmidt had drawn from the German government deposits in the National Park Bank and had given to Pavenstedt, who in turn checked it over to the French traitor. It was not the purchase of print paper which interested him, however, but the perversion, through purchase, of as many French newspapers as he could lay his slimy hands on; once in his possession, they could be made to carry out a sinister propaganda for a separate peace between France and Germany. Germany had offered, through Abbas Hilmi, to yield Alsace-

Lorraine in return for certain French colonies, and to evacuate the occupied portions of French soil, and by painting such a settlement in bright colors to the people of France Bolo could have served Germany's ends effectively either by actually accomplishing some such settlement, or by weakening the morale which was so largely responsible for holding the German drive against Verdun, then in the first stages of its fury.

On March 17, the Deutsches Bank wirelessed to Schmidt:

"You may dispose on Fred Hooven (the Guaranty Trust Company) on behalf Charles Gladhill (von Bernstorff) $1,700 (which meant $1,700,000)."

Bolo had his million and three-quarters, which he had asked. He had made disposition of it through the Royal Bank, setting a portion aside to his wife's credit, depositing another portion to the credit of Senator Charles Humbert (part-owner with Bolo of *Le Journal*) and holding a reserve of a million dollars in the Royal Bank subject to his call. Then he took ship for France.

His final arrangements with Pavenstedt prompted von Bernstorff to send the following message on March 20 to the Foreign Office:

"No. 692, March 20.

"With reference to telegram No. 685 please advise our

Minister in Berne that some one will call on him who will give him the password Sanct Regis who wished to establish relations with the Foreign Office. Intermediary further requests that influence may be brought to bear in France so far as possible in silence so that things may not be spoiled by German approval.

"(Signed) BERNSTORFF."

Von Bernstorff had been cautious enough during Bolo's sojourn in the United States to negotiate with him only through Pavenstedt, in order that the Embassy might not be compromised in an exceedingly hazardous undertaking if any suggestion of Bolo's real designs leaked out.   He was fully prepared in such an event to repudiate Pavenstedt, and to state honestly that he had never seen or heard of Bolo, for until the day before he left, when Pavenstedt asked the Ambassador for the telegram of introduction quoted above, Bernstorff did not know Bolo's name.   That he did know it then, and that he discussed Bolo with Berlin during April and May is evident from the following cable, sent from the Foreign Secretary to the Embassy at Washington on May 31:

"Number 206.   May 31st.   The person announced in telegram 692 of March 20th has not yet reported himself at the Legation at Berne.   Is there any more news on your side of Bolo?

"JAGOW."

There was not, although Bolo was keeping the cables hot with messages directing the further transfer of the nest-egg of $1,700,000 which he had acquired in his month in New York. He wanted the money credited to the account of Senator Humbert in J. P. Morgan & Co., then through Morgan, Harjes & Co. of Paris he directed the remittance of his funds to Paris, then cancelled those instructions and directed that his million be credited to him in Perrier & Cie., in which he was interested. What twists and turns of fate occasioned the juggling of these funds after he returned to France is not known, but certainly no bag of plunder ever passed through more artful manipulation. The explanation of its hectic adventures may lie in the fact that the spectacle of Bolo, commissioned to go to the United States to spend money for news print, and returning with nearly two millions of dollars, would have interested the French police.

For more than a year he covered his tracks. Shortly after his return the *Bonnet Rouge*, the declining publication which served ex-Premier Joseph Caillaux as mouthpiece, began to attract attention for its discussion of peace propaganda. A strain of pessimism over the conduct of the war began to make itself apparent in other journals. The arrest of Duval and Almereyda of the *Bonnet Rouge* disclosed certain of Bolo's activities and a search of his house in February revealed papers covering certain of his financial transactions in America. The United States was requested to investigate, and refused, as the affair was considered political, and it was not until we joined France in the war that the request was repeated, this time with better success.

Attorney-General Merton Lewis of New York State conducted an investigation which revealed every step of Bolo's operations in New York. His search of the records of the banks involved indicated that a fund of some $50,000,000 in cash and negotiable securities lay on deposit in America which the Deutsches Bank could place at the disposal of von Bernstorff and his fellow conspirators at any time for any purpose, and which was adequate as a reserve for any enterprise which might present itself. The evidence against Bolo was forwarded to Paris, and he was arrested. On October 4, 1917, Secretary Lansing made public the correspondence which the State Department had intercepted.

The French public became hysterically interested in the case. Senator Humbert promptly refunded the 5,500,000 francs which he had received from Bolo for 1,600 shares in *Le Journal*. Almereyda of the *Bonnet Rouge* committed suicide in prison; his death dragged Malvy, Minister of the Interior under Ribot, out of office under suspicion of trading with the enemy; the editor of a Paris financial paper was imprisoned on the same charge; "Boloism" became a generic term, and the French government, feeling a growing restlessness on the part of the public, encouraged the new diversion of spy-hunting which resulted in the exposure of negotiations between Caillaux and German representatives in Buenos Aires. Russia had been dissolved by similar German propaganda, Italy, after vigorous advances into Italia Irridenta, had had her military resistance sapped by another such campaign as Bolo proposed for France, and had retreated to the Po valley; the sum total of "Boloism" during the autumn and winter of 1917-1918 was an increased conviction on the part of the Allied peoples that the line must be held more firmly than ever, while the rear was combed for prominent traitors.

Thus, a year before she entered war, the United States supplied the scene of one of the outstanding intrigues of the war. How voluble was Adolph Pavenstedt in confessing his services as intermediary for the Kaiser; Pavenstedt was interned in an American prison camp . . . a rather comfortable camp. Hugo Schmidt, who on his own testimony was the accredited manipulator of enormous sums for the German government, was ingenuous to a degree in his denial of any knowledge of what the money paid Bolo was to be used for; Schmidt was interned. Bolo was shot.

Revolution in India, a battle royal on the Central American isthmus, a revolution in Mexico, uprisings in the West Indies, a separate peace in France—these were ambitious undertakings. For three years they were cleared through Washington, D. C. We must accept that fact not alone with the natural feeling of chagrin which it evokes, but with an eye to the future. We should congratulate our smug selves that our country was concerned only with the processes of these intrigues, and was not subject directly to their results. And then we Americans should ask ourselves whether it is not logical that, our country having served as the most fertile ground for German demoralization of other nations, we should be on our guard for a similar plot against ourselves.

That plot will not come noisily, obviously. It will be no crude effort to suggest that "American troops are suffering at the hands of the French high command." It will not be phrased in terms which reek of the Wilhelmstrasse—earnest, plodding, grotesque German polysyllables. The

German knows that an army must depend upon
the hearts of its people, and he reasons: "I shall
attack the hearts of the people, and I believe that
if it is a good principle to attack my enemy from
the rear through his people, it is also a good principle to attack his people from the rear. The
heart is as near the back as it is the front, *nicht
wahr?*" The plot will seem, in its early stages,
part and parcel of our daily life and concern; we
shall not see the German hand in it; the hand
will be so concealed as not even to excite the
enthusiasm of the German-American, often a
good danger-signal. It will involve institutions
and individuals whom we have trusted, and we
shall take sides in the controversy, and we shall
grow violently pro-this and anti-that. We shall
grow sick of the wretchedness of affairs, perhaps, and we shall lose heart. That is precisely
what Germany most desires. That is what Germany is striving for. That is why the nobility
of our citizenship carries with it the obligation
of vigilance. It is in the hope that each one of us
Americans may learn how Germany works
abroad, that we may be better prepared for her
next step here, that this narrative has been
written.

# CHAPTER XVIII

## AMERICA GOES TO WAR

Bernstorff's request for bribe-money—The President on German spies—Interned ships seized—Enemy aliens —Interning German agents—The water-front and finger-print regulations—Pro-German acts since April, 1917— A warning and a prophecy.

On January 22, 1917, President Wilson set forth to the Senate of the United States his ideas of the steps necessary to secure world peace. On the same day Count von Bernstorff sent his Foreign Office this message:

"I request authority to pay out up to $50,000 (Fifty thousand dollars) in order, as on former occasions, to influence Congress through the organization you know of, which perhaps can prevent war. I am beginning in the meantime to act accordingly. In the above circumstance a public official German declaration in favor of Ireland is highly desirable in order to gain the support of Irish influence here."

The money did not have the desired soothing effect. Nine days later Germany announced unrestricted submarine warfare as her immediate future policy and the head of the German spy system in America received his passports for return to Germany. He was succeeded by the head of the German spy system in America.

The real name of this successor is not known to the authorities at this date. If it were he would be arrested, and punished according to whatever specific crime he had committed against a set of American statutes created for conditions of peace. Then, with the head of the German spy system in America in prison, he would be succeeded, as Bernstorff was, by the head of the German spy system in America.

And so this absurd progression would go on, until finally there would be no more spies to head the system on the American front. How much the system would be able to accomplish during the painstaking pursuit and capture of its successive heads would depend upon America's swiftness in pursuit and capture. Who the individual in authority over the system is, and what is his structure of organization, cannot be answered here. But it is vitally necessary for every citizen who has the free existence of this republic at heart to decide, basing his judgment on certain events since the declaration of war, what measure of accomplishment the German spy system shall have, and what it has already effected against a nation with which it is now openly and frankly at war.

Let him first recall that in his Flag Day speech of June 14, 1916, President Wilson said in part:

"There is disloyalty in the United States, and it must be absolutely crushed. It proceeds from a minority, a very small minority, but a very active and subtle minority. . . . If you could have gone with me through the space of the last two years and could have felt the subtle impact of intrigue and sedition, and have realized with me that those to whom you have intrusted authority are trustees not only of the power but also of the very spirit and purpose of the United States, you would realize with me the solemnity with which I look upon the sublime symbol of our unity and power."

Let him then refer to the President's Flag Day address of one year later (quoted at the beginning of the book). With those admirable expressions in mind, let him recapitulate the activities of German sympathizers or agents since February, 1917.

Ninety-one vessels flying the German flag were in American harbors. Their displacement totalled nearly six hundred thousand tons—the equivalent of a fleet of seventy-five of the cargo carriers on which the United States later began

construction to offset the submarine.   Months in
advance of the severance of diplomatic relations,
orders had been issued from the Embassy to the
masters of all these vessels in case of war between
Germany and the United States to cripple the
ships.   With the break in relations imminent,
German agents slipped aboard the vessels and
gave the word: the great majority of the ninety-
one ships were then put out of commission by the
368 officers and 826 men aboard.   The damage
was performed with crowbars and axes.   Vital
parts had been chalk-marked weeks in advance,
so that the destruction might be effected swiftly:
delicate mechanisms were mashed beyond recognition, important parts removed and smuggled
ashore or dropped overboard, cylinders cracked,
emery dust introduced in the bearings of the engines, pistons battered out of shape, and the machinery of the ships generally destroyed as only
skilled engineers could have destroyed them.
Out of thirty ships in New York harbor, thirty
ships were damaged—among them the liners,
*Vaterland,* of 54,000 tons, the *George Washington,* of 25,000 tons, the *Kaiser Wilhelm,* the *President Lincoln,* and the *President Grant,* of about
20,000 tons each.   In the harbor of Charleston,
S. C., lay the *Liebenfels,* of 4,525 tons; her crew,
led by Captain Johann Klattenhoff, scuttled her

on February 1, in the navigating channel of Charleston Harbor; Klattenhoff, with Paul Wierse, a Charleston newspaper man, and eight of the *Liebenfels'* crew were tried and convicted of the crime, fined and sentenced to periods averaging a year in Atlanta. The discovery of the damage forced the Government to take over the vessels at once. The Department of Justice hastened on February 2 to notify all of its deputies "to take prompt measures against the attempt at destruction or sinking or escape of such ships by their crews" which those crews had already done; and the customs authorities who boarded the ships in San Francisco, Honolulu, New York, Boston, Manila, and every other American port came ashore with rueful countenances. The combined damage served to tie the vessels up for at least six months more, and to require expensive repair. To return to the comparison: a fleet of seventy-five 8,000 ton cargo vessels, such as have since been built, would have been able to make, during those six months, at least four round trips to France each, or 300 voyages.

When the German fleet put into neutral American ports of refuge in 1914 the personnel of its ships totalled 476 officers and 4,980 men. When the ships were seized in 1917, there were 368 officers and 826 men aboard. Of those who had been discharged or allowed indefinite shore leave a considerable number were active German agents, by far the great majority were German citizens, and the United States was on the horns of a dilemma: either each of the sailors ashore must be watched on suspicion, or else each was free to go about the country as he pleased. Thus more than 4,000 potential secret agents from an active auxiliary arm of the German navy were dumped on the hospitality which our neutrality entailed. When war was declared those men came within the troublesome problem of the status of the enemy alien.

What was an enemy alien? The United States, on April 6, declared war against Germany. "Meanwhile," reads the report of the Attorney-General for 1917, "prior to the passage of the joint resolution of Congress of April 6, 1917, elaborate preparation was made for the arrest of upward of 63 alien enemies whom past investigation had shown to constitute a danger to the peace and safety of the United States if allowed to remain at large." These "alien enemies" were male Germans. Not Austrians, for the United States did not go to war with Austria until December 7. Not Bulgars, nor Turks, for the United States has not declared war upon Bulgaria or Turkey. Not female Germans, in the face of the full knowledge of the predilections of Bernstorff, Boy-Ed, and von Papen for employing women in espionage. Of the thousands of Germans in the United States whose sympathies were presently to be demonstrated in numerous ways against the successful prosecution of America's war, sixty-three had been deemed worthy of arrest. By June 30 this number had risen to 295, and by October 30 to 895. "Some of those interned," continues the report, "have been paroled with the necessary bonds and restrictions." Although the United States went to war on April 6, Karl Heynen, who managed the Bridgeport Projectile Company for Bernstorff and Albert, and who had previously earned the good will of the United States by gun-running in Mexico, was not arrested until July 6, in his offices in the Hamburg-American Line at 45 Broadway. At the same time F. A. Borgemeister, former adviser to Dr. Albert, and latterly Heynen's lieutenant, was arrested. Both were interned at Fort Oglethorpe and during December, Borgemeister was allowed three weeks' liberty on parole. Rudolph Hecht, confidant of Dr. Albert, who had sold German war loan bonds for the Kaiser, and who had also been interned, was released for a like period of liberty in December. G. B. Kulenkampf, who had secured false manifest papers for the supply-ship *Berwind* in August, 1914, was arrested on May 28, 1918, more than one year after America had entered the war; on the same day Robert J. Oberfohren, a statistician employed by the Hamburg-American, was arrested and in his room were captured compiled statistics covering the exports of munitions from the United States during the two years past: Oberfohren said he expected to turn the figures in to the University of Munich after the war.

Bernstorff himself left an able alien enemy in the Swiss Legation in Washington. He was Heinrich Schaffhausen, and had been one of the brightest attachés of the German Embassy. As a member for three months of the Swiss Legation he might readily have sent (and no doubt did send) information of military value to his own people in code, under protection of the Swiss seal. The State Department on July 6 ordered his deportation. Adolph Pavenstedt was arrested on January 22, 1918, in the Adirondacks, after having enjoyed nine months' immunity; Otto Julius Merkle was not interned until December 7; Gupta, the Hindu, was finally caught in New York in 1917, gave bail, and escaped; Dr. John Ferrari, alias F. W. Hiller, a German officer who had escaped from a British detention camp in India and had joined the German intrigue colony, was interned in January, 1918; Baron Gustave von Hasperg was arrested only after he had displayed undue interest in the National Army cantonment at Upton in the same month; Franz Rosenberg, a wealthy German importer, convicted in 1915 of having attempted to smuggle rubber in cotton bales into Germany, and fined $500 for that offense, was allowed at liberty until February 9, 1918; in a round-up which took place in January, 1918, the Federal authorities collected such celebrities as Hugo Schmidt, Frederick Stallforth, and Baron George von Seebeck (the son of General von Seebeck, commander of the Tenth Corps of the German army).

The cases cited are picked at random out of a mass. They illustrate the breathing periods given to Germans who had been active under Bernstorff in disturbing America's peace and defying her laws. They serve also to illustrate the contrast between the methods employed by the United States, and those adopted by her Allies, from whom she has taken other lessons in the business of warfare. France gave alien enemies forty-eight hours in which to leave the soil of the country, and any such person found at large after that date was to be interned in a detention camp. To have interned all of the Germans in the United States would have been impossible and the Government took some time to find a second best method. By May 2 the Department of Justice was in a position to announce that it had plans for internment camps for three classes of aliens: prisoners of war, enemy aliens, and detained aliens, and it announced on that date there were some 6,000 in those classes already detained. By February 17, 1918, however, there were actually no more than 1,870 aliens interned under the war department and under military guard at Forts McPherson, Oglethorpe and Douglas, and some 2,000 at Hot Springs, North Carolina, in the Department of Labor's detention camp.

At both camps the prisoners were fed and housed at the expense of the Government, and it was not until the early spring of 1918 that they were put to work.

From April 6 to July 10, 1917, an enemy alien could be employed by any shipbuilder, tug-boat captain, lighterage firm or steamship line; he could go about any waterfront at will, provided he did not enter the so-called "barred zones" in the vicinity of Government military or naval property, and he could make unmolested such observations as his eyesight afforded of the shipping upon which the United States depends for its share in this war. After that date he was forbidden such employment, and denied approach to all wharves and ships. On July 9 the Government discharged from its employ 200 German subjects who for weeks past had been loading transports at the docks in an "Atlantic port." A raid on the Hoboken waterfront in the following winter rounded up 200 more enemy aliens who had calmly ignored the "barred zone" regulations.

The Government was confronted with a stupendous problem. How to handle with its normal peace-time police force the great unwieldy flow of the alien population presented a constantly baffling question, yet it was absolutely essential to the control of internal affairs that the Government know the comings and goings of the enemies within its gates. The date of February 13, 1918, was eventually set as the last on which citizens of enemy countries living in the United States might set down their finger prints and names and file their affidavits of residence and condition.

What facilities had the United States provided for transacting this great volume of additional protective duty? There existed, first of all, the Department of Justice, whose chief function in peace-time had been the enforcement through its investigators and prosecutors of acts of Congress, such as the so-called Mann "White Slave" Act, and the Sherman "Anti-Trust" Act. There was the United States Secret Service, a bureau of the Treasury Department, whose chief function had been the detection of smuggling and counterfeiting and the protection of the person of the President. There was the Intelligence Bureau of the War Department, and a similar Bureau of the Navy Department, both undermanned, as was every other branch of our military forces at that time. The advent of war brought a complicated necessity for coordination of these four branches and of several other Federal investigating bureaus.

The German did not wait for coordination. He inspired food riots among the poorer classes of the lower East Side in New York. He opposed the draft law, rallying to his support the Socialist, the Anarchist, and the Industrial Worker of the World, under whose cloak he hid, not too well concealed. He celebrated the declaration of war by blowing up a munitions plant at Eddystone, Pa., on April 10, 1917, and killing 112 persons, most of whom were women and girls. He sneaked information into Germany through the Swedish legation. He tried to promote strikes in Pittsburg, but his agent,

Walter Zacharias, was arrested. He tried to dynamite the Elephant-Butte dam on the Rio Grande, but his agent, Dr. Louis Kopf, was caught. He caused a serious revolution in Cuba until his agents were expelled. He tried to block the Liberty Loans, in vain. He tried to obstruct the collection of Red Cross funds. He caused strikes in the airplane-spruce forests of the Northwest. He assisted Lieutenant Hans Berg of the captured German prize *Appam* to escape from Fort McPherson with nine of his crew in October, 1917. He erected secret wireless stations at various points, to communicate to Berlin via Mexico, whither thousands of his army reservists had fled on false passports at the outbreak of war. He smuggled information of military importance in and out of the country in secret inks, on neutral vessels, and even wrote them (on one occasion) in cipher upon the shoulder of a prima donna. He burned warehouses and shell plants. He sawed the keel of a transport nearly through. He placed a culture of ptomaine germs in the milk supply of the cadets' school at Fort Leavenworth. He invented a chemical preparation which would cause painful injury to the kidneys of every man who drank water in a certain army cantonment. He received Irish rebellionists and negotiated with them for further revolution. He made his way into our munitions plants and secured data which he forwarded to Berlin; he worked in our aeroplane plants and deliberately weakened certain vital parts of the tenuous construction so that our aviators died in training; he kept track of our transports, and of the movements of our forces, and passed them on to the Wilhelmstrasse. He sold heroin to our soldiers and sailors. He supplied men for the motor boat *Alexander Agassiz* which put to sea from a Pacific port to raid commerce. In short, he continued to carry out, with multiplied opportunity, the same tactics he had employed since August, 1914.

The German spy in America continues to attack our armies in the rear. He is here in force. A word to him may mean that within twenty-four hours Kiel will know of another transport embarking with certain forces for France. He is here to take the lives of Americans just as certainly as his kinsman is firing across a parapet in Lorraine for the same purpose. Whatever provision will save those lives must be made swiftly. The Departments, already overtaxed with the magnitude of their task, ask simply that they be given the weapons to make their splendid battle on the American front successful.

Whatever aid and comfort the enemy may find in this recitation of his disgraceful achievements and graceless failures, he may have and welcome. He has imposed upon the hospitality of the United States, has dragged his clumsy boots over the length and breadth of their estate, has run amuck with torch and explosive, and has earned a great deal of loathing contempt, hardly amounting to hatred. But no fear—and that is what he sought. The spectacle of what the disloyalists of America have done, and the easily conjurable picture of what they would do if Germany should win, are graphic enough for loyal America. The United States must proceed with incisive vigor to cut out this poisonous German sore. And the United States will remember the scar. It is so written.

# APPENDIX

## A GERMAN PROPAGANDIST

In 1915 Fritz von Pilis came to America. He had been a member of the colonization bureau of the German Government maintained to Prussianize Poland, and later an emigration agent of the North German Lloyd.

He posed here as an anti-German Austrian who desired to give the American public the "true facts" of Germany's intentions in the war. He approached the *Sun,* offering it the following brief of a volume written in late 1914 by a Prussian Pan-German, provided he (von Pilis) be allowed to write a commentary to accompany the outline. His offer was not accepted, for the *Sun* saw him in his true light of Prussian propagandist sent here to spread the gospel of might which is preached in the book.

The brief is offered here as an authoritative platform of Germany's aims by conquest as the Pan-German party saw them after a few months of war. Many of these aims have already been achieved.

(The phraseology and spelling is von Pilis'.)

### *Denkschrift, etc.*

*General War Goal.* Weakening of foes: discard all "world citizen" sentiment and dangerous objectivity in favor of strangers. We want peace terms based solely on our interests.

Severity: Let's hear no more of "considerations of humanity," "cultural demands." Must impose indemnities on foes and take land in Europe and overseas to lessen political power:

(a) In Europe for healthy colonization.

(b) Colonial: to supply raw materials and take finished products.

(c) Indemnities to be devoted to common social betterment of German people.

*Internal.* Rehabilitation of farmer class by providing ample land. Combat city evils.

(1) Opportunity provided by fate in this attack by our foes.

(2) France and Russia must cede land near our gates as punishment; estates to German farmers.

(3) City evils to be remedied by better housing conditions; by war indemnities, not single tax. (Cheap rents, tenants become owners.) (Gift of fate through foes.) Old age pensions larger and at lower period of age (65 years instead of 70).

*Overseas.* Take over colonies and settle by Germans to give economic independence for imports and exports. This will give opportunities to eliminate "intelligent proletariat" by use elsewhere.

*Belgium.* Conspiracy and conduct of people and Government show Belgium not entitled to independence.

(1) All well-informed people in Germany say: "Belgium must cease to exist."

(2) Impossible to take into German people with equal rights.

Rather leave with indemnity which must pay anyway. But we need the coast against England.

Belgium to be property of Empire, Kaiser its Lord:

Belgium to lose its name.

Belgium to be divided into 2 parts: Walloons and Flemish.

Kaiser's officials to govern as dictators of province.

Belgians taken into Empire to have no political rights. All who object may emigrate. Walloons unworthy of being "Germanized."

*France.* Must "bleed it white" so as never to be attacked again:

(1) i.e., indemnity and land. Land from Switzerland via Belfort, Moselle, Epinal, Toul, Meuse, Verdun, Sedan, Charleville, St. Quentin to Somme and Channel at Cayeux.

(2) France to take over and indemnify the present inhabitants. We get the land sans dangerous people. Such expulsion immoral? Retribution. Not bricht evisen! France'll be thankful for the population. Needs it.

(3) Ceded area to become military frontier, administered by dictator. To be settled by Germans: discharged soldiers or war veterans' families.

(4) Toulon and environs to be made impregnable fortress on land and seaside for base on the Mediterranean.

Rather forego all French territory than take with it the hostile French population. Walloons to be kept in land only to furnish mass of laborers, lest new German settlers become industrial laborers again.

*England.* Its world-rule must be ended! Can't formulate demands until naval warfare decided. *Build ships with all your might!*

*Japan.* Must be punished for white race. Revenge.

*Russia.* Must be put *hors de combat* by permanent

weakening. We must forcibly once more turn Russia's face towards East by curtailing its frontiers as before Peter I's time. Then its pressure vs. Asia.

(1) A new Poland (off G. territory) including Grodno, Minsk and part of Mohilen to Dnieper. Probably a kingdom with personal connection to Hapsburg House.

(2) G. to seize hegemony of Baltic; take Kniland, Livona, Esthonia and Lithuania safeguarded by territories to rivers that were frontiers of R. before Peter.

(3) To take Suwalki and military strip of Poland to strengthen Thorn and Silesia, Soldau, Wloclanek Kolo.

(4) Finland to be independent or go to Sweden?

(5) R. to lose most of Black Sea coast.

(6) Ukraine Empire under Hapsburg for "Small Russia." Bessarabia to Rumania. Austria to get good part of Serbia and Montenegro.

How avoid clash of nationalities in newly formed territories? Ans.: By forced migration. No home feelings in Russian farmer; R's precedents Siberia. Exchange of G. settlers in New Russia for R's in new G. (several years). Possibly so exchange Poles in Posen too? Lithuanians may readily be incorporated into Poland and Letts and Esthonians to be left or transferred to Russia according to treatment of G's in this war. R. Jews unthinkable in G. Empire: Bar their migration westward. Remedy (1) Bind R. to remove restrictions vs. Jews and then Jews back there.

(2) Zionism: Palestine to be ceded through G. and A-Hung, influence. This—safe wall vs. Jews and stimulate migration of Jews to Russia.

Prussia to get New Territory in East or else form "Marks" for Germanization.

Tenants to be settled by public grant in return for enhanced realty values.

We must never be without enemies strong enough to compel defensive militia. Fr. and Eng. made powerless, let R. always threaten us and be our foe; that'll be our luck.

*The Colonies.* French Morocco, Senegambia & Congo. Egypt freed from England; England's colonies in Africa depend on developments.

Tunis to Italy.

Bizert and Damietta (with Italy's and A-H's consent), Djibuti, Goa, Ceylon, Sabang, Saigon, Azores, Caperdon (?), Isls, Madagascar.

*Austria-Hungary.* Heavy indemnity from Russia.

New Poland and Ukraine Empire personally united to A-H. North half of Serbia. South ½ to Bulgaria. Guarantees to be given to Germanic minority by Slavs. West Galicia to Poland. East Galicia to Ukraine Empire. German to be Reichsprache?

*The Neutrals.* Luxemburg to win G. Statehood (too weak to control B. Luxemburg).

Holland. Avoid pressure politically. Not to receive Flemish Belgium. These need strict masters.

Italy, if neutral, Corsica, Lower Savoy, Nizzia, Tunis.

Rumania: Bessarabia (Odessa, if she joins G. in war).

Bulgaria: South ½ of Serbia (more if she joins G. in war).

Turkey, if enters war, heavy indemnity and land in Caucasus. Integrity guarantees by G. and A-H: spheres of influence economically.

Sweden may get Finland if both willing.

Economic unity of territories and G. and A-H., Switzerland, Holland, Italy, Scandinavia, Rumania and Bulgaria probably join.

Offensive and Defensive Germanic Alliance: Scandinavia. Maybe and voluntarily restore settlements of N. Schleswig to Denmark, if necessary. New Germanic blood needed to make good war losses.

*Special Demands.* Exclusion of all East people from G. soil; rights to expel Letts, Esthonians and Lithuanians for 25 years.

No colored person on G. soil.

G. high schools for G's and foreigners of G. descent; special exceptions.

Only allied officers to be in G. army.

Only mature and fortified G. youth to study abroad.

Only G. language, G. fashions, G. Geographical names.

Steady supply of grain.

Subsidies to married officers out of war indemnity.

G. nobles to marry only Germans.